TREASURES OLD AND NEW

Reading through the Scriptures as One Story

ERNEST CLARK, JR.

Treasures Old and New: Reading through the Scriptures as One Story
cc 2013 Ernest Clark, Jr.

Address requests for information to epcj@st-andrews.ac.uk.

Cataloging-in-Publication Data

Clark, Jr., Ernest
    Treasures old and new : reading through the Scriptures as one story /
    Ernest Clark, Jr.
    ISBN: 1478348186 / ISBN-13: 978-1478348184
    1. Bible – Reading.
    220.6 – dc21

For Catherine, Ben and Ana

जैसे वीर के हाथ में थीर

Contents

Preface

One day, at the end of a series of parables about the kingdom of heaven, Jesus explained to his disciples, "every teacher of the law who has become a disciple in the kingdom of heaven is like the owner of a house who brings out of his storeroom new treasures as well as old" (Matthew 13:52, NIV). A teacher of the law or scribe knows the law—the Old Testament—well. A scribe who now follows the kingdom of heaven understands how the reign of King Jesus fulfills the expectations of the Law and the Prophets.

I began writing this book for my daughter Catherine when she started grade five. As a disciple of Jesus, I wanted to instruct Catherine in the Law, the Prophets and the Kingdom. I wanted to give her a "way of seeing" the Holy Scriptures.

Why I Wrote This Reading Guide

God's word gives us his account of why he made this world and us in it. In lesson two (Genesis 1-2) you'll read that God made humans in his image, to be like him and to rule for him on his good earth. He made us to serve him and to serve and keep his world and each other. God taught the first man and woman how to live and showed them how to work. Over the centuries he spoke by his Spirit through his prophets, shaping the people he loved to live faithfully. In his Son, he himself came and lived among us as one of us, showing us his grace and teaching us his truth. The Scriptures are God's words to instruct his people to live by faith that shows itself in love. We read God's word so that we can know him and love him and become like him and live and work for his glory in his good earth.

God's account is, of course, a story—the most real and most true of all stories, but a story nonetheless—with a beginning, a middle and an end, a plot and lots of characters. And it makes the most sense when we read it as a story.

In the final month of this book's gestation, Trevor Hart, the minister at St Andrews Church, painted a compelling picture of what happens when we read the Scriptures this way. Reading from Luke 7:11-17, Rev. Hart noted how Jesus copied Elijah when he raised the widow's son and gave him back to her. It is important, he said,

> for each of us to become better versed not just in the gospel stories but in the *whole* of Scripture, familiarising ourselves not only with its major themes, characters and plot lines, but with the many by-ways and sub-plots and hidden recesses too, and some of the relatively unsung heroes (and heroines) in the stories it tells. Because, like any good novel or well told story, the whole is much more than the sum of its parts, and we become faithful readers of it by allowing its deep patterns and sustained characterizations to shape our imagination and take it captive, soaking into us through repeated reading and re-reading, until we can hardly any longer draw a clear line between the world of this book and the world we live in from day to day. I know people (perhaps you do too) who are such avid watchers of Star Trek ... that they could tell you exactly what happened to whom in which episode and in what year, and what they themselves were doing when it happened. In fact, their imagination is completely saturated with and populated by the characters and events of their favourite show or series of novels, or whatever, so that it colours and begins to seep into the way they see the world itself. ... I really wish that those of us who are Christians would give the Bible even *half* the chance to gain such imaginative purchase in our lives, so that its stories and characters and events and expectations might begin to seep imperceptibly into the way we see the world itself.
>
> Because, of course, the world to be found within the pages of the Bible and the world in which we lives are the *same* world, whether as believers we recognise it as such, and look expecting to see signs of God at work in its midst; or else, as unbelievers or just those who aren't really sure, we look at it wondering how to make sense of its often bewildering plethora of events, and where on earth God *might* be found in the midst of it all. Either way, if we're going to notice him when he confronts us or hear him when he calls us, we need to know what sort of thing to look and to listen out for. And having eyes to see and ears to hear takes more than a working familiarity with our Old and New Testaments alone, it certainly takes nothing less.

I have no better words to say why I've written this book.

How This Guide Works

I have arranged the Scriptures chronologically into 600 readings of about the same length: 450 readings cover the Old Testament and 150 the New Testament. Middle and high school students can read one lesson for each school day and work through all 600 lessons in four school years. Others may want to read six days a week right through the year. Doing so, you should be able to study through the whole Bible in two years.

Each day you will follow the guidelines on the bookmark to (1) pray, (2) read through and mark the assigned passage, (3) think through questions and write answers, (4) write your own ideas, questions, application and summary and (5) pray again. You can tear out one of the bookmarks at the end of this book and use it to mark your place in the book.

My goal with these questions is to help you understand the flow of the Bible's one story. You will understand this by reading through the Scriptures in a mostly chronological (rather than canonical) order. You will make connections with earlier parts of the story as that story spirals forward. The questions emphasize a narrative and literary approach and focus on the Scriptures as God has given them to us.

Finally, this book will help you develop the skills of Bible study using a study Bible. Questions will tell you to look at its book introductions, textual and study notes and cross-references. I recommend most the *ESV Study Bible* (Crossway) or the *NIV Study Bible* (Zondervan). Zondervan has published the notes from its Study Bible with the KJV and NASB as well.

As you work through the guide, I would love to hear from you. What are you learning? What do you have questions about? Or even, what typographical mistaks have you found?

In writing these questions, I have found the most help in Gordon Fee and Douglas Stuart's outstanding *How to Read the Bible Book by Book: A Guided Tour*. I thank God also for other teachers who have opened my eyes to see and my ears to hear what the Spirit shows and says to the churches. I list them in the bibliography.

I wrote much of this book while discipleship director at Rocky Bayou Christian School. I thank Mike Mosley, the superintendent, whose confidence in me was a profound encouragement; Adam Rhoads, fellow scribe in the scriptorium, and Lisa Eaves who labored patiently and faithfully beside me; and my students, both the eighth graders at Rocky and the "youth" at Trinity Church, gracious subjects of the book's field testing. I thank Trevor Hart for faithfully keeping me and the rest of the flock at St Andrews Church and for sharing his words in this preface. Last I thank my wife Tiffany for refracting through her words and her life the truth of God's word and the beauty of his Spirit. Never tasted coffee so rich nor shone truths so bright as when read at your side ere dawn's first light.

This book is dedicated to my children Catherine, Ben and Ana, for whom the project was conceived in the first place. Did ever a foe so rejoice in his defeat as do I, when in triumphal glee you find a "connection" I have not spied? *Touché!*

May God grant you eyes to see, ears to hear and a heart to understand.

By his grace,

Ernest
St Andrews, Scotland
Feast of Thomas the Apostle, 2013

PART ONE

OLD TESTAMENT HISTORY
Adam to Amaziah

Genesis

I. Genesis — Introduction

Pray. Then Read, Think and <u>Mark</u>.

An introduction gets you ready to read a book. It usually tells you who wrote the book, when and for whom. It points out the important themes you should look out for and summarizes the book's message.

Read your study Bible's introduction to Genesis. Think about the questions for each of the following sections. <u>Mark</u> the answers and other things that seem important.

If you're reading the ESV Study Bible, use the following questions.

- "Author, Title, and Date" (on page 39)
  - Read the first paragraph. What does *Genesis* mean?
  - Read the second paragraph. God is the main author of Genesis. Through which human did he write?
- "Place in the Pentateuch" (on p. 40)
  - With which other books does Genesis belong?
  - What is that set of books called?
- "Arrangement of the Book" (p. 40)
  - Read the third paragraph. Which phrase is a hallmark in Genesis? Underline it.
- "Theme" and "Key Themes" (41)
  - <u>Mark</u> each of the key themes in Genesis.
- Now skip to the end of the lesson and follow the instructions to write an introduction to Genesis.

If you're reading the NIV Study Bible, use the following questions.

- "Title" (on page 1)
  - What does *Genesis* mean?
- "Author and Date of Writing" (on p. 2)
  - Read the first two paragraphs.
  - God is the main author of Genesis. Through which human did he write?

- o   With which other books does Genesis belong?
- o   What is that set of books called?
- •   "Theological Theme and Message" (p. 3)
    - o   Read the first paragraph. What is a key word in Genesis? Underline it.
    - o   Read the second paragraph. Mark each of the key themes in Genesis.

Write

Write your own introduction to Genesis. Tell who wrote the book, when and for whom. State the important themes. Summarize the book's message.

2. Genesis 1:1-2:25

Follow your bookmark. Then answer these questions:
-   a.   What four things are not yet good with the earth at the beginning? Read Genesis 1:2. What does God do to turn the chaos into goodness? Read Genesis 1:3, 9, 22, 28, 31.
-   b.   What does God create humans to be like and to do? Read Genesis 1:26. What does God do to them? Read 1:28.
-   c.   What does God tell the humans to do (Genesis 1:28; 2:15-16)? What does he tell them not to do (2:17)?

Return to your bookmark and do d through g.

3. Genesis 3:1-5:32

Follow your bookmark. Then answer these questions:
-   a.   Who controls and speaks through the serpent? What all goes wrong in 3:1-6?
-   b.   "Seed" or "offspring" is an important word in Genesis. What promise of hope does the LORD God give the man and woman (3:15)? In 5:1-3, who is in whose likeness?
-   c.   Genesis 4:17-24 tells us about Adam's line of offspring through Cain. Genesis 5:1-32 tells us about his line through Seth. How are these two lines alike? How are they different?

Return to your bookmark and do d through g.

4. Genesis 6:1-9:29

Follow your bookmark. Then answer these questions:
-   a.   What have humans become like (6:5)? What is "human nature" (6:5)? What happens to the ground when humans spill

blood (kill other humans) on it (6:11-12)? Also look back to 4:10-12.

b. Why does God flood the whole earth (6:11-13)? After all the rains, what does the earth look like again? Compare 7:18 with 1:2. How does Genesis 8 remind you of Genesis 1? Compare 8:1-2, 11, 17-18; 9:1 with 1:6-10, 12, 25-26, 28.

c. Whom does Noah curse? Whom does he bless? Read 9:24-27.

Return to your bookmark and do d through g.

5. Genesis 10:1-12:20

Follow your bookmark. Then answer these questions:

a. What do the people at Babel do wrong? Why does the LORD stop their work and scatter them? See 9:2; 11:2, 4.

b. What does the LORD promise Abram in 12:2-3? Mark the key words. What does the LORD promise Abram in 12:7? Mark the key words.

c. While the Israelites were living as slaves in Egypt, how would the story of Abram in Egypt have encouraged them? See 12:10-13:2.

Return to your bookmark and do d through g.

6. Genesis 13:1-16:16

Follow your bookmark. Then answer these questions:

a. What does the LORD promise Abram in 13:14-17? Mark the key words.

b. Why does the LORD declare Abraham righteous (15:6)?

c. A covenant is an agreement between two people, often kings. In a covenant, the Lord says who he is, what he has done and what he will give. Who is the Lord in 15:7? What has he done? What does the Lord promise in 15:18?

Return to your bookmark and do d through g.

7. Genesis 17:1-19:38

Follow your bookmark. Then answer these questions:

a. What is the name of the Lord of the covenant in 17:1? (Look at the translation note.) What does the Lord promise (17:4-8)?

b. What must Abraham do so that the LORD will bring about for him what he has promised him (18:19)?

(3) Think about and answer the questions. (4) Return to your bookmark.

    c.   What does Abraham do about Sodom (18:22-33)? What does Lot want with Sodom? Which two nations are descended from Lot and his daughters (19:36-38)?

8. Genesis 20:1-22:24

    a.   How is Sarah able to bear a son even though she is so old (21:1-2)?

    b.   Just as trees cast shadows on a sunny afternoon, there are shadows of Jesus throughout the Old Testament. Isaac is a shadow (or type) of Jesus. Isaac does things that look like the things Jesus will do. How is Jesus' death like Isaac's death (22:1-14)? How is it different or better, more real than "the shadow"?

    c.   What does the LORD promise Abraham in 22:17-18?

9. Genesis 23:1-24:67

    a.   Why does Abraham want to bury Sarah in Canaan? Read the study note for 23:19 or 20.

    b.   Why must Isaac's wife not be a Canaanite (24:3-4; look ahead to 26:34-35)? Why must Isaac not go back to Aram-Naharaim (Mesopotamia) (24:6-8)?

    c.   Who provides a wife for Isaac? What does the chief servant do before the wife is provided (24:12)?

10. Genesis 25:1-26:35

    a.   Who provides children for Isaac's wife? What does Isaac do before the children are provided (25:21)?

    b.   Which of Rebekah's two sons does the LORD choose to bless (25:23)? How does that son get the birthright?

    c.   A series of events happens in 26:24-25. This series is similar to Abraham's relationship with the LORD. What happens in the series?

11. Genesis 27:1-29:14

    a.   What does Isaac promise Jacob in 27:27-29?

    b.   What does *Jacob* mean? See translation note for 25:26. In these chapters, whom does Jacob deceive?

    c.   What does the LORD promise Jacob in 28:13-15? Do all of the "good guys" in the Scriptures always do what is right, or even worship the LORD? What does Jacob promise God (28:20-22)?

12. Genesis 29:15-31:21

    a. Who deceives Jacob (29:23, 25)?

    b. How does Jacob try to get more streaked, spotted or speckled animals (30:37-41)? Who was with Jacob and made his plan work (31:5-9)? What does he call himself, and where does he tell Jacob to go (31:13)?

    c. Draw the following chart. Write the names of the sons in order, with each son in the column headed by his mother.

Jacob's Wives and Sons				
	Leah	*Zilpah*	**Rachel**	*Bilhah*
1	Reuben			
2				
3				
4				
5				Dan
6				
7		Gad		
8				
9	Issachar			
10				
	Dinah			
11				

13. Genesis 31:22-33:20

    a. When Jacob fears Esau, on whom does he call (32:7-12)? What does Jacob call him (32:9)? What does Jacob call himself (32:10)? What does God call Jacob (32:28)?

    b. What Hebrew words does Moses play with in 32:22-24? Read the study note for 32:24.

    c. *El* (rhymes with "tell") is another ancient (Semitic) name for God. The Hebrews often used *El* as a part of a name for a person or a place. From today's reading, list the names that include *El*. Then list their meanings beside them. See 32:28, 30; 33:20.

14. Genesis 34:1-36:43

    a. What does Jacob build on the land he has bought in Shechem (33:20)? What does God do in chapter 34?

    b. What does God tell Jacob right after the trouble with the men of Shechem (35:1)? How does Jacob respond (35:1-4)? Is he changing?

(3) Think about and answer the questions. (4) Return to your bookmark.

    c.   As Jacob obeys God, what does God do for him (35:5)? What does God promise Israel (35:11-12)? How many sons does Jacob have (35:22)?

15. Genesis 37:1-38:29

    a.   Do Joseph's dreams have a meaning (37:5-10; see the study note for 37:5)? What is the meaning? Who rescues the dreamer (37:21)? Which number brother is he?

    b.   What kind of woman does Judah marry (35:2)? Who else settled among Canaanites (13:10-13)? Who else married a Canaanite woman (26:34-35)? Who else treats an Israelite woman like a prostitute (38:15-19; see 34:31)?

    c.   When a man dies before his wife has a son, what should the dead man's brother do (38:8)? What do Onan and Judah refuse to do (38:9, 11)? Who does what is righteous (38:26)?

16. Genesis 39:1-41:36

    a.   What does Yahweh do for Joseph (39:2-3)? What does Yahweh do through Joseph (39:5)? What promise is Yahweh fulfilling (12:2-3)?

    b.   Compare the situation between Judah and Tamar with the situation between Joseph and Potiphar's wife. In each story,

        o   What does the woman do with her eyes (38:14-15; 39:7)?

        o   How does the man respond (38:16; 39:8-10)?

        o   What does the woman have in hand (38:18, 25; 39:13)?

    c.   Similar things happen to Joseph with three different men: Potiphar, the prison warden and Pharaoh. List the series.

17. Genesis 41:37-43:34

    a.   Do Joseph's dreams come true (41:53-54; 42:6-8)? How does the LORD fulfill his promise to bless the nations through the offspring of Abraham (41:57)?

    b.   Why does Joseph treat his brothers as he does (42:9-20)? Is he taking vengeance on them (42:25)? What is he trying to figure out? Why do the brothers think these bad things are happening to them (42:21-22)?

    c.   Who do the brothers think controls the bad things that are happening to them (42:28)? How does their father feel (43:6,

14)? With whom does Israel wrestle (43:14)? In whose name does Joseph's steward comfort Joseph's brothers (43:23)?

18. Genesis 44:1-46:27

    a.   Though Reuben is Jacob's firstborn, Judah (the fourth-born) manages to convince Jacob to let him take Benjamin to Israel. What sort of man has Judah become? What is he willing to do for the rest of his brothers (44:33)?

    b.   Who all sent Joseph to Egypt (45:4-8)? Can two different people do the same thing for different reasons? *Remnant* is an important word in the Scriptures. Why did God send Joseph to Egypt (45:5-8)?

    c.   Beersheba means "the well of the oath." What does God promise Jacob in Beersheba (46:1-4)? How many members of Jacob's family went to Egypt (46:27)?

19. Genesis 46:28-48:22

    a.   What is the occupation of Jacob and his sons (46:32-34)? Who is Jacob's shepherd (48:15)?

    b.   What do the Egyptians do with their land (47:20)? What do the Israelites do with property (47:11, 27)? What else do the Israelites do (47:27)? What blessings are they fulfilling (see 1:28; 9:1)?

    c.   What does Jacob do to Pharaoh (47:7, 10)? What does he do to Joseph, Manasseh and Ephraim (48:9, 15-16, 20)? What blessing is Jacob fulfilling (see 12:2-3)?

20. Genesis 49:1-50:26

    a.   How does Jacob treat Reuben, his firstborn (49:3-4)? Whom does Jacob treat as his firstborn (49:25-26; see 48:22)?

    b.   Which of Jacob's sons will rule over the others (49:8-10)? Which tribe do David and his descendants come from? Does another king come from that tribe too? Who? See study notes for 49:9-10.

    c.   Where does Jacob tell his sons to bury him (49:29-31)? Where will Joseph be buried? See the translation note for 48:22. What does Joseph twice promise the Israelites in 50:24-25?

21. Genesis — Review

You've now read all of Genesis. Well done! Today you will think back over the book.

Pray. Think through the following points.

    a.   Reread your own introduction to Genesis.

    b.   What were important themes in Genesis? How did Moses put his stories together to emphasize these themes? For example, where did you find the themes of creation, sin and recreation or the themes of relationships?

    c.   Flip through Genesis, looking for the verses you marked. What seemed important to Moses?

    d.   What was important to you?

    e.   Look back at your answers to question *d* each day. What were some things you discovered on your own?

    f.   Think back through your answers to question *f* each day. What are some key ways God is telling you to change the way you love, think or live?

    g.   Jesus told his disciples that everything written about him in the Law of Moses had to be fulfilled (Luke 24:44). Which stories made you think about the Messiah and long for him to come? You might think about what the LORD God told the woman, what he promised Abram, what Isaac did on Mt. Moriah, what Jacob promised Judah or something else.

Write

Write a review of Genesis. In the first paragraph, state Moses' key theme and describe a couple ways it shows up in the book. In the second paragraph, write about the things that seemed most important to you and how God is changing you. In the third paragraph, explain one of Jesus' "shadows" in Genesis and how it made you think of him. Finally, end your review with a prayer to Jesus: Address him by one of his titles in Genesis, and thank him for the way he fulfilled one of Genesis' prophecies about the Messiah.

This reading guide follows the story of Israel straight from Genesis into Exodus. If you would like to read each part of the Old Testament when it was written, this is a good place to read through Job (see lessons 378-406).

Exodus

22. Exodus — Introduction

Pray. Then Read, Think and <u>Mark</u>.

Read your study Bible's introduction to Exodus. Think about the questions for each of the following sections. <u>Mark</u> the answers and other things that seem important.

for the ESV Study Bible
- "Title"
  - What does "Exodus" mean?
- "Author"
  - Read the second paragraph.
  - Through which human did God write Exodus?
- "Date and Historical Context"
  - Read the second paragraph.
  - What verse in the Bible helps us date the exodus?
  - When may the exodus have been?
- "Theme"
  - What is the overarching theme of Exodus?
  - What two things does Exodus highlight?
- "Purpose, Occasion, and Background"
  - In which book does Exodus' narrative (or story) begin? In which books does its story continue?
- "Key Themes"
  - Read the first paragraph.
  - What are five key themes in Exodus?

for the NIV Study Bible
- "Title"
  - What does "Exodus" mean?
  - In which book does its narrative (or story) begin? In which books does its story continue?

- "Author and Date of Writing"
  - Through which human did God write Exodus?
- "Chronology"
  - Read the first paragraph.
  - What verse in the Bible helps us date the exodus?
  - When was the Exodus?
- "Themes and Theology"
  - Read the first sentence. The first sentence is the thesis statement for this whole section. It summarizes what the author will tell you in the section.
  - In the thesis statement, underline each of the things God reveals.
  - The author explains each of these things in the following paragraphs. Up the margin beside
    - the second, third and fourth paragraphs write "Name";
    - the fifth paragraph write "Redemption";
    - the sixth paragraph write "Law"; and
    - the seventh paragraph write "Worship."
  - Read the last paragraph. What three great things does God do through Moses in the book of Exodus? Underline them.

Write

Write your own introduction to Exodus. Tell who wrote the book and when. Tell the important themes of Exodus and summarize its message.

23. Exodus 1:1-4:17

a. Moses' birth alludes to (reminds us of something we have read already) the flood and foreshadows (hints at something we have not yet read) the exodus. What is the Hebrew word for basket (2:3)? Read the NIV's translation and study notes for 2:3. When next will Moses be among the reeds? See 13:18 and the translation and study notes there.

b. What is God's name? Read the study notes for 3:14 and 3:15.
  - The Hebrew word for *I am* is HYH'. Read the letters right-to-left. The word is pronounced "ehyeh."
  - The Hebrew word for *He is* is HWHY. It is pronounced "yahweh."
  - In English translations, *the LORD* stands for Yahweh.
  What does God call himself (3:14)? What do we call him (3:15)?

    c.   What had Yahweh told Abraham and Jacob he would do (Genesis 15:13-21; 46:3-4)? Why does he call himself "the God of your fathers—the God of Abraham, Isaac and Jacob" (Exodus 3:16-17)?

24. Exodus 4:18-6:27

    a.   What do the elders of the Israelites do when they see the signs Moses performs (4:30-31)? What will Pharaoh do when he sees them (4:21)? Why will Pharaoh respond that way (4:21)?

    b.   How do Moses and Aaron describe Yahweh when they meet Pharaoh (5:1, 3)? What does Pharaoh think of Yahweh (5:2)?

    c.   Yahweh gives several reasons for coming to help his people in Egypt (6:2-8). List them.

25. Exodus 6:28-9:7

Today and tomorrow you will make a chart of Yahweh's Signs. You will list the sign (or plague), whom Yahweh was scorning with the plague, what the Egyptians would know, how the magicians responded and who hardened Pharaoh's heart.

Get a plain sheet of paper and turn it sideways (landscape). Title it "Yahweh's Signs." Divide the paper into five columns. Head the columns: "Plague," "Scorned," "Will Know," "Magicians" and "Pharaoh."

The table below lists the verses you should check for the information you will put in that cell. If there is an asterisk (*) after the verse, check the study note for that verse in the *NIV Study Bible*. In the *ESV Study Bible*, see the table "The Battle between Yahweh and the Rulers of Egypt." If there is no verse, you may leave the cell blank.

Plague	Scorned	Will Know	Magicians	Pharaoh
7:8-13	4:3*		7:11-12	7:13
7:14-24	7:19*, 20*	7:17	7:22	7:22
7:25-8:15	8:2*	8:10	8:7	8:15
8:16-19			8:18-19	8:19
8:20-32		8:22		8:32
9:1-7	9:3*			9:7

(3) Think about and answer the questions. (4) Return to your bookmark.

26. Exodus 9:8-11:10

Complete the chart from yesterday.

Plague	Scorned	Will Know	Magicians	Pharaoh
9:8-12			9:11	9:12
9:13-35	9:23-24	9:14		9:34-35
10:1-20		10:2		10:1, 20
10:21-29	10:21*			10:27
11:1-10	11:5; 12:12, 29, 30	11:7		

27. Exodus 12:1-13:16

a. What must Israelites remove from their homes (12:15, 18-20)? What is it a symbol of? See the study note for 12:15 (*NIV*).
b. Which people did Yahweh spare (12:21-23)? What does the Passover lamb foreshadow? See the study notes for 12:21, 46.
c. What and who belong to Yahweh (13:12)? Why (13:14-16?

28. Exodus 13:17-15:21

a. Add this sign to your chart (14:4, 8, 17-18). What did Yahweh do for the Israelites (14:30)? How did they respond (14:31)?
b. On what occasions in Genesis did Yahweh make dry land appear and set his people on it (14:21-22)? See Genesis 1:9-10; 2:8-9; 8:13-18.
c. Whom did Yahweh defeat at the Red Sea (15:3-4, 11)? Whom will he attack next (15:14-16)?

29. Exodus 15:22-17:16

a. Is Yahweh unable to give the Israelites water (15:22-24)? Why does he not give them water (15:25b)? How many springs and palm trees does Yahweh provide at Elim (15:27)?
b. Why might Yahweh let the manna rot the next day? What do you think he wants the Israelites to do?
c. How do the Israelites test Yahweh (17:7)?

30. Exodus 18:1-20:26

a. Jethro is a high priest of Midian, a different nation. How does he respond when he hears "all the good things Yahweh had done for Israel" (18:9-12)?

b. Describe what things sound, look and feel like when Yahweh comes down on the mountain (19:16-19). What has happened to the mountain (19:23)? What must happen to anyone who touches the mountain (19:12)?

c. How do the people feel (20:18)? What will their fear of God do (20:20)? What will Israel be if they obey Yahweh fully and keep his covenant (19:5-6)?

31. Exodus 21:1-23:19

a. What is God more concerned with: the action or the intention (21:12-14)? What is the punishment for unintentional killing (21:13)? What is the punishment for intentional killing (21:12, 14)? What other sins are punished with death (21:15, 16, 17, 22-23, 29; 22:3, 18, 19, 20)?

b. What is "restitution" (22:3)? Give an example of a law that requires restitution (21:18-19, 33-34, 36). Sometimes restitution is 1 for 1, sometimes 2 for 1 and sometimes 4 or 5 for 1. What makes the difference (22:1, 4, 14, 15)?

c. Whom does Yahweh himself defend (22:22-27)? How must Yahweh's people treat the poor (22:26-27; 23:3, 6)?

32. Exodus 23:20-26:37

a. Whom does Yahweh send to lead the people (23:20-23)?

b. What is the Book of the Covenant (24:7)? See study note. How do the people and Yahweh seal the covenant (24:7-8)?

c. When Moses and the elders go up to see God, what do they see (24:9-11)? What is the Israelites' tabernacle to look like (25:40; 26:30; 27:8)?

33. Exodus 27:1-28:43

a. Look at Stephen Tam's three-dimensional (3D) model of the tabernacle (www.3dbibleproject.com). Use the next viewpoint triangle for a tour of the tabernacle.

b. On a plain sheet of paper, draw the courtyard, the tabernacle and its furnishings. Use the pictures in your study Bible to help you.

c. Now color it, following the instructions carefully.

(3) Think about and answer the questions. (4) Return to your bookmark.

34. Exodus 29:1-31:18

a. When Yahweh came down to Mt. Sinai, could the people go up to meet with him (19:20-23)? Why not? Read 29:42-46. How will Yahweh live among his people Israel? Where will he dwell? Who will go between Yahweh and the Israelites? What must be done to his dwelling and to the mediators (people who go between)?

b. Whom does the Spirit choose to make the tabernacle and its furnishings (31:2, 6)? How does he prepare them (31:3, 6)?

c. Why are there two tablets of stone? See the study note for 31:18. Who writes on the tablets (31:18)? What word in 31:18 sounds like "Scriptures"? How do the Israelites know that the Law really is God's Word (24:9-18; 31:18)?

35. Exodus 32:1-33:23

a. What do the Israelites want gods to do (32:1)? What name does Aaron give the gods, and what does he say they have done (32:4-5)?

b. What does Yahweh want to do to the Israelites because they worshiped the calf (32:10)?

c. How serious is Yahweh about idolatry and his holiness (32:26-29)? What does he demand of his people?

36. Exodus 34:1-36:7

a. When Yahweh proclaims his name, he tells Moses what he is like and what he does. Write out and memorize Yahweh's description of himself (34:6-7). (Write "the LORD" as "Yahweh.")

b. When did Moses' face become radiant (34:34-35)? What happens to us when we turn to the Lord and are in Christ (2 Corinthians 3:13, 16-18)?

c. When his people had to build him a tent, what (or whom) did Yahweh give them (35:30, 34)? How did he prepare these men (35:31, 34)?

37. Exodus 36:8-38:31

a. *Cherubim* is the plural form of *cherub*; so it means "cherubs." What are cherubim (36:8; see also Genesis 3:24; Ezekiel 10:18-20)? What metal does Bezalel use to make them (Exodus 37:7)?

b. What metal do Bezalel and Oholiab cover all the wooden items and even the frames with (36:34; 37:2, 4, 11, 26, 28)? What metal does he use for the lampstand and the rings (37:3, 13, 17, 24, 27)? What color cloth do they use to make the curtains (36:8)? Where else are there cherubim in a house of gold surrounded by blue? What is the Tabernacle?

c. How much silver, gold and cloth did the Israelites bring for the sanctuary (36:3-7; 38:24, 25, 29)? Where had this stuff come from (3:21-22; 12:35-36)?

38. Exodus 39:1-40:38

a. What phrase is repeated in 39:1, 5, 7, 21, 27, 29, 30? What work in Genesis does Exodus 39:32; 42-43 remind you of?

b. Why does Aaron wear "Holy to Yahweh" on a plate on his forehead? Look back at the section in Exodus where Yahweh described how and why to make the plate. Why does Aaron wear bells on the hem of his robe (28:33-35)?

c. What does Moses do when all the work is finished (39:42-43)? What does Yahweh do when all the work is finished (40:34-35)? How would you feel if you had been there?

39. Exodus — Review

Pray. Think through the following points.

a. Reread your own introduction to the book.

b. What were important themes in Exodus? How does Yahweh fulfill his covenant promises to Abraham, Isaac and Jacob? What all does Yahweh do to set up a kingdom in which he lives among and rules his obedient people as their holy king?

c. Flip through Exodus, looking for the verses you marked. What seemed important to Moses?

d. What was important to you?

e. Look back at your answers to question *d* each day. What were some things you discovered on your own?

f. Think back through your answers to question *f* each day. What are some key ways God is telling you to change the way you love, think or live?

g. Jesus told his disciples that everything written about him in the Law of Moses had to be fulfilled (Luke 24:44). Which stories in Exodus made you think about the Messiah and long for him to come? You might think about the Passover, the giving of God's law on the mountain, the Tabernacle and high priest or something else.

(3) Think about and answer the questions. (4) Return to your bookmark.

Write

Write a review of Exodus. In the first paragraph, state Moses' main themes and point out where those themes show up as Yahweh sets up his kingdom. In the second paragraph, write about the things that seemed most important to you and how God is changing you. In the third paragraph, explain one of Jesus' "shadows" in Exodus and how it made you think of him. Finally, end your review with a prayer to Jesus: Address him by one of his titles in Exodus, and thank him for the way he fulfilled one of Exodus's prophecies about the Messiah.

Leviticus

40. Leviticus — Introduction

Pray. Then Read, Think and Mark.

Read your study Bible's introduction to Leviticus. Think about the questions for each of the following sections. Mark the answers and other things that seem important.

for the ESV Study Bible

- "Theme"
  - ○ What is Leviticus an unfolding of?
  - ○ Why must the Israelites deal with sin and impurity?
- "Interpretive Issues"
  - ○ Read the paragraph *Ritual and ethical commands.* What is the whole of the book of Leviticus concerned with?
  - ○ Read the paragraph *Unclean, clean, holy.*
  - ○ Read the paragraph *How ritual purity relates to moral purity.* What do the ritual states represent or symbolize? How does the Lord remind the people to seek moral purity?
- "Key Themes"
  - ○ What are the key themes of Leviticus?

for the NIV Study Bible

- "Title"
  - ○ Read from "Exodus gave the directions ..." to the end of the paragraph.
  - ○ When did Yahweh give Leviticus to his people?
- "Theological Themes"
  - ○ Read the first paragraph.
  - ○ What has Yahweh set his people apart to be?
  - ○ What does he teach them in Leviticus?

- o What does "holy" mean in Leviticus?
- o What is the key thought of the book?
- o In Leviticus, what does physical perfection symbolize?

Write

Write your own introduction to Leviticus. Tell who wrote the book, when, where and for whom. Identify the key word in Leviticus and explain the key themes. Describe what Yahweh demands of his peo-ple in their relationships with him and with each other.

Complete the following outline and write it after your introduc-tion.

- A. Holy _____ (1-7)
- B. Holy Priests (8-10)
- C. Clean and _____ (____)
- D. Yahweh Makes You Clean (____)
- E. _____ Living (17-26)
- F. Vows (27)

41. Leviticus 1:1-5:13

- a. What does the burnt offering do (1:4)? What does it act as? (See the study note for 1:3.)
- b. Who eats the grain offering (2:2-3)? Who eats the fellowship offering (3:3-5)? Who eats the rest? See 7:15-17.
- c. What do you think the altar area of the tabernacle would look like (1:5, 11, 14-16; 3:2, 8, 13; 4;25, 30, 34)? What do you think Yahweh is trying to show? (Look back at your introduc-tion.)

42. Leviticus 5:14-7:38

- a. What is the difference between the sin and the guilt offer-ings? Compare 5:13 with 5:16. What extra requirements are in the rules about the guilt offering that are not in the rules about the sin offering? (See the study note for 5:15.)
- b. What happens if you do not know you have sinned (5:17)? Why does Yahweh give his people this system of sacrifices? What are the last five words in 5:16, 18?
- c. What happens to Aaron and then to the son who will follow him (6:20, 22)? Whom else will that happen to? (The Hebrew word here is *mashiyakh*.)

43. Leviticus 8:1-10:20

a. What all must Moses do to make Aaron and his sons ready to serve Yahweh as priests? List the steps in chapter 8.
b. What must Aaron do before he goes into the tent to meet with Yahweh? List the steps in chapter 9.
c. How does Yahweh respond when Nadab and Abihu offer fire against God's command (10:1-3)? Why? Look for the keyword in 10:3.

44. Leviticus 11:1-13:46

"Unclean" does not mean dirty. It means something that God will not accept in worship. People and things can be clean or unclean.

a. What happens when a clean person or thing touches something unclean (11:31-40)? Which spreads, cleanness or uncleanness?
b. Write out 11:44-45 and meditate on it. Why must Yahweh's people keep clean? What does their cleanness show (11:44-45)?
c. Who checks for uncleanness (13:1-3)? What do those people normally do? Why do you think Yahweh has chosen them to check?

45. Leviticus 13:47-14:57

a. What happens to unclean people (13:46)? What happens to unclean things (13:52)?
b. Do you recall a time when defilement was spreading within a "house," God emptied it, the people from the house did something with two birds (one over water and the other over land) and then Yahweh cleansed the house and let the people and animals return to live in it? Think about Leviticus 14 and Genesis 6-9.
c. Who will put a spreading mold or leprous disease in a house (14:34)? Who provides a way for the house to be cleansed (14:53)?

46. Leviticus 15:1-16:34

a. How is a man or woman cleansed from an unusual discharge (15:13-15, 28-30)? How are they cleansed from usual things like sex or a period (15:18)?

    b.   Where may Aaron the high priest not go (16:2)? Why not (16:2)? How often may Aaron go there (16:29-30, 34)?

    c.   Why must the priest make atonement for the Most Holy Place (16:16)? What and whom does the atonement cleanse from all their sins (16:30, 33-34)? What did our high priest do (Hebrews 9:11-14)?

47. Leviticus 17:1-19:37

    a.   What is in a creature's blood (17:11)? When someone gave an animal to the priest and he splashed its blood on the altar, what was the priest showing?

    b.   When people do detestable things, what happens to them and to the land they live on (18:24-25)? Then what does Yahweh do to the land (18:25)? And what does the land do to the people (18:28)?

    c.   What is the second great command (19:18)? Write it out and meditate on it.

48. Leviticus 20:1-23:44

    a.   Must the Israelites try all by themselves to be holy (20:7-8)? Why must Israel make a distinction between clean and unclean things (20:24-26)? How does Yahweh make something holy (20:24-26)?

    b.   What sort of animals must the Israelites offer as sacrifices (22:18-20, 25)? Why must the Israelites keep Yahweh's commands about sacrifices (22:31-33)?

    c.   You're going to draw something like a clock. Draw a circle, but start numbering by writing 1 where you would normally see 3. (The month that the Israelites counted as first happens during the time when our third month happens.) Working clockwise around the outside of your clock-shaped calendar, write the date and name of each festival and draw a line from its date to the point on the clock where that date would fall. Include the following festivals: Passover, Unleavened Bread, Firstfruits, Weeks, Trumpets, Day of Atonement, Tabernacles, Sacred Assembly.

49. Leviticus 24:1-25:55

    a.   When the man blasphemed the Name, what did he do (24:11, 15-16)? What does Yahweh say the punishment for blasphemy is (24:16)? For what other sin does Yahweh prescribe this same punishment (24:17, 21)?

b. What do Israelites do on the Sabbath day (23:3)? What does the land do in the Sabbath year (25:1-5)?

c. What happens in the Jubilee Year (25:10)? To whom does the land belong (25:23-24)? How should the Israelites help the poor and foreigners (25:35-38)?

50. Leviticus 26:1-27:34

a. Use one word to describe each type of blessing in 26:4-5 (& 10), 6, 7, 9, 11-12, 13.

b. The word *if* introduces five types of curses, each worse than the former. Use one word to describe each level of curse in 26:16-17, 19-20, 22, 25-26, 29-33. When Yahweh causes his people pain and suffering, what does he want them to do (26:18, 21, 23, 27, 40-41)?

c. How much must the Israelites pay to redeem, or buy back, something they dedicate to Yahweh (for example, a house, 27:15)? Can the Israelites redeem something devoted to Yahweh, something that is set aside to be purged (27:28)?

51. Leviticus — Review

Pray. Think through the following points.

a. Reread your own introduction to the book, including your outline.

b. What is the keyword in Leviticus? Why must the Israelites be holy? In what ways does Yahweh demand that his people be holy? How can they be holy?

c. Flip through Leviticus, looking for the verses you marked. What seemed important to Moses?

d. What was important to you?

e. Look back at your answers to question *d* each day. What were some things you discovered on your own?

f. Think back through your answers to question *f* each day. What are some key ways God is telling you to change the way you love, think or live?

g. Jesus told his disciples that everything written about him in the Law of Moses had to be fulfilled (Luke 24:44). Which stories or laws in Leviticus made you think about the Messiah and long for him to come? You might think about the sacrifices, laws of clean- and uncleanness or the Day of Atonement.

(3) Think about and answer the questions. (4) Return to your bookmark.

Write

Write a review of Leviticus. In the first paragraph, state the keyword and summarize what Yahweh teaches his people about it. In the second paragraph, write about the things that seemed most important to you and how God is changing you. In the third paragraph, explain one of Jesus' "shadows" in Leviticus and how it made you think of him. Finally, end your review with a prayer to Jesus: Address him by one of his titles in Leviticus, and thank him for the way he fulfilled one of Leviticus's prophecies about the Messiah.

Numbers

52. Numbers — Introduction

Pray. Then Read, Think and <u>Mark</u>.

Read your study Bible's introduction to Numbers. Think about the questions for each of the following sections. <u>Mark</u> the answers and other things that seem important.

for the ESV Study Bible

- "Author, Date, and Title"
  - o Read the first paragraph. Who wrote Numbers?
- "Theme"
  - o What does Numbers show being fulfilled gradually?
- "Purpose, Occasion, and Background"
  - o Read the first paragraph.
  - o Where does the book begin? Where does it end? What happens in between?
- "Key Themes"
  - o Read the first paragraph.
  - o What four things (elements) did God promise Abraham, Isaac and Jacob (the patriarchs)?
- "Outline"
  - o Read the first paragraph and the Roman numerals.
  - o How many major sections (blocks of material) does Numbers consist of?
  - o Where does each section happen?

for the NIV Study Bible

- "Title"
  - o What does Numbers present?
- "Author and Date"
  - o Read the first paragraph. Who wrote Numbers?

- "Theological Teaching"
  - Read the first paragraph. What does the Lord lead Israel to do?
  - Read the second paragraph. In the book of Numbers, what frightening, new truth (sobering reality) does Israel learn about the God who made a covenant with them and has delivered them from Egypt to be his people?
  - Read the next to last paragraph. What is God still determined to do?
- "Structure and Outline"
  - Read the first paragraph and the Roman numerals.
  - How many major divisions does Numbers have?
  - Where does each division happen?

Write

Write your own introduction to Numbers. Tell who wrote the book and what it is about. Explain the important themes: God's plan for Israel and what gets in the way. Outline the book under five or six headings.

53. Numbers 1:1-2:34

a. Whom does Yahweh tell Moses and Aaron to count (1:2-3)? How many total men are there (1:46)?
b. Draw a map of Israel's camp. (See the map under chapter 2 in the NIV Study Bible.) Within each division (or tribe), write the number of its soldiers.
c. Outside each camp (group of three tribes), write the name of the camp. (See study notes on 2:3-7, 10-12, 14, 18-22, 25, 27, 29.) Beside each camp's name, write the number of its soldiers.

54. Numbers 3:1-4:49

a. To whom do all firstborn boys belong (3:13)? When did he set them apart (make them holy) for himself?
b. Whom does Yahweh take in place of the firstborn sons (3:40-41)? How many of them are there (3:39)? What is the ratio of soldiers to Levites?
c. Which colors of cloth does Yahweh say the Kohathites should use to cover the most holy things (4:6, 7, 8, 9, 11, 12, 13)? When else did Yahweh use these colors (Exodus 26:1, 31, 36; 28:6, 15, 31)?

55. Numbers 5:1-6:27

a. Yahweh tells Moses how to use an ordeal to test a woman's faithfulness and purity. What all is in the water she must drink (5:17, 23-24)? How does the ordeal work (5:27-28)?

b. Why would someone become a Nazir (6:1-2)? What is the symbol of his or her dedication and holiness (6:5)?

c. Write out and meditate on the blessing Yahweh gives Aaron to use (6:24-26). What does the blessing do (6:27)?

56. Numbers 7:1-8:26

a. What earlier chapter records the setting up of the tabernacle (7:1; follow the cross-reference)? Where is Israel at the end of Leviticus? Which chapters in the Bible record the events of the first month of the second year after the exodus (Exodus 40:17; Numbers 9:1)? (The *ESV Study Bible* has a helpful chart under Numbers 7.)

b. After Moses dedicates the altar, what does he hear (7:89)? Where?

c. What does Yahweh give as gifts (8:19)? What are they to do where (8:19)? What do they do first (8:21)?

57. Numbers 9:1-11:35

a. How does Yahweh lead the Israelites (9:15-24)? How do they respond?

b. How long is Israel in the Desert of Sinai (Numbers 10:11-13; Exodus 19:1)?

c. How does Yahweh respond when his people complain about the way he leads and cares for them (11:1, 33)?

58. Numbers 12:1-14:45

a. When Yahweh tells Moses to send the explorers, how does he describe the land of Canaan (13:2)?

b. How do the people respond to the explorers' report (14:1-4)? What does Yahweh say they have done wrong (14:11)? What do Caleb and Joshua say (14:8-9)?

c. When the Israelites presume that Yahweh is with them and that they can take the land, what happens (14:45)? What is the difference between believing and presuming (14:41-44)?

(3) Think about and answer the questions. (4) Return to your bookmark.

59. Numbers 15:1-16:50

a. After Yahweh says he will punish the rebellious Israelites with 40 years of suffering, what does he promise them again (15:2, 18)?

b. What may Israel do to atone for (cover) unintentional sin (15:22-29)? What is the punishment for defiant sin (15:30-31)? What example does Yahweh give (15:32-36)?

c. When Korah, Dathan, Abiram and 250 others rise up against Moses, whom are they opposing (16:11)? How does Yahweh respond (16:31-35)?

60. Numbers 17:1-19:22

a. When the whole Israelite community grumbles against Moses and Aaron, what does Yahweh do (16:49)? What do the Israelites fear will happen (17:12-13)?

b. Whom does Yahweh appoint to keep his wrath from falling on the Israelites (18:5)? How do they do that (15:25, 28; 16:46-48)?

c. What is one way people become unclean (19:14-16)? Is this happening often? How should the priest use the ashes (19:17-18)?

61. Numbers 20:1-21:35

a. What does Yahweh do when the Israelites grumble (21:6)? What does he do when they confess and pray (21:8-9)?

b. Who are the first kings the Israelites kill? Which is the first land they capture and settle in (21:21-35)?

c. Draw a map to show where Israel goes, whom they fight against and what land they take.
    - *ESV Study Bible*: Use the maps under Numbers 20 (The Journey to Canaan) and Numbers 22 (Israel Defeats Og and Sihon).
    - *Zondervan Study Bibles* (KJV, NASB, NIV): Use maps 3 (Exodus and Conquest of Canaan) and 4 (Land of the Twelve Tribes) in the back of your Bible.

   Label the following:
    - 20:14 – Kadesh, Edom
    - 21:3 – Hormah
    - 21:4 – Red Sea
    - 21:11 – Moab
    - 21:24 – Ammon, Arnon River, Jabbok River; shade in the area Israel took from Sihon

o   21:33 – Edrei

62. Numbers 22:1-23:30

a.   Where is Balaam from (22:5)? Is he an Israelite? Who does Balaam say is God (22:18)? Which God meets with Balaam and tells him what to say (23:3-5)?

b.   Balaam talks about curses, blessings and God (23:7-11). Which blessing does Yahweh tell Balaam to repeat (Genesis 12:2-3; 15:5-6)? What blessing does Balaam want to inherit (Numbers 23:10)?

c.   Who is king in Israel (23:21)? In all the Bible, who is the first person to call God king? Read the study note for 23:21.

63. Numbers 24:1-25:18

a.   Who is Israel's king (24:7)? What will he do to Agag and the Amalekites? What happened the last time the Israelites fought the Amalekites (14:39-45)?

b.   What do stars do (Genesis 1:17-18)? What type of person holds a scepter? Who is Jacob's star and Israel's scepter? Read the study note for Numbers 24:17.

c.   When Balaam could not curse Israel, what does he advise the Moabites and the Midianites to do to get God to be angry with Israel (31:16)? How do the Moabites and Midianites get the Israelites to be unfaithful to Yahweh (25:1-3, 18)?

64. Numbers 26:1-27:23

a.   How many men die in the wilderness (26:64-65; see also 1:46)? What does their death teach you about Yahweh?

b.   Who gives Moses power to lead (Numbers 11:25)? Who will help Joshua lead (27:18)?

c.   How does Yahweh tell Moses what to do (for example in 27:5-6, 11, 12, 18, 22; see also 12:8)? How will Yahweh tell Joshua what to do (27:21)?

65. Numbers 28:1-30:16

a.   What must the Israelites be sure to do (28:2)? What kinds of food does Yahweh tell them to offer him (28:4-5, 7)?

b.   On which occasions must the Israelites present offerings to Yahweh (28:3-4, 10, 14, 16, 26; 29:1, 7, 12)? How are the days of sacred assembly (holy convocation) different from the daily,

(3) Think about and answer the questions. (4) Return to your bookmark.

Sabbath and monthly offerings (28:18-19, 22)? What seems to be the most important assembly (29:12-38)?

c. What must you do if you make a vow to Yahweh (30:2)? Who may forbid a vow and nullify it, make it nothing (30:5, 8, 12)?

66. Numbers 31:1-32:42

a. Why must the Israelites kill the Midianite women (31:15-17; see 25:1-6, 16-18)? Why does Yahweh allow the girls who have not slept with a man to live (see the study note for 31:18)?

b. What happens to the Israelites when they obey Yahweh and kill the Midianites (31:19)? How must the Israelites and their spoils be cleansed (31:22-24)?

c. To which tribes does Yahweh give land on the east side of the Jordan (32:33)? What must those tribes do before they settle in their own land (32:28-30)?

67. Numbers 33:1-36:13

a. What must the Israelites do when they go into the land (33:52)? What will happen if they do not do it (33:55-56)?

b. Who should put a murderer to death (35:19)? What do the cities of refuge provide (35:10-12)?

c. What does bloodshed do (35:33)? How can the Israelites atone for (cover) polluted land (35:33)? But if someone is killed accidentally, whose death seems to cover the land (35:25)?

68. Numbers — Review

Pray. Think through the following points.

a. Reread your own introduction to the book, including your outline.

b. At the beginning of Numbers, what does Yahweh promise the people, and where does he send them? What do they do, and where do they end up? What happens along the way?

c. Flip through Numbers, looking for the verses you marked. What seemed important to Moses?

d. What was important to you?

e. Look back at your answers to question *d* each day. What were some things you discovered on your own?

f. Think back through your answers to question *f* each day. What are some key ways God is telling you to change the way you love, think or live?

g. Jesus told his disciples that everything written about him in the Law of Moses had to be fulfilled (Luke 24:44). Which stories or laws in Numbers made you think about the Messiah and long for him to come? You might think about water from the rock, the bronze snake or Balaam's messages.

Write

Write a review of Numbers. In the first paragraph, describe what happens in each of the three locations in Numbers. In the second paragraph, write about the things that seemed most important to you and how God is changing you. In the third paragraph, explain one of Jesus' "shadows" in Numbers and how it made you think of him. Finally, end your review with a prayer to Jesus: Address him by one of his titles in Numbers, and thank him for the way he fulfilled one of Numbers' prophecies about the Messiah.

Deuteronomy

69. Deuteronomy — Introduction

Pray. Then Read, Think and <u>Mark</u>.

Read your study Bible's introduction to Deuteronomy. Think about the questions for each of the following sections. <u>Mark</u> the answers and other things that seem important.

Important Words and Their Meanings

- Former Prophets: Joshua to 2 Kings, except for Ruth
- Prologue: an introduction
- Ratify: confirm. For example, "Yes, this is the covenant. Yes, we agree to it."
- Stipulation: a condition, what Yahweh demands of Israel
- Suzerain: a conquering king
- Vassal: a conquered servant

for the ESV Study Bible

- Author and Title
  - What does *Deuteronomy* mean?
  - Who does Deuteronomy say its author is?
  - Which passages in the New Testament say Moses wrote most of Deuteronomy?
- Structure
  - What is Deuteronomy's structure like?
- Purpose, Occasion and Background
  - Read the second paragraph. How does Moses motivate or encourage Israel to obey?
  - Read the third paragraph. What characteristics of God does Moses talk about?
- Function of Deuteronomy in the Bible
  - What themes does Deuteronomy bring together?

- o As we read Joshua-2 Kings, which book's words and language do we often find?
- Outline
  - o What are Deuteronomy's seven main sections?

for the NIV Study Bible

- Title
  - o What does *Deuteronomy* mean?
- Author and Date of Writing
  - o Who does Deuteronomy say its author is?
  - o Which people in the New Testament say Moses wrote most of Deuteronomy?
- Special Function in the Bible
  - o Read the first four sentences.
  - o After reading Numbers, what do we expect to happen next?
  - o Where are the Israelites at the end of Deuteronomy?
  - o Read the last paragraph ("But in that long pause ...").
  - o What does Moses remind the people of in Deuteronomy?
  - o What does Deuteronomy help us do as we read the history of Israel in the Former Prophets?
- Theological Teaching and Purpose
  - o Read the first paragraph. What form does Deuteronomy have?
  - o Read the second paragraph.
  - o What themes are important in Deuteronomy?
  - o As we read the Former Prophets, which book's style and themes do we keep running into?
- Structure and Outline
  - o Read the third and fourth sentences ("But it also bears ...").
  - o What is the structure of Deuteronomy like?
  - o What are the five main sections of Deuteronomy?

Write

Write your own introduction to Deuteronomy. Tell who wrote the book and what form (or structure) it has. State the important themes. Explain how those themes prepare Israel to settle in the land as Yahweh's people. Outline Deuteronomy under five or seven headings.

(3) Think about and answer the questions. (4) Return to your bookmark.

70. Deuteronomy 1:1-2:37

a. How did Yahweh keep his covenant with Abraham (1:8-10)? Read Genesis 22:17. What did he promise Israel's ancestors (1:21)? What tenses—past, present or future—did Moses use when he talked about Yahweh giving the land to Israel (1:20-21)?

b. What did Yahweh say when Israel refused to enter the land (1:34-35)? Then what did he do (2:14-15)? But what did he do for everyone else (2:7)?

c. Who are the descendants of Esau (2:8)? Why did Yahweh give Israel none of Esau's land or of Lot's land (2:4-6, 9-12, 17-22)? What did Yahweh do for the descendants of Esau and the descendants of Lot (2:21-22)?

71. Deuteronomy 3:1-4:43

a. Why will Moses not enter the land (1:37; 3:26; 4:21)? What did Yahweh tell Moses to do for Joshua (3:28)? What will Joshua do (3:28)?

b. What happened at Baal Peor (4:3-4)? What will happen if Israel does not obey (4:25-28)? Then what will Yahweh do if they seek him (4:29-31)?

c. Look back at your outline of Deuteronomy. Which section does today's reading come under? Throughout today's reading, who is the subject of most of the sentences, that is, who is the main character?

72. Deuteronomy 4:44-6:25

a. Which section of Deuteronomy does 4:44-45 begin? Which relationship are the first three commandments about (5:7-11)? Which relationships are the last six commandments about (5:16-21)?

b. Read 6:1-3 to explain why Yahweh gave his laws to Israel: What does Yahweh want Israel to do (6:2)? How (6:2)? Then what will happen (6:3)?

c. Deuteronomy 6:4-5 is called "The Great Shema" because it begins with the Hebrew word *Shema*, "Hear." It summarizes the whole Law in one command. Write out that command.

73. Deuteronomy 7:1-8:20

a. What must Israel do to the seven nations in the land (7:1-2)? Who are the Israelites (7:6)? If Israel does not destroy the nations, what will the nations become (7:4, 16)?
b. How did Yahweh treat Israel in the wilderness (8:5)? What did he do to them (8:2)? Why (8:3)?
c. The peoples of Canaan worship their gods to get babies, grain, wine, oil and animals. Who will give these things to Israel (7:13)? Why is Yahweh so kind to Israel (7:7-9)? What will Yahweh do if Israel is satisfied with the things he gives them and forgets Yahweh himself (8:10-14, 19-20)?

74. Deuteronomy 9:1-11:32

a. Why will Yahweh drive out the nations before Israel (9:4-5)? What is Israel like (9:6)? When did Israel make Yahweh their God angry (9:7, 8, 22, 23)?
b. Yahweh asks five things of Israel. What five things must they do (10:12-13)? What must Israel do to stop being stiff-necked (10:16)?
c. What does Moses set before the people (11:26-28)? What will the Suzerain do if the vassal is faithful to obey and love him (11:8-9, 14-15, 22-23)? What will the Suzerain do if the vassal serves other suzerains (11:16-17)?

75. Deuteronomy 12:1-14:29

a. Where must the Israelites sacrifice animals (meat) (12:5-7)? When the Israelites eat meat at home, what must they not eat (12:23)? Why (12:23)?
b. What must the Israelites do to anyone who calls them to follow other gods (13:5, 9)? What must they do before destroying a town that they have heard is worshiping other gods (13:14)?
c. To whom does the tithe of the crops belong (14:22-23)? To whom does he feed it (14:23)? What must the Israelites do when they eat with Yahweh at his house (14:26)?

76. Deuteronomy 15:1-17:20

a. How did Yahweh treat the Israelites when they were poor slaves (15:14-15)? How must Israelites treat the poor (15:7-8, 10-11)? How will Yahweh treat those who care for the poor (14:29; 15:10, 18)?

(3) Think about and answer the questions. (4) Return to your bookmark.   45

b. What principle (or idea) must the judges follow as they lead the people (16:20)? What does a bribe lead judges to do (16:19)?

c. What would a king do with many horses or much gold (17:16-17; see 20:1)? What will many wives do (17:17)? What must the king do with the law (17:18-19)?

77. Deuteronomy 18:1-21:23

a. How does Yahweh use a prophet (18:18)? Name a few prophets whom Yahweh our God raised up after Moses (18:15). Who was *the* Prophet he raised up? Follow the cross reference for "I will raise up for them a prophet" in 18:18.

b. Why should Israel not be afraid of enemies greater than them (20:1)? What rules should Israel follow when they fight against a faraway city (20:10-15)? What rules must they follow when they fight against a city of one of the seven nations (20:16-18)?

c. What does it show if someone is hung on a tree (21:23)? Can you name someone who was hung on a tree? Follow the cross-reference for "under God's curse" in 21:23.

78. Deuteronomy 22:1-24:22

a. What must the Israelites not mix, but keep separate (22:5, 9, 10, 11)? Which types of people may not enter Yahweh's assembly (23:1, 2, 3)? Why must Israel keep their camp holy (23:14)?

b. What is the punishment if someone has sex with someone he or she is not married to (22:21, 22, 24)? What is the punishment for rape (22:25-26)? What is the punishment for kidnapping (24:7)?

c. Yahweh commands Israel to live justly. Make a list of the things and people they must look out for and take care of (22:4, 6-7, 8; 24:1-4, 6, 7, 10-11, 12-13, 14-15, 17, 19-21; 25:3, 4, 5).

79. Deuteronomy 25:1-28:14

a. How must Israel protect (1) a guilty person (25:3), (2) a widow who has no son to care for her (25:6) and (3) people who buy things (25:13-16)? How must Israel provide for Levites, foreigners, the fatherless and widows who live in their towns (26:12)?

b. In Yahweh's covenant with Israel, what do Israel and Yahweh call each other (26:17, 18)? What has Israel now become (27:9)? What must Israel do (27:10)?

c. Fold a sheet in your notebook in half from top to bottom. Label the left half "Blessings" and the right half "Curses." You will fill in the first column today and the second tomorrow. In the left column, list the blessings from 28:3-6.

80. Deuteronomy 28:15-29:29

a. Yesterday, you began filling in a table of blessings and curses. You listed the blessings in the left column. Now in the right column, list the curses in 28:16-19.

b. Who will send a nation against Israel to destroy them (28:49-51)? What will the nation do (28:52)? How bad will the siege be (28:53)?

c. What three things do the Israelites not have (29:4)? What will Yahweh do to rebellious people who still expect him to bless them (29:20)? In the end what will Yahweh do to the nation of Israel (28:64; 29:27-28)?

81. Deuteronomy 30:1-31:29

a. After Yahweh scatters Israel among the nations, what must they do (30:2)? Then what will Yahweh do (30:3-4)? How will Yahweh help Israel love him (30:6)?

b. Whom does Moses call as witnesses to Yahweh's covenant with Israel (30:19)? Whom did people normally call as witnesses to their covenants? See the study note for 30:19. What must Israel do as these witnesses watch (30:19)? Who is that (30:20)?

c. What four things did Yahweh and Moses do to make sure the Israelites listened to the law, learned the law and kept the law? Read (1) 31:9, 24; (2) 31:26; (3) 31:10-13; (4) 31:19, 21-22.

82. Deuteronomy 31:30-32:47

a. What did Yahweh do for Israel (32:10, 13)? What did Israel do to Yahweh (32:15-18)? How did Yahweh respond (32:19, 21, 23)?

b. What did the nations think (32:27)? What will Yahweh do to the nations and Israel (32:41, 43)? How important are the words of Moses' song (32:47)?

    c.   In this song (32:1-43), what does Moses call Yahweh in 4, 15, 18, 30, 31; in 6; in 8; in 15; and in 39? Moses says the 'sons of gods' are not God (32:8, 17, 21, 31, 39). Instead, what four things does Yahweh call them (32:12, 16, 16, 17)?

83. Deuteronomy 32:48-34:12

    a.   Who is the hero of Moses' blessing? How does Moses describe him at the beginning of the blessing (33:2-3, 5)? At the end (33:26-27, 29)?

    b.   What did Levi do for Yahweh (33:9)? What do the Levites do in Israel (33:10)? Which tribe was Moses from (Exodus 2:1, 10)?

    c.   Follow the cross-reference for "like Moses" (34:10). Who did Moses promise would come (18:15, 18)? Had he come when Deuteronomy 34 was written (34:10-12)? Has he come yet?

84. Deuteronomy — Review

Pray. Think through the following points.

You've now read all of Deuteronomy and all of the Books of Moses. Well done! Today you will think back over the book.

    a.   Reread your own introduction to the book, including the outline.

    b.   Think about Deuteronomy's context, main theme and form. Context: Where is Israel, and what are they about to do? Main theme: What is the most important idea that Moses emphasizes over and over again? Form: How does Moses use the form of a suzerain-vassal treaty to encourage Israel to be faithful to Yahweh their God as they prepare to possess the land? What does Moses say in each section of the treaty?

    c.   Flip through Deuteronomy, looking for the verses you marked. What seemed important to Moses?

    d.   What was important to you?

    e.   Look back at your answers to question *d* each day. What were some things you discovered on your own?

    f.   Think back through your answers to question *f* each day. What are some key ways God is telling you to change the way you love, think or live?

    g.   Jesus told his disciples that everything written about him in the Law of Moses had to be fulfilled (Luke 24:44). Which parts of Moses' speeches made you think about the Messiah? You might think about the laws for the king or the prophet Moses said Yahweh would raise up after him.

Write

Write a review of Deuteronomy. In the first paragraph, explain *how* Moses uses the form of a suzerain-vassal treaty to encourage Israel to be faithful to Yahweh their God as they prepare to possess the land. In the second paragraph, write about the things that seemed most important to you and how God is changing the way you love, think and act. In the third paragraph, explain one of Jesus' "shadows" in Deuteronomy and how it made you think of him. Finally, end your review with a prayer to Jesus: Address him by one of his titles in Deuteronomy, and thank him for the way he fulfilled one of Deuteronomy's prophecies about the Messiah.

Joshua

85. Joshua — Introduction

Pray. Then Read, Think and <u>Mark</u>.

Read your study Bible's introduction to Joshua. Think about the questions for each of the following sections. <u>Mark</u> the answers and other things that seem important.

for the ESV Study Bible

- Theme
  - o Who is the Lord, and what does he do?
- Purpose, Occasion, and Background
  - o Read the first paragraph.
  - o What is the purpose of the book of Joshua?
  - o What does the book emphasize?
  - o Read the second paragraph. What did the Lord promise Abraham and his descendants?
- The Destruction of the Canaanites
  - o Read the fifth paragraph.
  - o What is a "fundamental OT conviction," an important, basic belief in the Old Testament?
  - o Since God is the Creator of the universe, what else is he?
  - o What rights does God have?
  - o Read the sixth paragraph ("Since all people are sinners"). Why does God remove the Canaanites?
  - o Read the eighth paragraph ("Further, the Sinai covenant"). What will happen if Israel allows Canaanites to stay in the land?
- Key Themes
  - o Read the last paragraph. How is *Joshua* written in Greek?

- Literary Features
    - o Read the first paragraph.
    - o What section of the Hebrew Bible is Joshua included in?
    - o What other books are also in that division?
    - o How do these books tell Israel's history?
- Outline
    - o What are the four main sections of Joshua?

for the NIV Study Bible

- Title and Theological Theme
    - o Read the first paragraph. What is Joshua a story of?
    - o Read the second paragraph. What is the theme of the book?
    - o Read the fourth paragraph. How would you write *Joshua* in Greek? That is, what is the Greek form of *Joshua*?
    - o Read the last paragraph.
    - o What division of the Hebrew Bible is Joshua in?
    - o What other books are also in that division?
    - o How do these books tell Israel's history?
- Now look at the article "The Conquest and the Ethical Question of War." It's just before the introduction to Joshua.
    - o Read the third paragraph.
    - o What belongs to God?
    - o What did the Canaanites do?
    - o What does God use his people Israel to do?
    - o Read the fourth paragraph.
    - o What does the Lord's triumph over the Canaanites show the world?
    - o Read the fifth paragraph.
    - o Whose wars are the battles for Canaan?
    - o Why does Israel have to cleanse the land?
- Now turn to the Outline at the end of the introduction to Joshua.
    - o What are the four main sections of Joshua?

Write

Write your own introduction to Joshua. Tell which division of the Bible this book begins and how those books tell Israel's history. State Joshua's theme and summarize how Yahweh fulfills his promise to Abraham. Then explain why God uses the Israelites to kill the Canaanites. Last, outline Joshua under four headings.

86. Joshua 1:1-5:12

a. When Yahweh promises to be with Joshua, Yahweh says that he will be with him just like he was with whom (1:5)? Yahweh our God dried up the Jordan River just as he had dried up what (4:23)?

b. Many of these early events of Joshua's leadership are just like the early days of Moses' leadership. What other similarities can you find? Read the verses in parentheses if you are having a hard time remembering.
  - 1:17
  - 2:2-6 (Exodus 1:15-19)
  - 2:14-21 (Exodus 12:21-23)
  - 3:5 (Exodus 19:10-11)
  - 3:10 (Exodus 3:17)
  - 3:13 (Exodus 15:8)
  - 3:17 (Exodus 14; also Genesis 1:9-10; 8:13)
  - 4:24 (Exodus 7:5, 17; 8:10, 22; 9:14, 29; 14:18)

c. Who is the living God, God of heaven and earth, Lord of all the land (2:11; 3:10, 13)? To whom does the land of Canaan belong? Read the study note for 3:10.

87. Joshua 5:13-8:35

a. Who conquers Jericho (5:13-15; 6:16)? What does Joshua command Israel to do with the city (6:17-19)? What does the Hebrew word for "devoted" mean? See the translation note for 6:17.

b. Who takes some of the devoted things (7:1)? Against whom does Yahweh's anger burn (7:1)? Can Israel defeat Ai and conquer Canaan without Yahweh's help (7:4-5)?

c. Where does Joshua lead the people to build an altar (8:30)? What does Joshua read to the people (8:34)? Who all assembles to listen to the covenant (8:35)?

88. Joshua 9:1-10:43

a. How could the Israelites have known if the Gibeonites lived near them (9:7, 14)? The Israelites want to destroy the Gibeonites, but they have sworn a treaty with them. How do they solve their dilemma (9:21)?

b. What does Israel do in the battle against the five Amorite kings (10:8-10)? What does Yahweh do in the battle (10:11)? What else does Yahweh do (10:12-14)?

c. Trace the map "Conquest of Canaan: Southern Campaign." (It's under chapter 10 in the *ESV Study Bible* and under chapter 13 in the Zondervan *Study Bibles*.) Label the cities that Joshua and the Israelites totally destroy (10:10, 29, 31, 33, 34, 36, 38, 40-41).

89. Joshua 11:1-13:33

a. What land did Yahweh promise to give Abraham (Genesis 10:15-18; 15:8-12; Exodus 3:8)? Which nations unite to attack Israel (Joshua 11:3)? Who brings them to fight against Israel (11:1, 20)?
b. Trace the map "Conquest of Canaan: Northern Campaign." (It's under chapter 11 in the *ESV Study Bible* and under chapter 14 in Zondervan's study Bibles.) Label the cities that Joshua and the Israelites attacked (11:1-3, 5, 8, 10, 16-17, 21).
c. To which four nations does the land remaining to be taken over belong (13:2-3)? What does Yahweh promise to do (13:6)? So why do the people of Geshur and Maakah continue to live in their towns (13:13)?

90. Joshua 14:1-17:18

a. How was Caleb different from the other spies (14:8, 14)? For which territory does Caleb ask (14:9, 12)? What does Caleb believe Yahweh will help him do (14:10-12)?
b. Does Yahweh help him (15:14)? How does Caleb encourage his family to have faith like his (15:15-17)? Who else have faith to ask according to what Yahweh commanded (17:3-4)?
c. What do Judah, Ephraim and Manasseh fail to do (15:63; 16:10; 17:12-13)? What do the Canaanites do when Manasseh attacks them (17:12)? What must Ephraim and Manasseh believe (17:17-18)?

91. Joshua 18:1-19:51

a. Where does Israel assemble and set up the tent of meeting (18:1)? What has Yahweh done (18:3)? What must Israel do (18:3)?
b. What does Dan fail to do (19:47)? How should Dan have followed Yahweh (14:12, 14)?
c. Trace a map of the twelve tribes in the land. (The map "The Allotment of the Land" is beside chapter 14 in the *ESV Study Bible*. You may also find Map 4 in the back of the *ESV Study*

Bible helpful. Map 4 "Land of the Twelve Tribes" is in the back of Zondervan study Bibles.)

- Outline and label the Great (Mediterranean) Sea, the Sea of Kinnereth (Galilee), the Jordan River and the Salt (Dead) Sea.
- Outline and label the territory of each tribe.
- Draw a triangle and label Mounts Ebal, Gerizim and Hermon.
- Draw dots and label the towns of Beersheba, Hebron, Jerusalem, Jericho, Bethel, Shiloh, Shechem and Dan.

92. Joshua 20:1-22:34

a. Who may find safety in a city of refuge (20:3)? When may he leave the city (20:6)? Go back to the map you drew yesterday. Draw a dot for and then label each of the cities of refuge (20:7-8).

b. In which tribes are the descendents of Aaron (the priests) given towns (21:4)? Where are those tribes? To which tribe do the cities of refuge belong (21:13, 21, 27, 32, 38)?

c. What does Yahweh do, and what must his people do (21:43-45; 22:5)? What four steps does Israel take when they hear that the Reubenites, the Gadites and the half-tribe of Manasseh have built an altar (22:12, 13-14, 15-18, 18-20)? How do the two and a half tribes reply to the heads of the clans of Israel (22:22)?

93. Joshua 23:1-24:33

a. Where does Joshua summon the tribes to meet (24:1)? What did Israel do the last time they were at Shechem (8:30-35)? What had the suzerain Yahweh promised at Shechem (Genesis 12:6-7)?

b. In Joshua 24, Joshua leads Israel to make a covenant with Yahweh. In which verses are (1) the historical prologue (which retells the good things the suzerain has done for the vassal), (2) the stipulations (what the vassal must do), (3) the ratification (the vassal's pledge), (4) the curses, (5) the recording of the covenant and (6) the witness?

c. What must Israel do (23:11; 24:14)? Can they (24:19)? Will they (24:16-18, 21, 31)?

94. Joshua — Review

Pray. Think through the following points.

You've now read all of Joshua. Today you will think back over the book.

a. Reread your own introduction to the book.

b. What was Joshua's main theme? How did you see this theme in the book?

c. Look back through the book. Note the words and verses you marked. What are the main things God was showing and teaching Israel?

d. What things seemed important to you?

e. Look back at your answers to question *d* each day. What were some things you discovered on your own?

f. Think back through your answers to question *f* each day. What are some key ways God is telling you to change the way you love, think or live?

g. Jesus told his disciples, "Everything must be fulfilled that is written about me in the Law of Moses, the Prophets and the Psalms" (Luke 24:44). What parts of the book of Joshua made you think about the Messiah? For example, how are Joshua, his name, his character and his actions a shadow of Jesus?

Write

Write a review of Joshua. In the first paragraph, state Joshua's theme and describe how you saw it throughout the book. In the second paragraph, write about the things that seemed most important to you and how God is changing the way you love, think and act. In the third paragraph, explain one of Jesus' "shadows" in Joshua and how it made you think of him. Finally, end your review with a prayer to our Lord Joshua Messiah. Thank him for the way he has saved and led you. Praise him. Tell him how you will believe and obey him.

Judges

95. Judges — Introduction

Pray. Then Read, Think and <u>Mark</u>.

Read your study Bible's introduction to Judges. Think about the questions for each of the following sections. <u>Mark</u> the answers and other things that seem important.

for the ESV Study Bible

- Theme
    - o What is the theme of Judges? (Chaos is mess or disorder. Apostasy is unfaithfulness.)
- Purpose, Occasion, and Background
    - o Read the first paragraph (*Purpose*).
    - o What was the book of Judges written to show and to point the way to?
    - o What does Israel do time and again?
    - o Read the second paragraph (*Occasion*).
    - o What might Israel have done if they had a (godly) king leading them?
- Key Themes
    - o Summarize the second, third and fifth themes in one sentence each.
- Literary Features
    - o In the second paragraph, read the first two sentences ("The pattern ...").
    - o Like spokes on a wheel that goes round and round, there is a "recurring cycle" in Judges. What four things keep happening in that cycle?

for the NIV Study Bible

- Themes and Theology
    - o Read the third paragraph ("But in Canaan ...").
    - o What did God choose and call Israel to be?

- ○ How did Israel live?
- ○ Read the fourth paragraph ("Throughout Judges ...").
- ○ What is the fundamental (or most basic) issue throughout Judges?
- ○ Instead of obeying their king, what do the Israelites do?
- ○ Read the fifth paragraph ("Out of the recurring ..."). What is another important theme?
- Literary Features
  - ○ Read the first paragraph. What are the three main sections of Judges?
  - ○ Read the third paragraph ("The second part ...").
  - ○ Like spokes on a wheel that goes round and round, there is a "recurring cycle" in Judges. What four things keep happening in that cycle?
  - ○ What are the author's "formulas," that is, what phrases will he use again and again?
  - ○ Read the sixth paragraph ("The arrangement of ..."). What is the central story in Judges? What is the crucial (important) issue?

Write

Write your own introduction to Judges. State the crucial or fundamental issue in Judges. Tell who the Israelites are and how they should have lived. Describe how they do live and what happens to them. Draw a chart that shows the four things that happen again and again in the cycle. Outline Judges under three headings (include chapter numbers).

96. Judges 1:1-3:6

a. What does Yahweh tell the Israelites about the land (1:2)? Which tribes believe Yahweh, drive out the Canaanites and take possession of their land (1:3-4, 17, 22-25)? Which tribes do not drive out Canaanites (1:21, 27, 29, 30, 31, 32, 33)?

b. Yahweh's angel brings a "covenant lawsuit" against Israel (2:1-5). What does he remind them (2:1-2a)? What does he say they have done wrong (2:2b)? What will the nations and their gods become for the Israelites (2:3)?

c. Which three Canaanite gods do the Israelites worship (2:11, 13; 3:7)? Read the study notes for 2:13 and 3:7 to learn more about them. When and where have the Israelites worshiped Baal before (Numbers 25:1-5)? Why does Yahweh leave some

nations in the land and let them fight against the Israelites
(2:20-3:4)?

97. Judges 3:7-5:31

a. Look back at your introduction. What are the four phases of
the recurring cycle in Judges? List them in a column, one
above the other. Beside each phase, write the number of the
verse in Othniel's story in which that phase happens (3:7-11).
b. Which two men does Yahweh bring to Israel (3:12, 15)? What
reason does Ehud give when he orders Israel to follow him
(3:28)? Who is Shamgar's "parent" (see the study note for
3:31)?
c. Who tells Barak that Yahweh is sending him to attack Sisera
(4:4-7)? How does Yahweh honor a woman instead of letting
Barak get the glory (4:18-22; 5:24-27)? What are some differ-
ences between the two ways of telling the story of Israel's
battle against Sisera (4:10-24; 5:1-31)?

98. Judges 6:1-7:25

a. What does the prophet bring against Israel (6:7-10)? (See lesson 96, question b.) Who has brought one before (2:1-5)?
What role and responsibilities does Yahweh give a prophet
(6:7-10)?
b. What name do the people give Gideon (6:32)? Why do they
give him a name with that meaning (see 6:31-32 and note)?
How is this event the central event in the book of Judges?
c. What sense is there in shrinking an army of 30,000 men to
just 10,000; in choosing the men who lapped with their hands
to their mouths rather than those who knelt down; or in attacking an army with trumpets and torches? Why does Yahweh tell Gideon to do these things (7:2)? Whose sword wins
the battle (7:20, 22)?

99. Judges 8:1-9:57

a. After he delivers them, what do the men of Israel ask Gideon
and his sons to do (8:22)? Why does he refuse (say "No")
(8:23)? These words are the central message of the book of
Judges.
b. How do the Israelites treat Gideon's ephod and the god they
call "Baal-Berith" (8:27, 33-34)? What does *Baal-Berith* mean,
and where is his temple (9:46; see note for 8:33)? What had

Joshua led Israel to do at Shechem and Mt. Gerizim (Joshua 8:30-35; 24:1, 14-27)?

c. What does *Abi-melek* mean (see study note for 8:29-31)? In Hebrew, 9:6 says literally, "The citizens of Shechem ... gathered ... to king-ify *My-Father-is-King* as king." What does King Yahweh do to the man who would be king (9:20, 52-57)?

100. Judges 10:1-13:25

a. Which nations' gods does Israel serve (10:6)? To which nations does Yahweh sell Israel (10:7)? Which two ways does Yahweh feel about Israel (10:13-14, 16)?

b. Whom does Jephthah call Israel's real Judge (11:27)? After living in the land for 300 years, what sort of people have the Israelites become (11:1, 3, 30-31, 39; 12:1)? How many of their own people does Israel kill (12:6)?

c. How does a Nazirite show that he is dedicated to God (13:5)? Why must Manoah's wife not eat anything that comes from the grapevine nor drink any fermented drink (13:4, 14; see study note for 13:5)? Who prepares Samson to lead Israel and save them (13:3, 8-9, 19-20, 24-25)?

101. Judges 14:1-16:31

a. How does Yahweh use Samson's wedding to confront the Philistines and fight against them (14:4, 19; 15:1-7)? In the end, which strong fighter gives the Philistines something to eat (14:14; 16:21)? What is sweeter than honey and stronger than a lion (14:18)?

b. In what ways does Samson break his vow to be a Nazirite, someone set apart for Yahweh (14:8-9, 19; 16:19)? Check back through Numbers 6:1-8. What must a Nazirite do when he breaks his dedication and defiles his hair (Numbers 6:9-12)? Instead of two birds, what two things does Yahweh take from Samson to cover over his sins (Judges 16:21)?

c. What is the symbol of Samson's strength (15:14; 16:17)? What happens after a Nazirite who broke his vow shaves his head and offers two birds (Numbers 6:11-12)? What happens to Samson in prison (16:22)?

102.   Judges 17:1-18:31

    a.   How far is Micah's house from the house of God (17:1; 18:31)? What does Micah's mother want to do with the silver (17:3-4, 24)? What else does Micah have (18:24)?

    b.   Who is the Levite whom Micah installs as his priest (17:7, 12; 18:30)? What sort of priest is he (18:4-6, 18-20)? What sort of tribe is Dan (Joshua 23:4-13; Judges 1:34; 18:1, 29-31)?

    c.   What does Israel need (17:6; 18:1)? What should he do (Deuteronomy 17:18-20)? Where should the Levites serve as priests (18:31)?

103.   Judges 19:1-21:25

    a.   Why does the Levite not want to spend the night in Jebus (Jerusalem) (19:12)? The wicked men of Gibeah in Benjamin are very like the men of which city (19:22; follow the cross-reference to Genesis)? How does even a "good Levite" treat his concubine from Judah (19:25)?

    b.   Are the Israelites right to execute the men of Gibeah for raping the woman (20:12-13)? Who has made a gap or breach in Israel (21:15)? Why is he allowing so many people to die (Deuteronomy 28:15, 20, 25)?

    c.   How does this final story begin and end (Judges 19:1; 21:25)? What does Israel need? Which other person from Bethlehem in Judah will go up toward Jerusalem and then be given over by Levites to be abused by wicked men (Matthew 20:17-19)?

104.   Judges — Review

Pray. Think through the following points.

You've now read all of Judges. Today you will think back over the book.

    a.   Reread your own introduction to the book.

    b.   What was the crucial issue in Judges? How did the recurring cycle in Judges show that issue again and again?

    c.   Look back through the book. Note the words and verses you marked. What are the main things God was showing and teaching Israel?

    d.   What things seemed important to you?

    e.   Look back at your answers to question *d* each day. What were some things you discovered on your own?

f. Think back through your answers to question *f* each day. What are some key ways God is telling you to change the way you love, think or live?

g. Jesus told his disciples, "Everything must be fulfilled that is written about me in the Law of Moses, the Prophets and the Psalms" (Luke 24:44). What parts of the book of Judges made you think about the Messiah? You may think about Israel's having no king, about Gideon and Abimelek or about the Levite's concubine.

Write

Write a review of Judges. In the first paragraph, state Judges theme and describe how you saw it throughout the book. In the second paragraph, write about the things that seemed most important to you and how God is changing the way you love, think and live. In the third paragraph, explain one of Jesus' "shadows" in Judges and how it made you think of him. Finally, end your review with a prayer to Jesus, our king and judge.

Ruth

105.   Ruth — Introduction

Pray. Then Read, Think and <u>Mark</u>.

Read your study Bible's introduction to Ruth. Think about the questions for each of the following sections. <u>Mark</u> the answers and other things that seem important.

for the ESV Study Bible

- Author and Title
    - Where is Ruth from?
    - Whose ancestor does she become?
- Purpose, Occasion, and Background
    - When does the book of Ruth take place?
- Theme
    - What does the book of Ruth highlight?
- Key Themes
    - What are two key themes in the book of Ruth?
    - Who shows kindness to whom?
    - What does their kindness reflect?
    - "To redeem" is to buy back or save. What does Boaz redeem?
    - Read the third paragraph. What contrasts does the book of Ruth highlight?

for the NIV Study Bible

- Background
    - When is the book of Ruth set?
    - What is that time like?
    - In the book of Ruth, what is this remnant like?
- Theme and Theology
    - Read the first paragraph.

- What important thing does the book of Ruth under-score (or underline)?
- Which two characters show this kind of love?
- What does their love reflect?
- Read the second paragraph.
- Where is Ruth from? But what does she act like?
- What kind of ancestors does King David have?
- Read the third paragraph.
- What is a key concept in the book of Ruth?
- What several things does Naomi change from and to?

Write

Write your own introduction to the book of Ruth. State the main themes of the book. Describe how different characters show those themes. Describe the contrasts between Naomi's life at the beginning of the book and at the end. In another paragraph, tell when the story is set and what that time was like. Explain how the book of Ruth connects with King David. Outline the book under seven headings.

106. Ruth 1:1-4:22

a. Who sends famine and food, aid and affliction (1:1, 6, 13, 21)? Who blesses whom in Yahweh's name (1:8-9; 2:4, 12, 19-20)? What has Yahweh done hundreds of years earlier to make sure people cared for widows and aliens (Deuteronomy 24:19-22)?

b. *Corner* (Ruth 3:9) and *wing* (2:12) stand for the same Hebrew word. Under whose wings does Naomi tell Ruth to seek refuge (3:2-4)? How does Boaz respond (3:10-11)? What kind of people are Boaz and Ruth (3:11 and study note)?

c. What does Yahweh tell the nearest relative he must do (Leviticus 25:25; Deuteronomy 25:5-10)? What does Boaz do (Ruth 4:9-10)? Whom does Boaz act like (see Isaiah 54:5)?

Samuel

107.   1 and 2 Samuel — Introduction

Pray. Then Read, Think and <u>Mark</u>.

Read your study Bible's introductions to 1 Samuel and 2 Samuel.
Think about the questions for each of the following sections. <u>Mark</u>
the answers and other things that seem important.

for the ESV Study Bible

- Theme
    - o   What is the central theme of the books of Samuel?
         To answer that question, think about these three: (1)
         Who is God? (2) What does he inaugurate? And (3)
         what does he elect?
- Purpose, Occasion, and Background
    - o   What principle does 1 Samuel establish?
    - o   What three transitions do 1 and 2 Samuel deal with?
    - o   What is the prophet Samuel the link between?
- 1 Samuel Key Themes
    - o   Read about the first theme, God's kingship.
    - o   What is the only way a human can be a king?
    - o   To whom does Hannah say God gives power?
    - o   What is a king, and what should he do?
    - o   Read the eighth paragraph ("Later, in 2 Samuel 7").
         What does Yahweh promise David?

for the NIV Study Bible

1 Samuel Introduction

- Title
    - o   Read the second paragraph. How many books were 1
         and 2 Samuel originally?

- Contents and Theme: Kingship and Covenant
  - o Read the first paragraph. What story does 1 Samuel relate or tell?
  - o Read the fifth paragraph ("All the material ..."). What is the tension or ambivalence in the Lord's attitude toward the monarchy? That is, what two ways does Yahweh feel about the king?
  - o Read the sixth paragraph ("Moses had anticipated ..."). What was Israelite kingship to be compatible with? That is, what did it have to fit with?
  - o Whom were the elders rejecting as their king?
  - o Read the eighth paragraph ("The question that still ..."). What two things did Samuel do when he called the people in chapter 10?
  - o What was the king to be?

2 Samuel Introduction

- Contents and Theme: Kingship and Covenant
  - o Read the first paragraph. What does 2 Samuel depict David as? That is, what does it show him to be?
  - o Read the second paragraph. What does the Lord promise to build for David? Who will be the perfect "theocratic king"?
  - o Read the first two sentences of the third paragraph. What does 2 Samuel 10-20 show?

Write

Write your own introduction to the book of Samuel (1 and 2 Samuel). Connect Samuel with the main theme in Judges. Describe what Israel's king is to be and what he should do. Name the three main characters in the book. Explain Yahweh's promise to David.

108. 1 Samuel 1:1-4:1

a. In today's reading, we meet two important words for the first time. *The* LORD *Almighty* or *the* LORD *of hosts* stands for the Hebrew title *Yahweh Tsava'ot* (1:3, 11). What does it mean? (See study note for 1:3.) Yahweh's king is called *mashiyakh* (2:10). What does it mean? (See study note for 2:10). What is the Greek word for *mashiyakh*? Look at the NIV study note again or find the ESV study note for Matthew 1:1.

b. When El Yahweh hears, what does Hannah name her son (1:20; see translation note)? You learnt this Hebrew verb (*shama'*) in Deuteronomy 6:4. It is also in the name *Ishmael* (Genesis 16-17). Underline each time this verb occurs in chapter 3: the *Samu* at the beginning of each *Samuel* and the verbs *listen* or *hear* (3:9-11).

c. What does Hannah's son do (1:28; 2:18, 21, 26)? What do Eli's sons not do (2:12, 25)? How does Eli treat his special role as God's chosen priest (2:29)?

109. I Samuel 4:1-7:17

a. How do the Israelites try to use Yahweh (4:3)? What does Yahweh do when they try to use him (4:10-11)? How has the glory (*kavod*) left Israel (4:21-22)?

b. What happens when the ark of Yahweh's covenant is near an idol, or near Philistines who do not worship him or near Israelites who do not fear him (5:2-3, 6, 9-12; 6:19)? What kind of God is Yahweh (6:20)?

c. How does Samuel tell Israel to seek Yahweh (7:3)? What does Israel do (7:4, 6)? Then what does Yahweh do (7:9-10)?

110. I Samuel 8:1-10:27

a. Whom do Samuel's two sons remind you of (8:1-3; see 2:12-25)? Why do the elders of Israel want a king (8:5, 20)? Does Israel have a king already (8:7; 10:18-19)?

b. By what two other titles do people call a prophet (8:6, 9)? How does Yahweh send Saul to Samuel (9:3-6, 16)? How does Yahweh tell Samuel and the people of Israel which man he has chosen to be king (9:16-17; 10:20-24)?

c. What does Samuel do to Saul to show that Yahweh has chosen Saul (10:1)? What will the Spirit of Yahweh do to Saul (10:6, 8)? How should Saul live when he has the Spirit of Yahweh and a changed heart (10:7)?

111. I Samuel 11:1-13:23

a. What does the Spirit of God do when he comes upon Saul (11:6)? Who rescues Israel (11:13)? In whose presence does Israel confirm Saul as king (11:15)?

b. Why does Israel want a king (12:12; see 8:20)? Who leads Israel into battle, rescues them and makes them safe (12:11)? What kind of acts are these (12:7)?

c. What must the king and the people do (12:24)? Whom do the king and the army fear (13:6-7)? What kind of man does Yahweh seek to lead his people (13:14)?

112.   I Samuel 14:1-52

   a. How does Jonathan lead his armor bearer to fight in faith (14:6)? How does the armor bearer respond (14:7)? What does God do when his people fight in faith (14:12-15)?

   b. Does Saul wait to hear from God before fighting (14:18-19, 36-37)? Whose enemies does Saul lead Israel to fight (14:24)? What does Saul make for the land of Israel (14:29)?

   c. Are Saul's men careful to obey Yahweh (14:31-33)? Had Saul been careful to follow Yahweh (14:35)? Which leader does Yahweh honor in the eyes of the men of Israel (14:45)?

113.   I Samuel 15:1-16:23

   a. What does Yahweh command Saul to do (15:3)? How does Saul describe what he has done (15:8-9, 13, 20-21)? What does Yahweh call it when someone gives him nice gifts but does not heed him (15:22-23)?

   b. What kind of man is Saul (10:22-23; 13:13; 15:24)? What kind of man does Yahweh want to choose to be king (13:14; 16:7)? How does Samuel show that David will be king (16:13; see 2:10)?

   c. What happens to David when Samuel anoints him (16:13)? What happens to Saul (16:14)? How does David fight against evil spirits (16:16, 18, 23)?

114.   I Samuel 17:1-18:30

   a. Whom does Goliath defy (17:10, 23, 25, 26)? How do Saul and the army feel, and how does David feel (17:11, 24, 26)? How did David, who was only a boy, have the power to kill a lion and a bear (17:36-37; see 16:13)?

   b. Why is David so confident Yahweh will help him (17:26, 36-37, 45)? Who controls the battle (17:47)? What will the whole world know when a boy with a sling kills a champion with armor (17:46)?

   c. Fill in the blanks: Saul's _____ loves David and makes a covenant with him (18:1-4). Saul's _____ praise David (18:6-7). Saul's _____ love David (18:16). Saul's _____ loves David (18:20). What happens after Saul becomes and stays very angry (18:8-11)?

115.   I Samuel 19:1-20:42

a.   Why does Saul try to kill David (19:1, 6, 9-10)? Which king is Saul acting like (19:11)? Follow the first cross-reference for 19:12. What does the Spirit of God make Saul do (19:23-24; see 18:10)?

b.   Why does Jonathan give David his robe, tunic, sword, bow and belt (see the study note 18:4; see also 20:31)? How does Jonathan try to protect David (19:3-7; 20:28-32)? Why does Saul try to kill even his own son (20:30-33)?

c.   What do Jonathan and David promise each other in their covenant (18:3; 20:8, 14-15, 17)? With whom do Jonathan and David make their covenant (20:15-16, 42)? Who is the witness to their covenant (20:42)?

116.   I Samuel 21:1-23:29

a.   Who may eat the holy bread (21:4)? Follow the cross-reference for bread in 21:4 to the verse in Leviticus. Why does Jesus say it was alright for the priest to share the consecrated bread with David, who is not a priest? Follow the cross-reference to Matthew. How else does Ahimelek help David (21:8-9, 15)?

b.   What sorts of people come to David for help (22:1-2, 20-22)? What two other sorts of people help David (22:3, 5)? Which prophecy does Doeg the Edomite fulfill without meaning to (22:18-19)? Follow the cross-reference to 1 Samuel 2.

c.   Whom does David follow and serve (23:2, 4, 9-12)? How does he lead David (23:6, 9)? Who saves whom (23:5, 14, 26-28)?

117.   I Samuel 24:1-26:25

a.   Why does David refuse to hurt Saul (24:6, 10)? Who will get even with Saul and avenge the wrongs Saul has done David (24:12)? What does Saul know (23:17; 24:20)?

b.   How does Nabal act like his name (25:3, 10-11, 25)? What sort of woman is Abigail (25:3, 18, 23-24, 30-33, 41)? Whose battles does David fight, and whose should he not fight (25:28, 31)?

c.   Who does Saul act like (26:21)? What will happen to him (25:26, 29)? Who values whose life (26:23-24)?

118.   I Samuel 27:1-29:11

a.   Whom do David and his men raid and destroy (27:8-9)? Whose work is David finishing? Read the study note for 27:8;

also read 28:18. Why does David kill all the people (27:9, 11; see Deuteronomy 20:16-18)?

b. Why is Yahweh not speaking to Saul (28:6, 15, 18)? Where is Samuel's body (28:3)? Who speaks to Saul (28:12, 14, 15, 16, 20)?

c. To whom has Yahweh been speaking (19:8; 22:5, 14, 20, 23; 23:1-4, 9-12)? What does Achish king of Gath say about David (29:6, 9)? How does Yahweh keep David from having to fight against his own people (29:2-5)?

119.   1 Samuel 30:1-2 Samuel 1:27

a. Why is David distressed (1 Samuel 30:4-6)? Where does David find strength (1 Samuel 30:6)? When David inquires of Yahweh, how does Yahweh respond (1 Samuel 30:7-8)? How does Yahweh fulfill his promise (1 Samuel 30:17-19, 23)?

b. How does Saul die (1 Samuel 31:3-6; 2 Samuel 1:5-10)? When the Israelites see that Saul has died, what do they do, and what do the Philistines do (1 Samuel 31:7)? What do David and all the men do when they hear the news about Saul, Jonathan and Israel (2 Samuel 1:11-12)?

c. Do you see how the beginning and "end" of David's lament (song of sadness) are almost the same (2 Samuel 1:19, 25)? Who is the gazelle or glory that lies dead on the mountains (2 Samuel 1:19, 25)? Why might David call this lament "The Bow" (2 Samuel 1:18, 22, 27)?

120.   2 Samuel 2:1-3:39

a. Whom does Abner know Yahweh has chosen to be the next king of Israel and Judah (3:9-10)? Several years after David has become king of Judah, whom does Abner make king over Gad, Ephraim and Benjamin, the northern tribes of Israel (2:8-9)? Follow the cross-reference for "Abner" in 2:8. How is Abner related to Ish-Bosheth?

b. How is Joab related to David? Follow the study note for 2:13 and read the study note for 1 Samuel 26:6. Why do Joab and Abishai murder Abner (3:30)? Is David happy they killed him (3:26, 28-29, 31-34, 37-39)?

c. Ish-Bosheth accuses Abner of sleeping with King Saul's concubine. What does Ish-Bosheth think Abner is trying to do (3:6-7)? See the study note for 3:7. When David makes peace with Abner, whose daughter does he demand (3:13-14)? What

(3) Think about and answer the questions. (4) Return to your bookmark.

does Yahweh think about David taking seven wives (3:2-5; see Deuteronomy 17:17)?

121. 2 Samuel 4:1-6:23

a. Why do Rekab and Baanah kill Ish-Bosheth (4:7-8)? Is David happy they killed him (4:9-12)? Look at the timeline in the front of your study Bible. When did David become king of Israel? Go back to 2 Samuel 5:4-5 and write that year in the margin.

b. Who do the elders know Yahweh said would be the "shepherd" of Israel (5:2-3)? What does David make with the elders of Israel (5:3)? How does David become strong and conquer his enemies (5:10, 12, 22-25)?

c. Who is enthroned between the cherubim (angels) on the ark (6:2)? Why does Yahweh kill Uzzah (6:6-7)? What does David do differently the second time he tries to bring the ark up (6:3, 13; see the study note for 6:3)?

122. 2 Samuel 7:1-9:13

a. What has Yahweh commanded David to do (7:7; see 5:12)? What does Yahweh promise David (7:9-10, 12-13, 16)? Who will build a house for whom (7:11-13)?

b. List the nations David defeats (8:1, 2, 3, 5, 12, 13). Find the map of David's conquests and kingdom in your study Bible. (It's with 2 Samuel 1 in the *ESV Study Bible* and with 2 Samuel 12 in the *NIV Study Bible*.) In your notebook or on a blank sheet of paper, trace the following: the shore around the Mediterranean (Great) Sea, the Euphrates River, the Jordan River, the Dead Sea and the eastern arm of the Red Sea. Label the following cities and nations: Amalek, Hebron, Jerusalem, Philistia, Moab, Syrians (Aram), Damascus, Edom and Ammon. What land has Yahweh promised to give Abraham and his offspring? See Genesis 15:18 and the study note for 2 Samuel 8:3.

c. What does David do to the chariot horses and with the silver and gold (8:4, 11)? What does he do for Jonathan's offspring (9:1, 7, 13)? What is David doing for Yahweh and his people (8:15; Genesis 18:19)?

Every day: (1) Follow your bookmark and pray. (2) Read and <u>mark</u> the passage.

123. 2 Samuel 10:1-12:31

a. Who leads the army to fight in the first battle and who in the second (10:7, 17)? What do David's enemies do when they face his army (10:13-14, 18)? What is Yahweh doing (see Genesis 49:8-10; Numbers 24:17-19)?

b. What should David have gone and done, and what is Uriah doing (11:1, 16)? What does David want to do, and then what does Uriah say he must not do (11:4, 11)? When his other schemes fail, what does David do (11:15, 16-17)?

c. How does Yahweh punish David for his sin (12:10-12, 14)? When David confesses his sin, what does Yahweh do (12:13)? When David loves his own wife, how does Yahweh feel about the child (12:24-25)?

124. 2 Samuel 13:1-14:33

a. Whom are Amnon and Absalom acting like (13:1-2, 6, 10-11, 26-29; see 11:1-4, 14-17)? Does David correct his sons (13:21-22, 38-39)? Which of Yahweh's punishments on David does Absalom fulfill (12:9-10)?

b. How does Tamar feel (13:19)? Does anyone protect or comfort her (13:19-20)? Which other fathers is David like (1 Samuel 2:11, 29; 8:1-2)?

c. Does Yahweh give the king the right to set a murderer free (2 Samuel 14:7-11; see Deuteronomy 17:18-20; 19:11-13)? Is the king really doing what is wise and just (2 Samuel 14:20, 24, 32-33)?

125. 2 Samuel 15:1-16:23

a. How does Absalom steal the hearts of the people (15:1-6)? Has David done what is just and right for his people (see 8:15)? Has David heard Absalom's case against Amnon and given him justice (15:4; see 13:21; 14:28)?

b. Whom does Shimei say David murdered (16:7-8)? Is David a murderer or a scoundrel (12:9-10)? To whom does David trust himself (15:25-26; 16:11-12)?

c. Which of David's people is helping Absalom, and who is secretly helping David (15:12, 31, 32-37; 16:15-19, 20-21, 23)? Who is Absalom acting like (16:21-22)? How does Absalom fulfill Nathan's prophecy (12:11-12)?

(3) Think about and answer the questions. (4) Return to your bookmark.   71

126. 2 Samuel 17:1-19:8

a. Whose advice would help Absalom defeat David and become the king (17:14)? Why do Absalom and the men of Israel listen to Hushai rather than to Ahithopel (17:14)? How do David and all the people with him feel (17:29; see Psalm 63)?

b. Even as his son tries to kill him, what does David tell his generals about Absalom (18:4)? How many Israelite men were killed that day (18:7)? Who could have prevented all this bloodshed (13:21-22; 14:32-33)?

c. Whom is David more concerned about, his nation, his army or his son (18:31-33; 19:6)? How do David's men feel when they hear he is grieving (19:2-6)? Meanwhile, where have the soldiers of Israel gone (18:17; 19:8)?

127. 2 Samuel 19:8-20:26

a. Who anointed Absalom to be their new king (19:9-10; see also 18:6-7)? After David gets the priests to persuade them, which tribe calls David to return (19:14-15)? Which tribe comes with that tribe to meet David (19:16-17)?

b. What is the "house of Joseph" (19:20)? How does Israel have ten shares (19:43; see study note)? How do the men of Judah and Israel feel about each other (19:43)?

c. Whom does David send to call the men of Judah (20:4; see 19:13)? Then whom does David choose to lead the warriors against Sheba (20:6-7)? By the end of the story, who is in charge of the army (20:22-23)? How does he become leader again (20:9-10)?

128. 2 Samuel 21:1-22:51

a. What part of the book of Samuel begins in 21:1 (see study note for 21:1-24:25)? Label each of the six sections in the outline below:

    a)   (21:1-14)

        b)   (21:15-22)

            c)   (22:1-51)

            c)   (23:1-7)

        b)   (23:8-39)

    a)   (24:1-25)

b. Why is there a famine (21:1)? Who are the Gibeonites (21:2; also follow the cross-reference for "Gibeonites" in 21:2)? How does Yahweh show that the bloodguilt of Saul's injustice has been washed from the land (21:6, 9, 10, 14)?

c. In what ways is David's song like Hannah's prayer (1 Samuel 2:1, 2, 10; 2 Samuel 22:2-3, 32, 47, 51)? What is the "sea" that David drowning in (22:5, 17-18)? What does Yahweh do for David and then David for Yahweh (22:48-49, 50)?

129. 2 Samuel 23:1-24:18

a. Why has God made a covenant with David and blessed him (23:3, 5)? Who brings about great victories (23:10, 12)? To whom does the lifeblood of the three mighty warriors belong (23:16-17)?

b. Why does David tell Joab to count the people (24:1-2)? To whom do the people belong, and to whom must each person give a half shekel (24:3; see Exodus 30:12-16)? When each person ransoms his life and gives atonement money to Yahweh, what will Yahweh not do (Exodus 30:12)?

c. What does Yahweh send on Israel (2 Samuel 24:15)? Where is his angel when Yahweh tells him to stop (24:16)? What does David sacrifice to Yahweh (24:24-25)? What does Yahweh do after David offers sacrifices (24:25)?

130. Samuel — Review

Pray. Think through the following points.

You've now read all of Samuel. Well done! Today you will think back over the book.

a. Reread your own introduction to the book. Look carefully at what you said a king is, what he should be like and what he should do.

b. Now look at Saul and David. Compare each of them with what you wrote. How did Yahweh treat each of them?

c. In his covenant with David, what does Yahweh say he will be to David's offspring (2 Samuel 7:14-15)? Compare Yahweh with the mother and the fathers in Samuel: Hannah, Eli, Samuel and David.

d. Yahweh promises David and his offspring several things in his covenant with them. As the book of Samuel ends, what are you waiting to see happen next?

e. When the Old Testament ends, what will you be waiting for?

f. Look back through the book. Note the words and verses you marked. What things seemed important to you?

g. Look back at your answers to question *d* each day. What were some things you discovered on your own?

(3) Think about and answer the questions. (4) Return to your bookmark.

h. Think back through your answers to question *f* each day. What are some key ways God is telling you to change the way you love, think or live?

Write

Write a review of Samuel. In the first paragraph, describe what Israel's king is to be like and what he should do. Briefly assess Saul and David as kings. In the second paragraph, talk about what kind of parents Yahweh, Hannah, Eli, Samuel and David were. In the third paragraph, write about the things that seemed most important to you and how God is changing the way you love, think and act. Finally, end your review with a prayer to Yahweh's Anointed and David's Son, our King Jesus. Thank him for being someone after God's own heart who learned obedience through suffering. Praise him for building a house for Yahweh's Name. Praise him because his kingdom and his throne are established over all forever.

This reading guide follows the Former Prophets straight from Samuel into Kings. If you would like to read each part of the Old Testament when it was written, this is a good place to read Psalms, Books I and II (see lessons 301-337).

Kings

131.   1 and 2 Kings — Introduction

Pray. Then Read, Think and <u>Mark</u>.

Read your study Bible's introduction to 1 and 2 Kings. Think about the questions for each of the following sections. <u>Mark</u> the answers and other things that seem important.

for the ESV Study Bible
- Author and Title
    - o   What period of Israel's history does the book of Kings narrate?
    - o   What book deeply influenced the authors? What were the authors trying to give Israel?
    - o   When the authors weighed (or assessed) the kings of Israel and Judah, what standard did they use?
- Theme
    - o   How does the book of Kings explain Israel's past?
    - o   How does it help Israelites live in the present?
    - o   What hope does it give them for the future?
- Purpose, Occasion, and Background
    - o   Read the third paragraph. What sorts of questions were the people of Israel and Judah asking?
    - o   Read the fourth paragraph. What answers does the book of Kings give?
- Key Themes
    - o   Read the second theme. How did Yahweh God use the prophets to show that he controls history?
    - o   Read the ninth and tenth paragraphs ("The *promise given to David* ..."). What did Yahweh promise David in his covenant with him?

for the NIV Study Bible

- Author, Sources and Date
    - o   Read the first paragraph. With what book were the prophets who wrote 1 and 2 Kings familiar?
- Theme: Kingship and Covenant
    - o   Read the first paragraph. How do 1 and 2 Kings describe the history of the kings? What is the guiding thesis (main point) of the book?
    - o   Read the second paragraph. What kind of history is the book of Kings *not*? How does the author assess each king?
    - o   Read the seventh paragraph ("While the writer ..."). What did Yahweh promise David in his covenant with him?
    - o   Read the eighth paragraph ("Another prominent feature ..."). How does the book of Kings present the history of the kingdom?
    - o   Read the tenth paragraph ("Reflection on ..."). What does the book of Kings explain?
- Content
    - o   What period of Israel's history does the book of Kings narrate?

Write

Write your own introduction to the book of Kings (1 and 2 Kings). Tell what period of Israel's history the book covers. State the purpose of the book, what the authors were trying to explain. State what book set the authors' perspective, and describe how they tell Israel's history from that perspective. Mention what Yahweh promised David in his covenant with him. Explain how the authors of Kings assess the kings of Israel and Judah. Finally, summarize the authors' reason for why Israel and Judah have been exiled from the land.

132.   I Kings 1:1-2:46

a.   Who is Adonijah (see the study note for 1:5)? Who all make Adonijah king (1:7, 9)? How does King David show that Solomon is the real king (1:32-35)?

b.   What was Yahweh's promise to David (2:4)? What must Solomon do so that Yahweh will establish his word and keep his promise (2:2-4)? Why does David tell Solomon to kill Joab (2:5-6, 31-33)?

c.   Why does Adonijah want to marry Abishag (2:17, 22)? Whom does Solomon execute (2:25, 34, 46)? Through Solomon's actions, what two things has Yahweh established (1:36-37; 2:4, 12, 27, 46)?

133. I Kings 3:1-4:34

 a. What one thing does Solomon want most (3:5, 8-9)? How does Israel see that Solomon has wisdom from God (3:16-28)? How wise is Solomon (3:12; 4:29-34)?

 b. What else does Yahweh give Solomon (3:13; 4:21-24, 27)? How does Yahweh fulfill his covenant with Abraham (4:20, 21; see study note for 4:21)? How does Yahweh fulfill the blessings of the covenant he gave Israel through Moses (4:20-21, 24-25; Deuteronomy 28:1-14)?

 c. How is Solomon like his father David (3:3, 6)? What makes you think Solomon may not stay faithful to Yahweh (3:1, 3; 4:26)? Read the ESV's note for 4:26 or follow the NIV's cross-reference to Deuteronomy. What must Solomon do for Yahweh to bless him fully (3:14)?

134. I Kings 5:1-6:38

 a. Why does Hiram make a treaty or covenant with Solomon (5:1, 7, 10-12)? What does Yahweh promise Solomon (6:11-13)? How much bigger is the temple than the tabernacle (6:2)? See the diagram of the tabernacle at Exodus 26.

 b. What does Solomon cover the inside of the temple with (1 Kings 6:20-22, 28, 30, 32, 35)? What creatures stand in the inner sanctuary and are on the walls and the doors (6:27-28, 29, 35)? If you stood inside the temple, where would you feel like you are?

 c. On a sheet of blank paper, begin to draw Solomon's temple. Use the drawing in your study Bible to help you.

135. I Kings 7:1-51

 a. In what year does Solomon begin to build the temple, and when does he finish it? See the study notes for 6:1, 38. Now write the year when he begins in the margin beside 6:1 and the year he finishes in the margin beside 6:38. How many years does Solomon take to build his own house (7:1)?

 b. Which earlier worker does Huram remind you of (7:13-14)? Follow the cross-references for 7:14. What plants and animals does Huram use in his work (7:18, 19, 25, 29, 36)? What kind

---

(3) Think about and answer the questions. (4) Return to your bookmark.

of metal does Huram use for the furnishings outside the temple (7:14, 45)?

c. Finish your drawing of Solomon's temple and its furnishings. Now color the drawing.

136.   I Kings 8:1-9:9

a. What is the cloud that fills Yahweh's temple (8:10-11)? Follow the cross-reference for "cloud." What promises has Yahweh kept (1 Kings 8:15-16, 19, 20-21, 24, 66)? Now that Yahweh's ark is in the land and his people have rest, what story does Solomon think has finally come to an end (8:9, 16, 21, 51, 53, 56)?

b. Will Yahweh God really dwell in the temple (8:13, 27, 29-30)? What does Solomon ask Yahweh to do (8:30, 32, 34, 36, 39, 42, 43, 45, 49)? Then what will the nations know (8:40, 43, 60)?

c. What does Solomon ask for (8:36, 58, 61)? What will Yahweh do if the people or Solomon keep sinning (8:33, 35, 37, 46; 9:6-9)? What must the people do for Yahweh to forgive them and uphold them (8:33, 35, 47-48)?

137.   I Kings 9:10-11:43

a. Why has Yahweh made Solomon so wise and wealthy (10:9)? What things about Solomon's power and wealth don't seem quite right (9:20-22; 10:14)? Which prophet said the king would act like this (see 1 Samuel 8:10-12)?

b. What did Yahweh tell the king of Israel to do and not to do? Follow the reference in the study note for 10:26 (Deuteronomy 17:16-20). Which of Yahweh's instructions is Solomon breaking (1 Kings 10:14, 26-28; 11:1-8)? Why does Solomon do these things (11:4, 6)?

c. How does Yahweh keep his covenant with David (see 2 Samuel 7:14-16; 1 Kings 11:13, 14, 23, 26, 36, 39)? How does Solomon lose his kingdom (11:9-11)? What does Yahweh offer Jeroboam (11:38)?

This reading guide follows the story of the Kings straight from Solomon to Rehoboam. If you would like to read each part of the Old Testament when it was written, this is a good place to read Proverbs, Ecclesiastes and the Song of Songs (see lessons 407-450).

Every day: (1) Follow your bookmark and pray. (2) Read and <u>mark</u> the passage.

138.   I Kings 12:1-13:34

a.   Who all choose the new king (12:1; see 2 Samuel 5:1-3)? How does a wise leader lead well (1 Kings 12:7)? Why does King Rehoboam not listen to the people and the older counselors (12:15, 24)?

b.   Then what do the tribes of Israel do (12:16, 18-20)? If people from Israel are going to worship Yahweh in the temple in Jerusalem, what will they pass by first (12:27-29; see the map beside chapter 12)? What does the man of God from Judah say will happen to the altar in Bethel (13:1-2)?

c.   Has Yahweh really sent an angel to give a message to the old prophet in Bethel (13:11, 18)? How does Yahweh show he is the one who judged the man of God from Judah for disobeying him (13:20-22, 24, 26, 28)? In this chapter, what could not be pulled back (13:4), who shouldn't have turned back (13:9-10, 16-17, 19, 22-23), and who turned back to the wrong thing (13:33)?

139.   I Kings 14:1-16:14

a.   How does Ahijah see even though he is blind (14:4-6)? What has Jeroboam done and also made Israel do (14:8-9, 16; 15:30)? What will Yahweh do (14:10-12, 14-16)?

b.   How does Israel act while Rehoboam is king (14:22-24)? What is Asa's heart like, and what does he do (15:11-14)? What happens to Yahweh's house while Rehoboam is king and while Asa is king (14:25-26; 15:15)?

c.   How does Baasha fulfill Yahweh's word against Jeroboam (15:27-30)? How does Zimri fulfill Yahweh's word against Baasha (16:1-4, 11-13)? Turn to the table of the Kings of the Divided Kingdom (near chapter 13). Find the year in which each king began to reign, and write that year in the margin beside 14:21; 15:1, 9, 25, 33; 16:8). Keep doing this for each of the kings as you read through 1-2 Kings.

140.   I Kings 16:15-18:15

a.   Which city does Omri build (16:24)? What does Ahab build in Samaria (16:31-33)? Why do two of Hiel's sons die (16:34)?

b.   When Israel starts to worship Baal, what does Yahweh do (see study note for 17:1)? Why else does Yahweh stop the rain (Deuteronomy 28:22-24)? How does Yahweh feed Elijah (1 Kings 17:6, 9)?

c. Where does Yahweh send Elijah (17:9; see 16:31)? What does Yahweh do (17:1, 12, 21-22; 18:10, 15)? What has Jezebel done to Yahweh's prophets (18:4, 13)?

141. I Kings 18:16-19:21

a. How do Ahab and Jezebel encourage the people to worship Baal and Asherah (18:19)? Why does Elijah choose fire as the way to figure out whether Yahweh or Baal is God (see the study note for 18:24)? How do Baal's prophets try to get him to send fire (18:26, 28-29)?

b. Why does Elijah tell them to pour water all over the altar (18:33-35)? How do the people know Yahweh is the real God (18:39-39)? Why does Yahweh send a great rain (18:45)? See question *b* in yesterday's reading.

c. How does Yahweh give Elijah strength (18:46; 19:5, 7-8)? Who else met Yahweh in the place where Elijah goes (19:8; see the cross-reference for 19:13)? How does Elijah show Elisha that he should become Elijah's assistant (19:16, 19, 21)?

142. I Kings 20:1-21:29

a. In each battle, how much bigger is Aram's (Syria's) army than Israel's army (20:1, 15, 27)? What do the Aramean officials think about Israel's gods (20:23, 28)? Why does Yahweh give the Arameans (Syrians) into Ahab's hand (20:13, 28)?

b. What does Ahab do with Ben-Hadad, and what should he have done (20:32-34, 42)? Why does Naboth refuse to give Ahab his vineyard (21:3)? Follow the cross-reference. Who leads Ahab into sin (21:7-10, 23, 25)?

c. What has Ahab done (21:20, 25)? How will Yahweh treat Ahab (21:21-24)? How does Ahab show that his humility and sorrow are real (21:27, 29)?

143. I Kings 22:1 – 2 Kings 1:18

a. Who is telling the prophets what to say to Ahab (1 Kings 22:6, 10-12, 22-23)? What three messages does Micaiah give Ahab (22:15, 17, 19-23)? Who plans Ahab's death (22:30, 34, 38; see 21:19)?

b. Does the author of Kings write more about Ahab's wicked-ness or his wealth (22:39)? What sort of king is Jehoshaphat (22:5, 8, 43)? Was Jehoshaphat as glorious as Solomon (follow the cross-reference in 22:48)?

  c. What does Ahaziah send his servants to do (2 Kings 1:2)? How does Yahweh show he is greater than Baal-Zebub (1:3, 10, 12, 14)? Why does Ahaziah die so young (1 Kings 22:53; 2 Kings 1:2, 16)?

144. 2 Kings 2:1-3:27

  a. Where does Yahweh send Elijah before he takes him to heaven (2:1-2, 4, 6, 8-9)? What does Elisha inherit from Elijah (2:9-10, 12-14)? What is a double portion (follow the study note for 2:9)?

  b. Why is the water in Jericho bad and the land unfruitful (see study note for 2:19)? How does Yahweh use salt (2:20-22)? Follow the study note for 2:20 to the verse in Numbers. How do the boys in Bethel treat Yahweh's prophet (2 Kings 2:23-24)?

  c. What are the people of Moab like (3:5, 27; see 1 Kings 11:7)? What does Yahweh tell Israel and Judah to do Moab (2 Kings 3:19; see Deuteronomy 20:16-20)? Who gives the Moabites and their land into Israel's and Judah's hands (2 Kings 3:18, 25-27)?

145. 2 Kings 4:1-5:27

  a. What has Yahweh promised his people (see Deuteronomy 7:12-13)? How does Yahweh give life and strength to the dead child (2 Kings 4:34-35; see study note for 4:34)? Which story about Jesus does 4:42-44 remind you of?

  b. What does Elisha tell Naaman to do (5:10)? What does Naaman do (5:14)? Look carefully at the verb in 5:14. (In Greek it's translated *baptize*.) What (or whom) does Naaman become like (5:2, 14)?

  c. What has Naaman come to know (5:8, 15)? Why might Naaman want dirt from Israel (see the cross-reference or study note for 5:17)? But what does Gehazi "worship" more than Yahweh (2 Kings 5:20, 24, 27)?

146. 2 Kings 6:1-7:20

  a. How does Elisha have the power to do such miracles (6:6, 12, 17, 18)? Who can see and who cannot see (6:17, 18, 20)? Who all are protecting Elisha (6:17-18; see 2:11-12)?

b. How does Ben-Hadad cause a famine in Samaria (6:24)? How bad is the famine (6:25-29; 7:13)? Why are these horrible things happening (6:33)? Follow the cross-references for 6:29.

c. Why does the Aramean (Syrian) army flee (7:6-7)? Do the chariots and horses belong to the Hittites and Egyptians (7:6; see 6:14, 17)? Who has more faith: the man on whose hand the king of Aram (Syria) leans or the one whose hand the king of Israel leans (5:17-18; 7:2, 17-20)?

147. 2 Kings 8:1-9:37

a. How does Yahweh care for a woman who obeys him (8:1-6)? What might Elisha be seeing as he fixes his gaze and stares at Hazael (8:11-12)? Why does Yahweh call for another famine and bring violent enemies against his people (8:1, 12; see Deuteronomy 28:15-17, 23, 25)?

b. What evil things does Jezebel do (2 Kings 9:22)? How does Jezebel, the queen of Israel, lead the kings of Judah to do evil (8:18, 26-27)? What did Yahweh tell Elijah to say against Ahab and Jezebel (1 Kings 21:21-24)?

c. How does Yahweh fulfill his prophecy against Jezebel (9:33, 36-37)? How does Elisha's servant fulfill Elijah's prophecy about Jehu (9:6-10; see 1 Kings 19:15-17)? Why does Jehu throw the body of Joram, Ahab's son, on the ground in Naboth's vineyard (2 Kings 9:25-26; see Genesis 4:10-11; Numbers 35:33)?

148. 2 Kings 10:1-11:21

a. Whom does Jehu wipe out in Israel and in Judah (10:1, 6-7, 11, 13-14, 17)? How does Yahweh wipe out Baal worship in Israel (10:19-28)? Why does Jehu do all these things (10:10, 16)?

b. Are the people of Israel worshiping Baal when they worship at the golden calves (10:28-29)? What does Yahweh promise Jehu (10:30)? But then what does Yahweh begin to do to Israel (10:31-33)?

c. Who all protect Joash from his grandmother Athaliah (11:2-4)? What does Jehoiada the priest give Joash (11:12)? How does Yahweh wipe out Baal worship in Judah (11:18)?

149. 2 Kings 12:1-14:22

a. Why does Joash (Jehoash) do what is right in Yahweh's eyes (12:1-2; see 11:3, 12)? Who does the work to repair Yahweh's house (12:6, 8, 11-12)? Which earlier king of Judah used gold from Yahweh's temple to buy peace with Aram (Syria) (12:17-18)? See the study note for 12:18.

b. For what reasons does Yahweh turn to Israel and have compassion on them (13:4-5, 23)? How many times does the savior Yahweh deliver Israel (13:5, 17-19, 25)? When Yahweh does banish Israel and throw them from his presence, whose message will give them hope of new life (13:20-21, 23; 17:20, 23; see Deuteronomy 30:1-6)?

c. How righteous is Amaziah (14:2-6)? What all does Jehoash king of Israel take from Jerusalem (14:13-14)? Remember to keep checking the table of the kings of Israel and Judah and writing the years of each king's reign in the margin beside his reign.

150. Old Testament 1 Review

Pray. Think through the following points.

You've now read all the way from Genesis 1 to 2 Kings 14 and finished Old Testament 1. Well done! Today you will think back over Yahweh's relationship with his people.

a. Reread your own introduction and review to each book.

b. At creation, what was God's plan for his people on his earth (Genesis 1:26-28; 2:15)?

c. What hope did Yahweh give the man and the woman when he judged them for their sin (Genesis 3:15)?

d. Why did Yahweh undo his creation, wash the whole earth and then redo his creation (Genesis 6-8)?

e. What covenant did God make with Noah, his offspring and every living creature (Genesis 8:20-9:17)?

f. What covenant did Yahweh make with Abraham and his offspring (Genesis 121-3; 15:1-20; 17:1-14)?

g. What did Jacob promise his son Judah (Genesis 49:8-12)?

h. In Exodus, what was Yahweh preparing his people to be (Exodus 19)?

i. What was the key word in Leviticus?

j. What went wrong in Numbers (Numbers 11-14)?

k. Who was the first person to see that Yahweh is king (Numbers 23:21)?

l. What was the structure of Deuteronomy? In Yahweh and Israel's covenant, who is the suzerain, and who is the vassal?

m. What were the final curses of the covenant (Deuteronomy 28:58-68)? And what hope did Moses give Israel (Deuteronomy 30:1-10)?

(3) Think about and answer the questions. (4) Return to your bookmark.

n. How do the Israelites conquer the land under Joshua's leadership?

o. What is the main problem in the book of Judges? Look at the very last verse of the book.

p. Why did Yahweh take the kingdom from Saul (1 Samuel 13:13-14)?

q. What covenant does Yahweh make with David (2 Samuel 7:1-17)?

r. How does the temple Solomon builds make you think of the Garden of Eden, Yahweh's kingdom and heaven (1 Kings 6-7)?

s. What is Solomon's sin, and what are the sins of the kings of Israel and Judah (1-2 Kings)?

t. What are some of the most important lessons you have learned as you've read Genesis – 2 Kings?

u. What are some key ways God has changed the way you love, think or live?

v. Jesus told his disciples, "Everything must be fulfilled that is written about me in the Law of Moses, the Prophets and the Psalms" (Luke 24:44). If you were living during the reign of Amaziah, and you read carefully through the Law of Moses and the Former Prophets, what kind of Messiah would you be expecting?

Write

Write a review of Genesis – 2 Kings 14. In the first paragraph, summarize Yahweh's plan for humans on the earth. In the second paragraph, describe Yahweh's covenant with Abraham and the promises he makes. In the third paragraph, explain how Yahweh uses the Law to set Israel apart as a kingdom of priests. In the fourth paragraph, write about the ups and downs of Israel in the Former Prophets. End your review with a prayer to King Jesus. Explain something he's taught you. Tell him how he's changing you. And thank him for something he has done for you as your king.

PART TWO

OLD TESTAMENT PROPHETS
Jonah to Nehemiah

Kings

151. Orientation; 2 Kings 14:23-29

Pray. Then Read, Think and Mark.

When you orient yourself, you figure out where things are around you and which direction you should head.

To orient yourself for Old Testament 2, go back and read carefully your review of Old Testament 1 (lesson 150). Then think about these questions.

- When Yahweh first created humans, what was his plan for us?
- How did Yahweh use his covenant with Abraham, his Law and his covenant with David to prepare his people to live faithfully in his kingdom?

Now go back and read your introduction to Kings (lesson 131) and think about these questions.

- What is the purpose of Kings? What are the authors trying to explain?
- Explain why Kings is one of the Former Prophets. How does the book of Kings tell the history of Israel?
- How do the authors of Kings assess the kings of Israel and Judah?
- What reasons do the authors give for why Israel and Judah have been exiled from the land?

Now read 2 Kings 14:23-29. Mark any words or sentences that seem important to you. Think about these questions.

- Look back at the table of the Kings of Israel and Judah (near 1 Kings 13). In what year did Jeroboam II begin to reign in Israel? Flip back to 2 Kings 14:23 and write that year in the margin. What great thing did Jeroboam do (see 14:25 and the study note)? How was he able to do that (14:26-27)?

Write

Write your own orientation to the Prophets. In the first paragraph, summarize the story of Yahweh God's plans for humans and how he used his covenants with Abraham, Israel and David to prepare his people to live faithfully in his kingdom. In the second paragraph state the purpose of Kings and describe the ups and downs of Israel and Judah from the time of Solomon to the time of Jeroboam II.

Jonah

152.   Jonah – Introduction

Pray. Then Read, Think and <u>Mark</u>.

An introduction introduces you to a book. It usually tells you who
wrote the book, when and for whom. It highlights important themes
and summarizes the book's message.

Read your study Bible's introduction to the book of Jonah. Think
about the questions for each of the following sections. <u>Mark</u> the answers and other things that seem important.

for the ESV Study Bible

- Theme
    - What is the theme of the book of Jonah?
- Purpose, Occasion, and Background
    - Read the first paragraph. What two things does God
      want you to reflect on or think about as you read the
      book of Jonah?
    - Read the second paragraph.
    - When did Jonah prophesy?
    - Because of Jehoahaz's sins, what were the Arameans
      (Syrians) doing to Israel?
    - Who delivered Israel from oppression by Aram?
    - Then what did Jehoash, king of Israel, do?
    - And what did his son Jeroboam do?
    - Who told the king of Israel he would have victories?
- Genre
    - Read the first paragraph. What does an allegory do?
      Is the story of Jonah an allegory?
    - Read the last paragraph. Is the book of Jonah just
      plain history, or does it do something else as well?
- Key Themes
    - Read both paragraphs. In this book, who is self-
      centered?

for the NIV Study Bible

- Background
    - o Read the first two paragraphs.
    - o What had Damascus (the capital of Aram) been able to do in Israel, the northern kingdom?
    - o Which nation defeated Damascus?
    - o Then what did Jehoash, king of Israel, do?
    - o And what did his son Jeroboam do while there were troubles within Assyria?
    - o Read the third paragraph.
    - o Who told the king of Israel he would have victories over Damascus?
    - o Who said Jeroboam would restore Israel's land and borders?
    - o What do the Israelites do after their triumph?

- Interpretation
    - o Read the first paragraph. Why do many people think the story of Jonah is not real, true history?
    - o Read the third paragraph. Is the book of Jonah just plain history, or does it do something else as well?

- Literary Characteristics
    - o Read the third paragraph ("Also as in Ruth ...").
    - o Read the fourth paragraph (The author uses ...").
    - o Whom does Nineveh represent or stand for? How does God feel about Nineveh and all people?
    - o Whom does Jonah represent? What do those people want to do about their special relationship with God?
    - o Read the last paragraph.
    - o What does God want Israel to rediscover?
    - o What does God want Israel to understand better?

Write

Write your own introduction to the book of Jonah. State when Jonah prophesied and refer to the verse in 2 Kings that mentions him. Tell the story of what had been happening in Israel. Describe how Israel felt about God, themselves and other nations. Now say whether the story of Jonah is real history or not and what the point of the story is. Finally, outline the book in two halves (1:1-2:10; 3:1-4:4) with an ending (4:5-11).

153.   Jonah 1:1-4:11

Follow your bookmark. Then answer these questions:

    a.   Why does Jonah not want to go to Nineveh (1:3; 3:10-4:2)? Who acts in a way that shows he really does fear Yahweh, the God of heaven (1:3, 9-10, 14-16)? Which people, who usually call on their gods, offer Yahweh a sacrifice and make vows to him (1:5-6, 16; 2:8-9)?

    b.   What do the people of Nineveh do when they hear Jonah's message (3:5-9)? What "wrong" does Yahweh do to make Jonah so angry (3:10-4:2)? Who turns away from God's gracious love (2:8; 4:1-4, 8-9)?

    c.   Whom does Yahweh care about (1:14-17; 2:9-10; 3:10; 4:1-2, 6, 10-11)? Who answers Yahweh's question at the end of the book (see the study note for 4:11)? Which other prophet will sleep through a storm at sea when he is going to the nations and then be "dead" for three days before coming back to life (Jonah 1:5-6, 17; see Matthew 8:23-28; 12:39-41)?

Return to your bookmark and do d through g.

Amos

154. Amos – Introduction

Pray. Then Read, Think and <u>Mark</u>.

Read your study Bible's introduction to the book of Amos. Think about the questions for each of the following sections. <u>Mark</u> the answers and other things that seem important.

for the ESV Study Bible

- Author
  - ○ Where was Amos from? Where was Tekoa (see the study note for 1:1)?
  - ○ What did Amos do for a living?
- Date
  - ○ During which kings' reigns did Amos prophesy?
  - ○ When did their reigns begin and end?
- Theme
  - ○ What is the theme of Amos?
- Purpose, Occasion, and Background
  - ○ Read the first paragraph.
  - ○ What happened to the kingdoms of Israel and Judah between 780 and 745 BC?
  - ○ Read the second paragraph.
  - ○ What did the Israelites their think their wealth was a sign of?
  - ○ How had the people breached or broken God's covenant with them?
  - ○ How had the people gotten their wealth?
  - ○ Was the people's worship true?
- Key Themes
  - ○ What all is Yahweh the Lord of?
  - ○ How do the Lord's people show their right relationship with him?

-       ○   What will the day of Yahweh be like?
-       ○   What hope did Amos give the people?

for the NIV Study Bible

- Author
  - ○ Read the first paragraph. Where was Amos from?
  - ○ What did Amos do for a living?
- Date and Historical Situation
  - ○ Read the first paragraph.
  - ○ During which kings' reigns did Amos prophesy?
  - ○ What were the years of each king's reign?
  - ○ What happened to the kingdoms of Israel and Judah during their reigns?
  - ○ What was life like in those kingdoms?
  - ○ Read the second paragraph?
  - ○ What did Israel feel sure about?
- Theological Theme and Message
  - ○ Read the first paragraph.
  - ○ What is the dominant theme of Amos?
  - ○ What did Amos speak vigorously for?
  - ○ Did the people's lives show they were committed to God's law?
  - ○ Whom does Amos condemn?
  - ○ How had the people gotten their wealth?
  - ○ Read the second paragraph.
  - ○ What would God's judgment be like?
  - ○ What hope did Amos give the people?
  - ○ Read the third paragraph.
  - ○ What all is God, the Great King, Lord over?

Write

Write your own introduction to the book of Amos. Tell where he was from, when he prophesied and who the kings of Israel and Judah were at that time. Describe what life was like in Israel then and how that made the Israelites feel about themselves. Explain how the Israelites were breaking God's covenant with them. And summarize what Yahweh said he would do to Israel.

155.   Amos 1:1-2:16

Follow your bookmark. Then answer these questions:

a.   If Yahweh roars from Jerusalem to Carmel, what cities in between hear his roar (1:2; 4:1, 4)? See the map in the ESV's Introduction to Amos (Israel and Judah at the Time of Amos) or Map 6 in the back of the NIV (Kingdoms of Israel and Judah). Find and write out the phrases in Yahweh's words against Gaza that he uses over and over again as he roars against each of the nations (1:6-8). Draw a simple map that shows each of the nations Yahweh judges: Damascus, Gaza, Tyre, Edom, Ammon, Moab, Judah and Israel. Then number them in the order Yahweh speaks against them.

b. Which nations does Lord Yahweh have the right to judge (1:3, 6, 9, 11, 13; 2:1, 4)? For what kind of sin does Yahweh punish each of the nations (1:3, 6, 9, 11, 13; 2:1)? How might the Israelites feel as they hear Yahweh's wrath against the other nations (1:3-2:5)?

c. What are the Israelites doing to poor and needy people (2:6-8)? What kind things has Yahweh done for Israel (2:9-11)? What will surely happen (2:13-16)?

Return to your bookmark and do d through g.

156. Amos 3:1-6:14

Follow your bookmark. Then answer these questions:

a. What wrong is Israel doing (3:9-10, 15; 4:1; 6:1, 4-7, 12)? Who are the cows of Bashan (see 4:1 and the study note)? What is more important to Yahweh, sacrifices and offerings or justice and righteousness (4:4-5; 5:7, 21-24)?

b. What is the answer to each of Yahweh's seven questions (3:3-6)? What things did Yahweh do to try to turn Israel back to him (4:6-11)? What will Yahweh do to Israel now (3:11; 4:2-3; 5:27; 6:7, 14)?

c. What does Yahweh still call Israel to do (5:4-6, 14-15, 24)? What were the Israelites hoping would happen for them on the day of Yahweh (5:18; see Deuteronomy 32:35-36, 41-43)? But whom will Yahweh be angry with on that day (Amos 3:14; 4:12; 5:18-23)?

Return to your bookmark and do d through g.

157. Amos 7:1-9:15

Follow your bookmark. Then answer these questions:

a. What does Lord Yahweh do when Amos asks him to forgive and stop (7:2-3, 5-6)? Does Amos get to choose where he prophesies or what he says (7:12-15)? What will happen to the king and the priest (7:11, 17)?

b. What do people do with ripe summer fruit (see 8:2 and study note)? What will Yahweh do to Israel (7:8-9; 8:7-10; 9:1-4, 8-10)? In the end, who will suffer for the sins of Israel (8:9-10; Luke 23:44-48; John 3:16)?
c. What will Yahweh do in that day (Amos 9:11; see 2 Samuel 7:15-16)? Which nations will Israel possess (Amos 9:12)? When did Yahweh begin to fulfill these promises (Amos 9:11-12; see Luke 1:30-33; Acts 2:32-36; 15:13-19)?

Return to your bookmark and do d through g.

158. 2 Kings 15:1-38

Follow your bookmark. Then answer these questions:

  a. What is Azariah's other name (15:1, 8, 13, 17)? Though Azariah and his son Jothan were both good kings, what do they not do (15:4, 35)? Why does Yahweh touch Azariah with a skin disease (15:5; 2 Chronicles 26:16-21)?

  b. What are the kings of Israel like (2 Kings 15:9-10, 14, 16, 18, 24-25, 30)? Who controls what kings do (15:12, 37)? What is Pul king of Assyria also called (see the translation note for 15:19)?

  c. How does Menahem save Israel from Pul, the king of Assyria (15:19-20)? What does Tiglath-Pileser do to people from many parts of Israel (15:29)? In the *ESV Study Bible*, see the map Assyria Conquers Northern Israel under 2 Kings 16; in the *NIV Study Bible* see the map Assyrian Campaigns against Israel and Judah in the middle of 2 Kings 15. Whose word does this exile fulfill (2 Kings 15:29; see Amos 3:11; 5:27; 6:7, 14; 9:9)?

Return to your bookmark and do d through g.

Isaiah

159.   Isaiah – Introduction

Pray. Then Read, Think and <u>Mark</u>.

Read your study Bible's introduction to the book of Isaiah. Think about the questions for each of the following sections. <u>Mark</u> the answers and other things that seem important.

for the ESV Study Bible

- Author and Title
    - ○ Read the first paragraph. What does Isaiah's name mean?
- Date
    - ○ Read the first paragraph.
    - ○ When did Isaiah begin his ministry?
    - ○ How long did Isaiah live?
    - ○ Read the second paragraph. What do many scholars think about the book of Isaiah?
    - ○ Read the fourth paragraph ("1. There is unified ..."). From which parts of Isaiah does John quote?
    - ○ Read the fifth paragraph ("2. There are many ..."). In what parts of Isaiah does the phrase "the Holy One of Israel" occur?
    - ○ Read the seventh paragraph ("However, the primary ..."). Where is the story of God's plan for Judah headed?
- Theme
    - ○ Read the first paragraph.
    - ○ What is the central theme of the book of Isaiah?
    - ○ Who is God, and what does he do?
- Purpose, Occasion, and Background
    - ○ Read the second paragraph. What is the purpose of Isaiah?
    - ○ Read the fifth paragraph ("This question ...").

- With which nation did King Ahaz of Judah make a treaty? In what year?
- Read the sixth paragraph ("The second crisis ...").
- In what year did that nation threaten Jerusalem?
- Read the eighth paragraph ("Second, Isaiah ...").
- To whom does Isaiah write in chapters 40–55?
- Who did Isaiah predict would free the Jews?
- Who would be an even greater liberator?

- **Key Themes**
  - Read theme 2. Who all will be part of God's people?
  - Read theme 7. Who is the only hope for the world?

for the NIV Study Bible

- **Author**
  - Read the first paragraph.
  - What does Isaiah's name mean?
  - When did Isaiah begin his ministry?
  - Read the second paragraph.
  - What do many scholars think about the book of Isaiah?
  - In what parts of Isaiah does the phrase "the Holy One of Israel" occur?
  - Read the last paragraph. From which parts of Isaiah does John quote?

- **Date**
  - How long did Isaiah live?

- **Background**
  - Read the first paragraph.
  - With which nation did King Ahaz of Judah make a treaty? In what year?
  - In what year did that nation threaten Jerusalem?
  - Read the second paragraph.
  - As Isaiah writes chapters 40–55, he looks forward and writes as though what event has happened already?
  - Who did Isaiah predict would deliver the Jews?
  - Who would be an even greater deliverer?

- **Themes and Theology**
  - Read the first paragraph. Who is God, and what must he do?
  - Read the second paragraph.
  - What will God do after that?
  - What is their restoration like?
  - Read the third paragraph ("Peace and safety ...").
  - Who all will come to Jerusalem?

- o Read the fourth paragraph ("The Lord calls ...").
- o Whom all does Isaiah call the Lord's "servant"?
- o Read the last paragraph.
- o Toward what goal does the book of Isaiah move?

Write

Write your own introduction to the book of Isaiah. Tell who wrote the book. Give references from both Isaiah and John's Gospel that say he wrote the book. State when the author ministered. Describe what was going on in and around Judah during those years. Say what Isaiah's name means. State the theme of Isaiah. Give Isaiah's special title for God and write about what God does. Explain how Isaiah writes chapters 40-55. End your introduction by describing what the whole book of Isaiah is moving toward.

160. Isaiah 1:1-2:5

a. Which earlier prophet called heaven and earth as witnesses against Israel (follow the first cross-reference for 1:2)? What does Yahweh charge Israel with; that is, what does he say they have done wrong (1:3-4, 21-23)? How does he feel about their many sacrifices (1:11-15)?

b. What does Yahweh tell them to do and promise them (1:16-20)? How will Yahweh purify his people (1:24-25, 27-28, 31)? Then what will Zion be like again (1:21, 26)?

c. Who all will come to Zion (2:2-3)? What will Yahweh do from Zion (2:3-4)? When did Yahweh begin to fulfill these promises (2:3-4; see Luke 24:45-49; Acts 2:5, 11, 17, 38)?

161. Isaiah 2:6-4:6

a. How has Israel made themselves low (2:8-9)? How will Yahweh Almighty humble proud people and bring their arrogance low (2:11-12, 17-19)? What do Jerusalem's words and deeds do to Yahweh (3:8)?

b. How are the elders and leaders treating Yahweh's people (3:14-15)? Whom is Lord Yahweh Almighty about to take away from Jerusalem (3:1-3)? What kind of leaders will Jerusalem have then (3:4-5, 12)?

c. What will happen to the women in Zion (3:16-4:1)? What will happen to the righteous people in Jerusalem (3:10; 4:2-4)? What earlier event in Israel's history will that day be like (4:5)? Follow the cross-reference to Exodus.

162.   Isaiah 5:1-6:13; 2 Kings 16:1-20

a.   What "grapes" did Yahweh look for in his vineyard (Isaiah 5:4, 7)? What have the "vines" done instead (Isaiah 3:14-15; 5:2, 4, 7, 8, 11-12, 18, 20-23)? How will Yahweh make his "vine-yard" a wasteland (Isaiah 5:1, 5-7, 13-14, 24-30)?

b.   Who is Yahweh, and what is he like (Isaiah 1:4; 2:10, 19, 21; 3:1, 8; 5:16, 24; 6:1-3, 5)? What does Yahweh do for those who repent (Isaiah 6:5-9)? What will Yahweh do to those who keep sinning (Isaiah 5:8, 11, 18, 20-22; 6:9-13)?

c.   What evil does Ahaz do (2 Kings 16:3-4, 7-8)? Whose prophecy does Yahweh use this evil to fulfill (2 Kings 16:9)? Follow the cross-reference for Kir. Whose pattern for worship does Ahaz follow (2 Kings 16:10-18; see Exodus 24:9-10; 25:8-9; 39:42-43)?

163.   Isaiah 7:1-10:4

a.   What will happen before the boy, who is not yet conceived, is old enough to reject the wrong and choose the right (7:14-16)? How will Yahweh do that (5:25-30; 7:16; 8:3-4, 21-22; 9:1; 9:8-10:4)? When will Yahweh do that (7:16)? See the ESV study note for 1 Kings 15:27-31 and the NIV study note for Isaiah 7:16.

b.   How should the boy's names encourage Ahaz to have faith in God (Isaiah 7:4, 9-14; 8:3-4)? What will life in Judah be like after the boy is old enough to reject the wrong and choose the right (7:14-15, 17-25; 8:5-8)? Even then, what hope does Immanuel's name still give Isaiah and his disciples (8:10, 13-14, 16-18)?

c.   Which virgin will conceive without a man and bear a son (7:14; 8:3; see Genesis 3:15; Matthew 1:18, 21-23, 25)? Where will she be (Isaiah 9:1-2; see Luke 1:26-27)? What will her son do (Isaiah 9:5-7; see Isaiah 2:4; Luke 1:31-35, 79)?

164.   Isaiah 10:5-12:6

a.   How does Yahweh use Assyria (8:4-8; 10:5-6, 15)? Why does Yahweh punish the king of Assyria (10:7-13)? What will it look like when Yahweh punishes Assyria (10:17-19, 33-34)?

b.   What will the son of David be like (11:1; see 6:13)? What will his reign be like (9:6-7; 11:2-5)? What will happen in the whole earth (11:6-9)?

c.   What will Yahweh stretch out his hand to do in that day (11:11-12)? What will the return from Assyria be like (11:16)?

When does Yahweh begin to fulfill these promises (Luke 3:22; Romans 15:8-12, 18-19)?

Hosea

165. Hosea – Introduction

Pray. Then Read, Think and <u>Mark</u>.

Read your study Bible's introduction to the book of Hosea. Think about the questions for each of the following sections. <u>Mark</u> the answers and other things that seem important.

for the ESV Study Bible

- Date
    - When did Hosea prophesy?
- Theme
    - What does Hosea depict or show?
    - What is greater than Israel's unfaithfulness?
- Purpose, Occasion, and Background
    - Read the third paragraph ("Within this chaotic ...").
    - What was life like in Israel (the northern kingdom) during these 30 years?
    - What was Hosea's priority?
    - Read the fourth paragraph ("Hosea's major concern ..."). What was Hosea's major concern?
    - Read the last paragraph ("Hosea's approach ...").
    - What was God's relationship with Israel like?
    - How did the Lord treat Israel?
- Outline
    - What is Hosea's own marriage a parable for?

for the NIV Study Bible

- Author and Date
    - When did Hosea prophesy?
- Background
    - What was life like in Israel (the northern kingdom) at that time?

- Theological Theme and Message
    - Read the first paragraph.
    - What was Hosea's family life a symbol of?
    - What was Hosea's wife Gomer like?
    - What did the Lord order Hosea to keep doing?
    - How did the Lord treat Israel?
    - Read the third paragraph.
    - What was God's relationship with Israel like?
    - When they were disloyal to God, what did they turn to?
    - What is the major purpose of the book?

Write

Write your own introduction to the book of Hosea. Tell when and where Hosea prophesied. Describe what life was like during that time. Summarize the story of Hosea's marriage and family. Explain how his family was a parable or symbol of Yahweh's relationship with Israel. Describe how the people of Israel were living at that time. State Hosea's priority or major purpose. Finally, outline the book of Hosea under two main headings:

A.   (1-3)

B.   (4-14)

166.   Hosea 1:1-3:5

a. Why does Yahweh tell Hosea to marry a promiscuous woman or a wife of whoredom (1:2)? Who is the father of each of Gomer's children (1:3, 6, 8-9)? What hope does Yahweh give the people to whom he shows no love or mercy (1:10; 2:1)?

b. Why does Israel worship the Baals (2:5, 12)? What will Yahweh do to Israel (2:6, 8-10; 3:4)? Then what will Israel say (2:7)?

c. When Israel returns and seeks Yahweh their God, how will Yahweh speak to them (2:14-15, 23; 3:5)? What will the relationship between Yahweh and Israel be like (2:19-20)? How does Hosea act out Yahweh's love for Israel (3:1-3)?

167.   Hosea 4:1-7:16

a. What is Yahweh's charge against Israel (4:1)? What all are the people doing wrong (4:10-14, 18)? Who rejects whom (4:6-7; 5:6)?

    b.   What will Yahweh do to Israel (5:2, 8-12, 14)? What is Yahweh waiting for (5:15)? Which person will Yahweh punish for Israel's sins, tear and then raise up on the third day (6:1-2; see Matthew 16:20)?

    c.   What does Yahweh desire, and what does Israel give him (Hosea 6:4, 6)? Whom is Israel devouring like a hot oven (see the study notes for 7:4-7)? From whom does Israel seek help (7:9-11, 14-16)?

168.   Hosea 8:1-10:15

    a.   Does Israel really know Yahweh (8:1-3, 12, 14)? Where has Israel looked for help (8:9-11)? Where will Yahweh send Israel (9:3, 6, 15-17; 10:6, 10)?

    b.   What did Israel do at Gibeah? Follow the study note for Hosea 9:9 to Judges. What did Israel do at Baal Peor? Follow the study note for Hosea 9:10 to Numbers. What did Israel do at Gilgal (Hosea 9:15; see 1 Samuel 13:1-15; 15:1-35)?

    c.   Which king does Israel have (Hosea 10:3)? Where do the people of Israel get their ideas for how to worship God (8:4-6, 12; 10:4-5, 13)? What will Yahweh do (8:13-14; 9:9, 12; 10:14-15)?

169.   Hosea 11:1-14:9

    a.   How did Yahweh treat Israel in Egypt (11:1)? Follow the first cross-reference for "my son" to Exodus (1:1). When again will Yahweh call his son out of Egypt (see 11:1 and the study note)? What kind things did Yahweh do for Israel (Hosea 11:3-4; 12:4-5, 10, 13; 13:4-5)?

    b.   What is Ephraim doing (11:2, 12; 12:7-8, 14; 13:1-2, 6)? Where does Israel seek help (12:1)? How will Yahweh treat Ephraim (11:5-7; 13:3, 7-9, 15-16)?

    c.   What does Yahweh call Ephraim to do (11:8-9; 12:6; 14:1-3)? What will Israel do (11:10-11; 14:7)? Then what will Yahweh do for them (11:11; 14:4-7)?

Joel

170. Joel – Introduction

Pray. Then Read, Think and <u>Mark</u>.

Read your study Bible's introduction to Joel. Think about the questions for each of the following sections. <u>Mark</u> the answers and other things that seem important.

for the ESV Study Bible

- Title and Author
    - Where did Joel probably live?

- Date
    - When may Joel have been written?

- Theme
    - What is the dominant theme of the book of Joel?
    - Who all will experience judgment on that day?

- Purpose, Occasion, and Background
    - What does Joel call everyone to do?
    - What precipitated this great calamity, that is, what made it happen?

- Key Themes
    - Read about the first theme.
    - What does the "day" refer to?
    - What happens on the "day of the Lord"?
    - Read about the second theme.
    - What may happen if the people repent?
    - Read about the third theme.
    - What will the Lord restore?
    - Read about the fourth theme.
    - What will the Lord give?

for the NIV Study Bible

- Author
  - ○ Where did Joel probably live?
- Date
  - ○ Read the first paragraph.
  - ○ When may Joel have been written?
- Theological Message
  - ○ What is happening to Judah?
  - ○ A harbinger is something that lets you know another thing is coming. When the people of Judah see those two things, what else do they know is going to happen?
  - ○ What does Joel call on everyone to do?
  - ○ Who all will be judged and punished on the day of Yahweh?
  - ○ What will come after judgment and repentance?

Write

Write your own introduction to the book of Joel. Identify when and where he may have lived. Describe what was happening in Judah when Joel prophesied. Say what other great judgment is going to happen. Explain what happens to whom on that day. Summarize Joel's call to everyone and the hope he gives them. Finally, outline the book of Joel under two main headings:

A.   (1:1-2:17)

B.   (2:18-3:21)

171.   Joel 1:1-2:17

a.   What is the invading nation doing in the land (1:4, 6-7, 10-12)? How do the priests and farmers and all the people feel (1:9-12, 16)? What does Joel call the people to do (1:13-14)?

b.   What is the day of Yahweh like (1:15)? Which army is destroying the land (2:2-9, 11)? Why do the heavens and earth tremble and the lights in the sky go dark (2:10)?

c.   How should the people return to Yahweh (2:12-13)? Why should the people return to Yahweh (2:13)? When the priests weep before Yahweh, what should they ask him (2:17)?

172.   Joel 2:18-3:21

a.   What does Yahweh do when the people return to him (2:12-14, 18-19, 25)? How does the restoration (when Yahweh makes things good again) make up for the judgment? Compare 2:19, 21-25 with 1:4, 7, 10, 12, 20. What will Yahweh do for all people (2:28)?

b. Whose wish does this prophecy fulfill (Joel 2:28; see Numbers 11:26-29)? When does the Lord fulfill this prophecy (Joel 2:28-32; see Acts 2:1-21)? Whom will the Lord save (Joel 2:23; see Acts 2:37-39; Romans 10:12-13)?

c. What do the signs in the heavens show is about to happen (Joel 2:30-31; 3:14-15)? How can Yahweh's people be safe on the day of Yahweh (2:26-27, 32; 3:16)? What will Zion be like (3:16-17, 20-21)?

Micah

173. Micah – Introduction

Pray. Then Read, Think and <u>Mark</u>.

Read your study Bible's introduction to Micah. Think about the questions for each of the following sections. <u>Mark</u> the answers and other things that seem important.

for the ESV Study Bible

- Author and Title
  - o Where was Micah from?
- Date
  - o During which kings' reigns did Micah prophesy?
  - o Which later prophet quotes from the book of Micah?
- Theme
  - o What is the theme of Micah?
- Purpose, Occasion, and Background
  - o Read the first two paragraphs. What sins does Micah catalog or make a careful list of?
- Key Themes
  - o Read the second theme. What will the Shepherd-King do?
  - o Read the fifth theme. Why does God forgive?
- Outline
  - o Read the first paragraph. What two things are in the pattern found throughout the book?

for the NIV Study Bible

- Author
  - o Where was Micah from?
- Date
  - o During which kings' reigns did Micah prophesy?
  - o Which later prophet quotes from the book of Micah?

- Literary Analysis
  - Read the first paragraph. What two things does Micah talk about in each cycle?
- Theme and Message
  - What is the theme of Micah?
  - What does God hate, and what does he delight in?
  - Who will lead the Davidic kingdom (the kingdom led by David's descendants) to greater glory?

Write

Write your own introduction to the book of Micah. Tell where Micah was from and when and where he prophesied. List the sins Micah spoke against. Summarize what Micah said about the Messiah. Finally, explain Micah's pattern of speaking about judgment and salvation and outline the book in three cycles.

174. Micah 1:1-2:13

a. Why does Yahweh come down (1:3-5)? Where does the disaster start, and how far does it reach (1:6, 9, 12)? What happens to the people who live in the cities of Judah (1:10-12, 14-16)?

b. Against whom do wicked oppressors plan and do evil (2:1-2, 8-9)? What will the oppressed people sing about their oppressors (2:4)? Who are the traitors or apostate people to whom Yahweh gives their fields (see the study note for 2:4)?

c. Where does all this disaster come from (1:12, 15; 2:3)? Afterward, what will Yahweh do for the remnant of Israel (2:12)? Who will be their shepherd and their king (2:12-13)?

175. Micah 3:1-5:15

a. How should a true prophet lead (3:1, 8)? How do the heads and prophets of Israel lead (3:1-3, 5, 9-11)? What will Yahweh do to them (3:4, 6-7, 12)?

b. What will happen to Zion now (4:9-11; 5:1)? What will Yahweh do to Jacob among the nations (5:10-14)? What will Yahweh do for the remnant (4:6-7; 5:3)?

c. Who will rule as king in Zion (4:7-8; 5:2, 4)? Follow the cross-reference for 5:2 to Matthew. What will the ruler do to the nations (Micah 4:3, 12-13; 5:5-9)? Why will the nations come to the mountain of Yahweh (4:2; 5:4-5)?

176.   Micah 6:1-7:20; 2 Kings 17:1-18:12

a.   In the historical prologue of his case or lawsuit, what kind things does Yahweh say he has done (Micah 6:4-5)? What does the suzerain king require (Micah 6:8)? What are the people doing (Micah 6:11-12, 16; 7:2-6)?

b.   What will Yahweh do to Israel (Micah 6:9, 13-15)? How will Yahweh save his people (Micah 7:7-9, 11-17)? How is El different from other gods (Micah 7:18-20)?

c.   Through which prophets did Yahweh warn his people about this judgment (2 Kings 17:13, 23; see Isaiah 8:1-4; 10:5-6; Hosea 9:15-17; 10:6; Amos 2:13-16)? Did the people whom the king of Assyria brought to Samaria fear Yahweh or not (2 Kings 17:25, 28, 32-33, 34-39)? What kind of king was Hezekiah (2 Kings 18:3-6)?

177.   Isaiah 13:1-16:14

a.   Who are the people Yahweh consecrates (sets apart as holy) and uses as his weapons against Babylon (13:3-5, 17-18)? What is the day of Yahweh like (13:6, 9)? What will Yahweh do for Israel after he destroys Babylon (14:1-2)?

b.   On the day of Yahweh, what is Yahweh against (13:11)? Follow the first cross-reference for "the day of the LORD" (13:6). Who is the day (or morning) star, the son of the dawn (14:4, 12, 16)? Why does Yahweh bring him down (14:12-15, 19-20, 22)?

c.   When Yahweh makes a plan, who can stop him (14:24, 27)? When Moab is attacked, where will the people run for refuge (see 16:3-4 and the study note)? What kind of king will Yahweh give Israel (16:4-5)?

178.   Isaiah 17:1-20:6

a.   When does Yahweh fulfill Isaiah's prophecy against Damascus (see the study notes for 17:1-3)? What will people in Israel start to do after they also are beaten (17:4-8)? How quickly will God protect them from the nations (17:13-14)?

b.   How does Yahweh judge Egypt (19:2-7, 12-14)? When are Egypt and Cush captured (see 20:1, 4 and the study note for 20:1)? Should other peoples look to Cush and Egypt for help (20:5-6)?

c.   At that time, what will the people of Cush do (18:7)? In that day, what will Egypt do (19:22)? In that day, who all will be Yahweh's people, those who worship him (19:18-25)?

179.   Isaiah 21:1-23:18

a.   When do the people of Jerusalem defend the city but not show sorrow as Lord Yahweh tells them to (22:8-14)? Follow the cross-reference for "the old pool" (22:11). Why does Yahweh give Eliakim the authority that Shebna had (Isaiah 22:15-23)? Is Eliakim able to lead Judah as he must (22:25)?

b.   What will happen to Jerusalem and Judah (21:10; 22:3-5)? Then what will happen to Babylon (21:9)? How would Isaiah's prophecy in 21:9 encourage the people of Judah when Babylon attacks them and when they are captives in exile in Babylon?

c.   What do the people of Tyre do (23:3)? What plan does Yahweh purpose for Tyre (23:9, 11)? How will Yahweh use even evil for good (23:17-18; see Ezra 1:1-4; 3:7)?

(3) Think about and answer the questions. (4) Return to your bookmark.

180. Isaiah 24:1-27:13

a. What have the people done to the earth (24:4-6, 20)? What will Yahweh do to the earth and its inhabitants (24:1-3, 17, 21-22)? What will the few people who are left do (24:6, 13-16)?

b. What has Judah failed to do (26:17-18)? How does Yahweh atone for Jacob's guilt and remove his sin (27:8-9)? What will Yahweh of hosts do for the poor and needy (24:23; 25:1-5, 10-12; 26:5-6)?

c. Where will Yahweh's people come back to (26:1-2, 15; 27:2-3, 6, 12)? What will Yahweh do there for all peoples (25:6-9; 26:19)? How should Yahweh's people live now (26:3-4, 8-9, 11-12)?

181. Isaiah 28:1-29:24

a. What will Yahweh of hosts be for the remnant of his people who are spared in that day (28:5-6)? What do the priest and prophet in Jerusalem think of Isaiah's message (28:7-10)? What will happen to them when Yahweh sends foreign people who speak a strange language to give them his message (28:11-13)?

b. What standard does Lord Yahweh use to judge the righteousness of his people in Zion (28:16-17)? Will the people who rely on the stone (or believe him) have to try anxiously to be in line with the stone (28:16; see Romans 9:30-10:4)? What will Lord Yahweh do to the land and to Ariel (28:21-22; 29:2-5)?

c. Then what will Yahweh do to the nations he used to fight against Ariel (29:5-7; see 2 Kings 19:34-35)? Yet what do the people say when the Lord tells them this vision (29:11-13, 15-16)? What will happen when Yahweh shows his people wonders (29:14, 18-19, 22-24)?

182. Isaiah 30:1-31:9

a. Where do Yahweh's children seek refuge (30:1-2)? How helpful will that protection be (30:3, 5, 6-7)? What does Lord Yahweh tell them to do to be saved and strong (30:15)?

b. But what do the people say (30:9-11, 16)? What will Yahweh do to those who trust Egypt for help (30:17; 31:1-3)? What does Yahweh want to do (30:18)?

c. After the afflicted people turn back to Yahweh, what will they see, hear and do (30:19-22; 31:6-7)? What will Yahweh do for them (30:23-26)? What will Yahweh do to their enemies (30:27-33; 31:8-9)?

183. Isaiah 32:1-33:24

a. What do fools and scoundrels do (32:5-7)? Why should the complacent women tremble (32:9-14)? What will life in the kingdom be like after the destruction (32:1-4, 15-18)?

b. What has Assyria done to Zion (33:1, 7-9)? Why do the faithful people in Zion wait and long for Yahweh (33:2, 5-6)? How will Yahweh treat the peoples (33:3-4, 10-14, 19)?

c. Who can survive Yahweh's consuming fire (33:14-16)? What will Yahweh make Zion like (33:5-6, 17, 19-21, 24)? Who do the people say Yahweh is (33:22)?

184. Isaiah 34:1-36:22; 2 Kings 18:13-37

a. Which armies or hosts will Yahweh destroy (Isaiah 34:2-4)? What will Yahweh do to Edom (Isaiah 34:5-17)? What will Yahweh do to the wilderness in Israel (Isaiah 35:1-2, 6-7)?

b. What will Yahweh do for his disabled people (Isaiah 35:5-6; see 6:9-10; 32:3-4)? Where will Yahweh's redeemed people come (Isaiah 35:8-10)? Who will prepare the way in the wilderness (Isaiah 35:8; see Isaiah 40:3; Matthew 3:1-3; Acts 9:1-2)?

c. Why might someone call the king of Assyria's question the most important question in the book of Isaiah (2 Kings 18:19; Isaiah 36:4)? Did Yahweh really tell the king of Assyria to destroy Judah (2 Kings 18:25; Isaiah 36:10)? Follow the cross-reference for "the LORD told me" in Isaiah 36:10 to Isaiah 10. Whom should the people of Jerusalem trust to deliver them (2 Kings 18:29-30, 33-35; Isaiah 36:14-15, 18-20; see Isaiah 14:24-27; 26:3-6)?

185. 2 Kings 19:1-37; Isaiah 37:1-38

a. How did Hezekiah try to save Judah at first (2 Kings 18:13-16)? What does he do now (2 Kings 19:14-19; Isaiah 37:14-20)? Whom has Sennacherib mocked and ridiculed (2 Kings 19:4, 16, 22-23; Isaiah 37:4, 6, 17, 23-24)?

b. How quickly does Yahweh answer Hezekiah (2 Kings 19:20; see Isaiah 30:19)? Now who despises whom (2 Kings 19:21; Isaiah 37:22)? Why was Sennacherib able to destroy fortified cities (2 Kings 19:25-26; Isaiah 37:26-27)?

(3) Think about and answer the questions. (4) Return to your bookmark.

c. Why does Yahweh save Jerusalem (2 Kings 19:19, 34; Isaiah 37:20, 35)? How does the angel of Yahweh kill 185,000 Assyrian soldiers (2 Kings 19:35; Isaiah 29:5-8; 30:27-33; 31:8-9; 37:36)? Which king's god fails him when he goes to his temple (2 Kings 18:29-30, 33-35; 19:14, 37; Isaiah 36:14-15, 18-20; 37:14, 38)?

186. 2 Kings 20:1-21; Isaiah 38:1-39:8

a. Does Hezekiah recover from his sickness and do the envoys come from Babylon before Yahweh delivers Jerusalem from Assyria or after (2 Kings 20:1, 6, 12; Isaiah 38:1, 6; 39:1; see the study notes for Isaiah 38:6; 39:1)? In this story what all goes down and turns and comes back (2 Kings 20:1-2, 5, 7, 9-11; Isaiah 38:1-2, 5, 8, 9, 21)? How is Hezekiah healed (2 Kings 20:5, 7-8; Isaiah 38:5, 7, 21)?

b. Why did Yahweh make Hezekiah so sick (Isaiah 38:13, 15, 17)? Why does Yahweh heal him (Isaiah 38:16-17)? Who sees and praises Yah (Isaiah 38:11, 18-20)?

c. Why may Marduk-Baladan have sent envoys with a gift to Hezekiah (see 2 Kings 20:12-13; Isaiah 39:1-2 and study notes)? When will Yahweh begin to fulfill this prophecy (2 Kings 20:17-18; Isaiah 39:6-7)? Follow the cross-references for Isaiah 39:6-7. But what does Hezekiah still think the prophecy means (2 Kings 20:19; Isaiah 39:8)?

187. Isaiah 40:1-41:29

a. What hard service or warfare will Jerusalem have to go through (40:2; see 39:6-7)? What is the gospel or good news for the towns of Judah (40:9-11)? Whose power and understanding are no match for Yahweh's (40:12-17)?

b. Do idols move and make things, or do humans move and make them (40:18-20; 41:7)? What does Yahweh move and make (40:21-26)? What should Israel do (40:27-31)?

c. What will Yahweh do for Israel when he stirs up one from the east (41:2-4, 8-10, 14)? How will Yahweh care for his people in the wilderness (40:3-5, 11; 41:17-20; see 35:1-10)? Who declares all these things long before they happen (41:21-26)?

188. Isaiah 42:1-43:28

a. What will Yahweh's servant do for the people and for the nations (42:1-4, 6-7)? Who is Yahweh's servant? See the study notes for 42:1-4, and follow the cross-reference for 42:1 or 42:4 to Matthew 12. Why did Yahweh hand Israel over to the plunderers (Isaiah 42:19-25; see 6:9-10; 42:8; 43:22-28)?

b. How does Yahweh act now (42:14-16)? What does he command his deaf and blind people to do (42:18)? <u>Underline</u> each time Yahweh says "I," "my" or "you" in 43:1-7. How does Yahweh feel about his people (43:1-7)?

c. What will Yahweh do for his people (43:8, 12, 14, 16-21)? What will this new thing make the people forget (43:16-19)? Why does Yahweh do all this to save his people (42:8, 12; 43:4, 7, 10-14, 21)?

189. Isaiah 44:1-45:25

a. After Yahweh pours his Spirit on Jacob's offspring, how will they feel about him (44:3-5)? Who makes what (44:9-20, 24)? Who is Yahweh, and what has he done for Israel (44:6, 22, 24)?

b. About how many years before Cyrus will become king does Yahweh call him by name (44:28-45:7)? See the study notes for Isaiah 39:1 and Ezra 1:1. Why does Yahweh send Cyrus to conquer (45:4-7)? Is it wrong for Yahweh to create this disastrous calamity (45:7, 9-13)?

c. Why will the nations come to Jerusalem (45:14-17)? What does El (God) command all nations on earth to do (45:20-23; see Philippians 2:9-11)? What will Yahweh do for all Israel's offspring (45:25)?

190. Isaiah 46:1-48:22

a. What does Yahweh do (46:4, 10)? Who carries the other: the idols or the people (46:7)? Who makes Bel and Nebo, the gods of Babylon, bow down (46:1-2, 11; see 45:1-7, 23; 48:14-16)?

b. What has Babylon done to Israel (47:6)? What will happen to Babylon (47:9-11)? When Babylon's astrologers and counselors keep doing their sorceries, will they be able to succeed and save Babylon (47:12-15)?

c. What kind of people are Israel (48:1-8; see 46:12)? Why does Yahweh preserve and purify Israel (48:9-11)? When Israel goes out of Babylon, where will Yahweh lead them (48:20-21; see 40:3-5, 11; 41:17-20; 43:19-21; 44:28; 45:13-14)?

191. Isaiah 49:1-50:11

a. Who is Yahweh's servant (49:1-3; see the study notes for 49:1-13; 49:3)? What will the servant do (49:5-6, 8)? How will Yahweh comfort his people (49:8-13)?

b. How does Yahweh show Zion that he has not forgotten her (49:14-16)? Who are the children that Zion does not recognize when they come to her (49:5-6, 19-23)? Why will Yahweh rescue his people (49:25-26)?

c. When and why did Yahweh divorce his wife and sell his children (50:1)? Follow the cross-reference for 50:1 to Hosea. What happens to Yahweh's servant when he listens and obeys (50:4-7)? What should those who fear Yahweh do (50:10)?

192. Isaiah 51:1-52:12

a. How does Yahweh comfort Zion (51:3, 11-12)? What does Yahweh do because he is righteous (51:5)? What does Yahweh do with his righteous law (51:4, 7, 16)?

b. Why did Yahweh afflict Zion and make his people suffer (51:13, 17-21)? Whom will Yahweh afflict now (51:22-23)? Why will Yahweh save his people (52:5-6, 10)?

c. How will Yahweh comfort his people and redeem Jerusalem (52:9-10)? Then what good news will the messenger run to tell Zion (52:7)? Who all will return to Zion (52:8, 11-12)?

193. Isaiah 52:13-55:13

a. Who is Yahweh's wise servant who is lifted up (52:13-14)? Why is the servant afflicted and crushed (53:4-6, 8)? Yet what do the people think of him (53:1-4)?

b. Whose will is it to crush the servant (53:10)? What does the righteous servant do with his knowledge (53:11)? What will their offspring do (53:10; 54:3)?

c. How will Yahweh treat his wife (534:5-8; see 50:1)? What covenant will Yahweh make with those who come and listen (55:1-7)? Where and how will Yahweh lead them (55:12-13)?

194. Isaiah 56:1-58:14

a. When he gave his law to Israel, what did Yahweh say about foreigners and eunuchs (see the study note for 56:3)? Whom all will Lord Yahweh gather (56:6-8)? When Jesus quotes

Isaiah 56:7, what are the people doing wrong? Follow the cross-reference for Isaiah 56:7 to the verse in Mark.

b. What have the Israelites done (Isaiah 57:5-8)? How are the wicked revived, and how are the lowly revived (57:10, 15)? What will the One who is high do for his people who are low (57:15-19)?

c. Do the people seek Yahweh (58:2)? Why does Yahweh not accept them (58:3-7)? What will Yahweh do when his people seek him, keep justice and do righteousness (56:1; 58:9-14)?

195.   Isaiah 59:1-61:11

a. At last, what do the people say about their sins (59:12-13)? What does it look like when Yahweh brings salvation and righteousness (59:16-20)? What does Yahweh do for those who turn from their sins (59:20-21)?

b. When the glory of Yahweh rises on Zion, what will Zion look like (60:1-2, 7, 9-11, 17)? What all will the nations bring to Zion (60:3-16)? What will the people of Zion be like (60:20-21)?

c. Whom will Lord Yahweh send to make these great things happen (61:1, 10)? To whom does he bring the good news of Yahweh's favor (61:1-3)? When does Yahweh send this anointed one? Follow the cross-reference for 61:1 to Luke.

196.   Isaiah 62:1-64:12

a. What should the watchmen who call on Yahweh do (62:1, 6-7, 10-11)? How will Yahweh feel about Zion (62:3-5)? How will the Redeemer save Zion (63:1-6)?

b. How does Yahweh feel about his people (63:7-9)? What does Yahweh do when his people sin (63:10)? What does Isaiah remember (63:11-14)?

c. What does Isaiah call Yahweh (63:15-16; 64:7)? What do the people say about their sin (64:5-7)? What do the people call on Yahweh to do (63:15; 64:1-2, 9-12)?

197.   Isaiah 65:1-66:24

a. Was Yahweh far away and not ready to answer his people (64:12-65:2; see 65:12, 24; 66:4)? What will Yahweh do to rebellious people whose worship is not true (65:2-7, 11-12)? Whom will Yahweh bless in the land (65:8-10, 13-16)?

b. What will Jerusalem be like in the new heavens and earth (65:17-25)? What will Yahweh do for his people in Jerusalem

(66:10-14)? What will Yahweh do to his enemies (66:3-6, 14-17, 24)?

c. What will the people who survive Yahweh's judgment do (66:19-20)? What will Yahweh do with his people's brothers from all the nations (66:20-21)? Why would Paul, the minister to the nations, want to go through Greece and Rome and on to Spain? See the study note for 66:19 and read Romans 15:16-24.

198. Isaiah – Review

Pray. Think through the following points.

You've now read all of Isaiah. Well done! Today you will think back over the book.

a. Reread your own introduction to the book (lesson 159).

b. What was the theme of Isaiah? How did Isaiah show that Yahweh is the Holy One of Israel?

c. What goal is the book of Isaiah moving toward? What will Yahweh's kingdom on earth be like?

d. Look back through the book. Note the words and verses you marked. What are the main things God was showing and teaching Israel?

e. What things seemed important to you?

f. Look back at your answers to question *d* each day (lessons 160-164, 179-194). What were some things you discovered on your own?

g. Think back through your answers to question *f* each day. What are some key ways God is telling you to change the way you love, think or live?

h. Jesus told his disciples, "Everything must be fulfilled that is written about me in the Law of Moses, the Prophets and the Psalms" (Luke 24:44). What parts of Isaiah made you think about the Messiah? You may think about the promise of the virgin's son and the meaning of his name, the promise of the nation's son and his names, the stump of Jesse or Yahweh's Servant.

Write

Write a review of Isaiah. In the first paragraph, state the key theme and Isaiah's special name for God. Describe some ways you saw that theme in the book. In the second paragraph, write about some of the things you discovered or that seemed important to you. Describe how God is changing the way you love, think or live. In the third paragraph, explain one of Jesus' "shadows" in Isaiah and how it made you think of him. Finally, end your review with a prayer to Jesus, the Holy One of Israel. Tell him how you feel about his holiness, his majesty and his mercy (especially if you are one of the people he has gathered from the nations and brought to Zion). Praise him for his holiness and his majesty. Thank him for his mercy gathering you from the nations and bringing you to be part of his people in Zion. Tell him how you want to live as one of his people.

199.   2 Kings 21:1-22:2

a.   In what year did Manasseh begin to reign (21:1)? Flip back to the chart of the rulers of the divided kingdom. The chart is near 1 Kings 12-14. Find the years Manasseh, Amon and Josiah began to reign. Now flip back to 2 Kings 21:1, 19; 22:1 and write those years in the margin.

b.   Which other nations is Manasseh even more evil than (21:2, 9, 11)? How will Yahweh treat Manasseh's kingdom Judah (21:11-15)? Does Manasseh listen to Isaiah and the other prophets (21:9-10, 16; see Isaiah 57:3-13; 59:3-8)?

c.   What sort of king is Josiah (22:2)? Which other kings' names does Josiah's mother's name remind you of (22:1-2; see 2 Samuel 12:24-25)? Which prophet's teaching does the author of Kings want you to think about when you read the phrase "to the right or to the left" in 22:2? Follow the cross-reference.

Every day: (1) Follow your bookmark and pray. (2) Read and mark the passage.

Zephaniah

200. Zephaniah – Introduction

Pray. Then Read, Think and <u>Mark</u>.

Read your study Bible's introduction to the book of Zephaniah. Think about the questions for each of the following sections. <u>Mark</u> the answers and other things that seem important.

for the ESV Study Bible
- Author and Title
  - From which king of Judah was Zephaniah descended?
- Date
  - Read the first paragraph. During the reign of which king of Judah did Zephaniah prophesy?
- Theme
  - What is the theme of Zephaniah?
  - What two things will God do on that day?
- Key Themes
  - When will God bless his people?
- Literary Features
  - Read the second paragraph. How does Zephaniah use poetry to show what the coming judgment will be like?

for the NIV Study Bible
- Author
  - From which king of Judah was Zephaniah descended?
- Date
  - During the reign of which king of Judah did Zephaniah prophesy?
- Purpose and Theological Theme
  - Read the second paragraph.

- What is Zephaniah's main theme?
- What will God do on the day of Yahweh?
- How does Zephaniah portray or show how horrible that day will be?
- What will God do for his people who repent?

Write

Write your own introduction to the book of Zephaniah. Tell who Zephaniah was descended from and when he prophesied. State Zephaniah's main theme. Explain the two sorts of things God does on that day. Finally, fill in the outline below:

A.   (1:1-18)

B.   (2:1-3:8)

C.   (3:9-20)

201.   Zephaniah 1:1-3:20

a.   Whom all will Yahweh punish (1:2-3, 17-18)? What is wrong with the way the people of Jerusalem worship Yahweh (1:4-6; see 3:4)? What does Yahweh say the day of Yahweh will be like (1:7, 8, 14-16, 18; 2:2)?

b.   What does Zephaniah call the people of Judah to seek (2:3)? In the middle of all the judgments, what hope does Yahweh give to humble Israelites (2:7, 9; see 3:12)? Does Jerusalem accept Yahweh's correction and draw near to him (3:1-2, 7)?

c.   What will Yahweh do to the nations (3:8)? Whom all will Yahweh gather and bring to Zion (3:9-10, 20)? What will Yahweh do for them (3:15, 17-20)?

Nahum

202. Nahum – Introduction

Pray. Then Read, Think and <u>Mark</u>.

Read your study Bible's introduction to the book of Nahum. Think about the questions for each of the following sections. <u>Mark</u> the answers and other things that seem important.

for the ESV Study Bible

- Author and Title
  - o   What does Nahum's name mean?
  - o   What would bring comfort to Judah?
- Date
  - o   Read the first paragraph.
  - o   Of which empire is Nineveh the capital city?
  - o   In what year did Nineveh fall?
  - o   When did Nahum prophesy?
- Theme
  - o   What is the theme of Nahum?
- Purpose, Occasion, and Background
  - o   Read the second paragraph. What did the people of Nineveh do when Jonah warned them of God's judgment?
  - o   Read the third paragraph. How did the Assyrians establish their empire?
  - o   Read the last paragraph. In the end, what happened to the Assyrians?
- Key Themes
  - o   Read the first theme. What is the Lord like? What does the Lord do?
  - o   Read the third theme. Why did Nineveh fall?
- Literary Features
  - o   Read the first paragraph. What are Nahum's oracles like?

for the NIV Study Bible

- Author
    - What does Nahum's name mean?
    - What would bring comfort to Judah?
- Date
    - In what year did Nineveh fall?
    - When did Nahum prophesy?
- Background
    - Read the first paragraph. What did the Assyrians and their army do when they fought?
    - Read the second paragraph.
    - Of which empire is Nineveh the capital city?
    - What did the people of Nineveh do when Jonah warned them of God's judgment?
    - In the end, what happened to the Assyrians?
- Literary Style
    - What are Nahum's oracles like?
- Theological Themes
    - Read the first paragraph. What is the focal point (or main theme) of the book of Nahum?
    - Read the second paragraph. What is the Lord like? What does the Lord do?
    - Read the third paragraph. What is God the Lord of?

Write

Write your own introduction to the book of Nahum. Say what Nahum's name means and how his message brings comfort to Judah. State the theme of Nahum. Tell how Yahweh had warned the people of Nineveh before and what they did. Describe how the people of that empire fought and made their empire bigger. Explain what the Lord is like, what he does and why he is judging Nineveh. Say what happened to Nineveh in the end and when that end was. Finally, outline the book under four main headings:

A.   (1:1-8)

B.   (1:9-15)

C.   (2:1-13)

D.   (3:1-19)

203. Nahum 1:1-3:19

a. Who is Yahweh, and what does he do (1:2-3, 7-8)? What is Yahweh for those who trust him and seek refuge in him (1:7; see 3:11)? What evil has Assyria done (1:9-11, 14)?

b. What is Yahweh doing for Israel (1:15; 2:2)? How does Yahweh use an overwhelming flood to destroy Nineveh and make the palace collapse like a sandcastle (1:8; 2:6, 8; see the study notes for 2:6, 8)? How does Yahweh's fiery anger destroy the lions' den (1:6; 2:11-13; see the study note for 2:11)?

c. What sort of evil has Assyria done (3:1, 4)? How will Yahweh show how shameful Nineveh's behavior has been (3:5-7)? Does Assyria deserve this punishment (3:19)?

Jeremiah

204. Jeremiah – Introduction

Pray. Then Read, Think and <u>Mark</u>.

Read your study Bible's introduction to the book of Jeremiah. Think about the questions for each of the following sections. <u>Mark</u> the answers and other things that seem important.

for the ESV Study Bible

- Author and Title
    - Read the second paragraph.
    - Does the book of Jeremiah arrange Jeremiah's oracles in chronological order?
    - Who was Baruch, and what did he do?
    - Read the sixth paragraph ("Jeremiah's difficult life").
    - When did Jeremiah's ministry as a prophet begin, and when did it end?
    - What did Jeremiah become?
    - Read the seventh paragraph ("Jeremiah had a ...").
    - What was Jeremiah's life like?
    - Did Jeremiah have many friends?
    - Read the eighth paragraph ("Many authors have ...").
    - What kind of follower of God was Jeremiah?
- Purpose, Occasion, and Background
    - Read the second paragraph. What was Jeremiah and Baruch's purpose when they wrote the book of Jeremiah?
    - Read the third paragraph ("Jeremiah lived ..."). What was life like during these times?
    - Read the fourth paragraph ("During Josiah's era ..."). Which country conquered Assyria?
- Key Themes
    - Read the second paragraph. How does Jeremiah present God?

- o Read the third paragraph ("God rules ..."). What is God like?
- o Read the fifth paragraph ("Since Israel ..."). What does the Creator become?
- o Read the sixth paragraph ("Given this situation ..."). What does Jeremiah ask the people to do?
- o Read the seventh paragraph ("Old covenant ..."). What had God made with Israel?
- o Read the ninth paragraph ("As time passed ...").
- o What will God do for Israel?
- o What will the king be like?
- o Read the eleventh paragraph ("God used ...").
- o What would God make with Israel and Judah?
- o In that covenant, what would God make his people like?

for the NIV Study Bible
- • Author and Date
  - o Read the first paragraph.
  - o What was Jeremiah's personal life like?
  - o When did Jeremiah's ministry as a prophet begin and end?
  - o Read the second paragraph.
  - o What kind of household was Jeremiah raised in?
  - o Did Jeremiah have many friends?
  - o Who was Baruch, and what did he do?
  - o Read the last sentence of the last paragraph. What was Jeremiah like?
- • Background
  - o Read the first paragraph.
  - o Who were the kings of Judah while Jeremiah was a prophet?
  - o What was life like for the countries of western Asia (the Middle East) during this period?
  - o Which countries conquered Assyria?
- • Theological Themes and Message
  - o Read the third paragraph ("Judgment is one ...").
  - o What is a theme that goes all through Jeremiah's writings?
  - o What did Jeremiah tell the people they must do?
  - o Read the fourth paragraph ("For Jeremiah, ...").
  - o How did Jeremiah conceive of (or think about) God?
  - o Of what is God the Lord?

- Read the seventh paragraph ("But God's judgment ...").
- What would God do for Israel after the judgment?
- What would God make with his people?
- What would God do in that covenant?
- What would the leaders be like?

- Outline
  - Read the first sentence. Does the book of Jeremiah arrange Jeremiah's oracles in chronological order?

Write

Write your own introduction to the book of Jeremiah. Describe what life was like in Judah and other countries during Jeremiah's lifetime. Describe Jeremiah and what his life was like. Say who Baruch was and what he did. Tell the story so far of God's relationship with his people and what is about to happen. State Jeremiah's command to the people. Summarize the hope God gives his people for the future, and explain what will happen in the new covenant.

205. Jeremiah 1:1-3:5

a. What does Yahweh set Jeremiah apart to do (1:5, 7, 10)? Will Jeremiah's work be easy (1:19)? How does Yahweh encourage Jeremiah (1:7-9, 18-19)?

b. How did Israel used to feel about Yahweh (2:2-3)? Then what did Israel do (1:16; 2:5, 7-8, 11)? What have the "lions" done to Israel (2:14-15, 18)?

c. What has Israel acted like (2:20, 23-24, 32-33; 3:1-3)? What else is Israel guilty of (2:34)? How do you think God feels (2:5, 7, 11-12, 20-21, 23-24, 27-30, 32, 35-36; 3:5)?

206. Jeremiah 3:6-4:31

a. What have Israel and Judah acted like (3:6-10)? What does Yahweh call them to do (3:10, 12-14)? What will Yahweh do for them when they return with their whole hearts (3:14-18, 22)?

b. What do the Israelites say when they return (3:22-25)? What does Yahweh tell them to do (4:1-2, 4)? What will the nations do when Yahweh restores Israel (3:17; 4:2)?

c. Who brings disaster against Jerusalem (4:5-8, 11-13, 16)? Why is this evil happening (4:14, 17-18, 22)? What does it look like after the disaster (4:23-26)? Follow the cross-reference for "formless and empty" or "without form and void" (4:23).

207. Jeremiah 5:1-6:30

a. Who all refuse to listen to Yahweh and repent (5:3-5)? How have Israel and Judah sinned against Yahweh (5:7-9, 11-12)? How completely will Yahweh destroy them (5:10, 17-18)?

b. How will the people become like the gods they have been serving (5:19, 21)? How else have they sinned against Yahweh (5:22-29)? Who all deserves Yahweh's punishment (6:11-15)?

c. What do the people do when Yahweh or Jeremiah talks to them (6:8, 10, 16-19)? Who tells the foreign nation to attack Jerusalem (5:15; 6:2-3, 6, 19, 21-23)? Are Yahweh's punishment and testing making the people change (5:3; 6:27-30)?

208. 2 Kings 22:3-23:37; Jeremiah 26:1-24

a. Who hears whom (2 Kings 22:11, 19)? What is written in the Book of the Law about Israel becoming desolate (a horror), accursed and laid waste (2 Kings 22:11, 13, 16, 19; see Deuteronomy 28:15, 37, 45)? In what ways is King Josiah's covenant like an earlier covenant (2 Kings 23:3)? Follow the cross-reference to Deuteronomy.

b. To which other gods have the Israelites given offerings (2 Kings 22:17; 23:4-14)? Whose prophecy does Josiah fulfill when he burns human bones on the altar in Bethel (2 Kings 23:15-17)? Follow the cross-reference to 1 Kings 13. Which command does Josiah keep (2 Kings 23:25; see Deuteronomy 6:5)?

c. How do the priests and the prophets feel when Jeremiah speaks against Yahweh's house (Jeremiah 26:2-11)? Which earlier event in their history do the elders say shows them how to respond to Jeremiah's message (Jeremiah 26:17-19)? Why might Shaphan's son Ahikam want to protect Jeremiah (see Jeremiah 26:24 and the cross-reference)?

209. Jeremiah 7:1-9:9

a. How do robbers feel when they are in their den (7:11; see 7:4, 8-10)? Follow the cross-reference for "den of robbers" to Matthew. Which commands are the people of Judah breaking (see the study note for Jeremiah 7:9)? What happened to Shiloh when the people thought they could do evil and still be safe because Yahweh and his house were among them (7:12-14; see 1 Samuel 4:2-11)?

b. How will Yahweh treat the people of Judah (Jeremiah 7:15)? Follow the cross-reference to 2 Kings. Which does Yahweh want more: obedient listening or burnt sacrifices (Jeremiah 7:21-26)? What did the people do when Jeremiah preached this sermon (7:27; see 26:1-24)?

c. What sin do the people of Judah keep doing (7:4; 8:5-6, 10; 9:2-6, 8)? How does Jeremiah feel (8:18-9:2)? Should Yahweh punish a nation like this (9:9; see 5:9, 29)?

210. Jeremiah 9:10-10:25

a. Which man has heard the words of Yahweh's mouth and is wise or skillful enough to explain this (9:13, 17, 20-22)? When a wise person has insight, what will he know Yahweh is like (9:24)? Are Judah's shepherds (leaders) wise and understanding (10:21; see 8:8-9; 9:3, 6)?

b. Why will Yahweh lay waste Jerusalem and Judah and empty them of people (9:10-16)? What part of a person's body most needs to be cut back and made clean (9:25-26)? What does Jeremiah ask Yahweh to do to the nations that have devoured Jacob (10:25)?

c. How are idols and the gods of the nations not like Yahweh (10:1-11)? What are idols and their makers like (10:14-15)? What is Yahweh like (10:12-13, 16)?

211. Jeremiah 11:1-13:27

a. How has Judah broken Yahweh's covenant with them (11:3-4, 6-8)? Who will listen when Judah cries for help (11:10-12)? What will Yahweh do to his beloved (11:14-17)?

b. How does Jeremiah feel about what the men of Judah are doing to him (11:18-20; 12:3)? How does Yahweh feel about what he has had to do to Judah (12:7-13)? What hope does Yahweh give to Judah and all nations (12:15-16)?

c. How is Judah to Yahweh like Jeremiah's loincloth is to him (13:11)? What will Yahweh do to the jars that are full of wine (13:13-14)? What will Yahweh do to his adulterous wife (13:22, 26-27)?

212. Jeremiah 14:1-15:21

a. Even before invaders come, how does Yahweh punish his people (14:1-6)? Why does Yahweh tell Jeremiah, "Do not pray for this people" (14:10-12)? Will fasts and offerings make him change his mind (14:12)?

    b. How do the other prophets prophesy (14:13-16)? When he prays for his people, to what does Jeremiah appeal (14:20-22)? Is Yahweh remembering his covenant with Israel (15:1-4)? Follow the cross-references to Leviticus and Deuteronomy.

    c. What does Yahweh do to his people (Jeremiah 15:7-9)? How does Jeremiah feel (15:10, 16, 18)? What does Yahweh promise him (15:19-21)?

213. Jeremiah 16:1-17:27

    a. How does Yahweh punish the people of Judah for serving other gods (16:11, 13)? What memorable rescue will the return from exile be even greater than (16:14-15)? Then what will the nations know (16:19-21)?

    b. What kinds of plants are the people who trust humans and the people who trust Yahweh like (17:5-8)? What is the human heart like (17:1, 9)? Who understands and heals it (17:9-10, 14)?

    c. How and why should the people of Judah keep the Sabbath day holy? Read 17:21-22 and follow the cross-reference to Deuteronomy. How will Yahweh bless the people of Judah if they obey him (Jeremiah 17:24-26)? How will Yahweh curse them if they disobey him (17:27)?

214. Jeremiah 18:1-20:18

    a. Why might Yahweh say the house of Israel is like clay in his hand (18:1-6; see Genesis 2:7)? Even after Yahweh has announced what he will do, why will Yahweh relent and do something different (18:7-10)? Since Yahweh's people have forgotten him, what will he do to them (18:15-17)?

    b. How have the people of Jerusalem forsaken Yahweh (19:4-5, 13)? How bad will the disaster be (19:6-13)? How do the people respond to Yahweh and to Jeremiah (18:12, 18; 20:1-2)?

    c. What did Jeremiah ask Yahweh to do for Jerusalem before (14:7-9, 19-22; 18:20)? What does Jeremiah ask him to do now (18:21-23; 20:11-12)? How does Jeremiah feel (20:7-9, 13, 14-18)?

Habakkuk

215. Habakkuk – Introduction

Pray. Then Read, Think and <u>Mark</u>.

Read your study Bible's introduction to the book of Habakkuk. Think about the questions for each of the following sections. <u>Mark</u> the answers and other things that seem important.

for the ESV Study Bible
- Date
  - o Read the first two sentences. About when did Habakkuk prophesy?
- Theme
  - o By the end of the book, what has Habakkuk learned?
  - o What does he realize?
- Purpose, Occasion, and Background
  - o Read the first paragraph.
  - o What is the book of Habakkuk?
  - o What are the first two chapters organized around?
  - o How does God's response puzzle Habakkuk?
  - o What does God make clear?
  - o How does the book end?
  - o Read the second paragraph ("The words ...").
  - o What were the righteous people in Judah probably wondering?
  - o How would God's words have reassured them?
- Key Themes
  - o Read the fourth theme. What does the key phrase summarize?

for the NIV Study Bible
- Date
  - o About when did Habakkuk prophesy?

- Theological Message
  - ○ Read the first paragraph.
  - ○ What does the book of Habakkuk contain?
  - ○ What is in the first two chapters, and what is in the third?
  - ○ Read the second paragraph.
  - ○ What were godly people in Judah probably struggling to understand?
  - ○ How would God's answers have helped them?
  - ○ Read the third paragraph ("Habakkuk expresses ...").
  - ○ What perplexed (or puzzled) Habakkuk?
  - ○ What perplexed him even more?
  - ○ Read the last paragraph.
  - ○ What does God make clear?
  - ○ In the end, what all does Habakkuk learn to do?

Write

Write your own introduction to the book of Habakkuk. Tell when Habakkuk probably wrote and what was happening in Judah at that time. Identify what sort of writing the book of Habakkuk contains. Explain what Habakkuk (and probably the godly people in Judah) was struggling with. Summarize God's answer, and describe how that answer puzzled Habakkuk even more. State what Habakkuk learned. Tell how the book ends. Finally, outline Habakkuk under three main headings:

A.	(1:1-11)
B.	(1:12-2:20)
C.	(3:1-19)

216. Habakkuk 1:1-3:19

a. What is Habakkuk's first complaint (1:2-4)? What kind of men is Yahweh raising up to do his work (1:6-11)? What does Habakkuk think about this (1:5, 12-13)?

b. In the middle of all this destruction, how will righteous people live (2:4)? How have righteous people always lived? Follow the cross-references for 2:4 to the New Testament. What will happen to the greedy Babylonians (Chaldeans) (2:6-8, 15-17)?

c. Who all will know that Yahweh judged the Babylonians and brought them to nothing (2:13-14, 20)? In what battles has Yahweh fought for his people before? Look at the study notes for 3:2-15. What will Habakkuk do now (3:16, 17)?

217.   2 Kings 24:1-7; Jeremiah 25:1-38; 35:1-36:8; 45:1-5; 36:9-32

a.   What all has Nebuchadnezzar king of Babylon been doing to Judah and other lands (2 Kings 24:1-7)? See the ESV study notes for 23:36-24:7 or the NIV study notes for 24:1. What does Yahweh call Nebuchadnezzar (Jeremiah 25:9)? In what year did the Babylonians defeat the Assyrians and the Egyptians who were trying to help them? See Jeremiah 25:19 and the study note for 2 Kings 23:29.

b.   How long will Judah and the surrounding nations serve the king of Babylon (Jeremiah 25:11)? Then what will Yahweh do to the Babylonians (Jeremiah 25:12-14). See the study note for 25:12. Which nations does Yahweh make drink the cup of his wrath (Jeremiah 25:15-33)?

c.   How does Yahweh use the Rekabites as an example for Judah (Jeremiah 35:13-16)? What does Yahweh keep telling the people of Judah (Jeremiah 25:3-7; 35:14-17; see 36:29-31)? How does Yahweh protect Baruch and Jeremiah (Jeremiah 36:19, 26; 45:5)?

Every day: (1) Follow your bookmark and pray. (2) Read and <u>mark</u> the passage.

Daniel

218. Daniel – Introduction

Pray. Then Read, Think and <u>Mark</u>.

Read your study Bible's introduction to the book of Daniel. Think about the questions for each of the following sections. <u>Mark</u> the answers and other things that seem important.

for the ESV Study Bible

- Author and Title
    - Who wrote the book of Daniel?
    - In what years did the first and last events recorded in Daniel happen?
- Theme
    - What is the central theme of the book of Daniel?
    - Whose kingdom will replace the others and never pass away?
- Purpose, Occasion, and Background
    - Read the first paragraph.
    - What genre or style of writing does the first half of the book of Daniel contain?
    - What do these stories show?
    - What genre does the second half of the book contain?
    - What are these apocalyptic visions designed to do?
- Literary Features
    - Read the first paragraph. What kind of images do apocalyptic visions use?

for the NIV Study Bible

- Author, Date and Authenticity
    - Read the first paragraph.
    - Who was the author of Daniel?
    - When was the book of Daniel probably completed?

- Theological Theme
  - What is the theological theme of the book?
  - Whose kingdom will last forever and ever?
- Literary Form
  - What style of writing does Daniel use in chapters 1-6?
  - What style of writing does he use in chapters 7-12?
  - What does the word *apocalyptic* mean?
  - What is apocalyptic writing like?
  - What does apocalyptic writing do?

Write

Write your own introduction to the book of Daniel. Tell who wrote the book of Daniel and when. Describe the writing in the first half of Daniel. State what style of writing is in the second half. Explain what that genre is like and what it is designed to do.

219.   Daniel 1:1-3:30

a. What does the king want to train the best young men from Judah to become like (1:4-7; see the study notes for 1:6-7)? Whose food and drink would defile Daniel (1:5, 8, 10, 13, 15)? What does God give Daniel, Hananiah, Mishael and Azariah (1:9, 17-20)?

b. What all has God given Nebuchadnezzar (2:37-38)? Which four empires do the four parts of the statue represent (2:31-45)? See the ESV's chart under chapter 2 ("The Traditional View of Daniel's Visions") or the NIV's chart under chapter 7 ("Visions in Daniel"). After Daniel explains God's message, what does Nebuchadnezzar do (2:28-30, 45, 46-48)?

c. Where is Daniel, and where are Shadrach, Meshach and Abednego (2:49)? How does God want his people to live when they live in an evil empire (3:16-18, 25-28)? What law does Nebuchadnezzar decree for all the peoples, nations and languages in his empire (3:29)?

220.   Jeremiah 46:1-48:25

a.   In what year did Nebuchadnezzar king of Babylon defeat Egypt at Carchemish (see the study note for 46:2)? Write that year in the margin beside 46:2. What is Egypt trying to do (46:7-8)? What is Yahweh doing as the Egyptian army is destroyed (46:10)?

b.   Whom is Yahweh bringing punishment upon (46:25)? What will Yahweh do for Israel (46:27-28)? Who is destroying Gaza and the Philistines (47:1, 4, 6-7)?

c.   What does Yahweh call himself (46:10, 18)? What must the conquering soldiers do to Moab (48:10)? Who is Chemosh, and what will Yahweh do to him (48:7, 13)? See the study note for 48:7.

221.   Jeremiah 48:26-49:39

a.   For what sins does Yahweh judge Moab (48:26-30, 35, 42)? Even as Yahweh is destroying Moab, how does he feel about Moab (48:31-33, 36, 38)? Whom all is Yahweh sending into exile (48:7, 46; 49:1, 3)?

b.   Though Yahweh destroys the people of Esau in every place, what group of people will he care for (49:10-11)? Which nations' fortunes will Yahweh restore (48:47; 49:6; 49:39)? After Yahweh destroys his enemies, what does he do (49:38)?

c.   Draw a map of the nations Yahweh judges through Nebuchadnezzar. (1) Trace over Map 7 (ESV) or Map 8 (NIV) in the back of your study Bible. (2) Label the following places: Egypt, Israel, Gaza, Moab, Ammon, Edom, Damascus, Euphrates River, Carchemish, Babylon and Elam. Check Map 6 for places you can't find on the map. Write "Kedar and Hazor" in northern Arabia. (3) Title the map "The Conquests of Nebuchadnezzar, Servant of King Yahweh of Hosts."

Obadiah

222.   Obadiah – Introduction

Pray. Then Read, Think and <u>Mark</u>.

Read your study Bible's introduction to the book of Obadiah. Think about the questions for each of the following sections. <u>Mark</u> the answers and other things that seem important.

for the ESV Study Bible

- Date
  - When was Obadiah likely written?
- Theme
  - What is the theme of Obadiah?
- Purpose, Occasion, and Background
  - Read the first paragraph. With what other scripture passages does Obadiah exhibit (or show) several parallels?
  - Read the second paragraph.
  - How are the Edomites related to the Israelites?
  - What should the Edomites have done?
  - What did they do?

for the NIV Study Bible

- Date
  - When was Obadiah likely written?
  - With what other scripture passage does Obadiah 1-6 have striking parallels?
- Unity and Theme
  - Read the first paragraph.
  - What is the theme of Obadiah?
  - Read the second and third paragraphs.
  - How are the Edomites related to the Israelites?
  - What should the Edomites have done?
  - What did they do?

Write

Write your own introduction to the book of Obadiah. Describe the setting of Obadiah's prophecy: Explain how the Edomites are related to the Israelites; say what the Edomites should have done; and tell what they did. Summarize the theme of Obadiah. Mention the other prophecy that Obadiah has several parallels with.

223.   Obadiah 1-21; 2 Kings 24:8-17

a.   Who attacks Edom (Obadiah 7-8)? Why will Yahweh attack Edom (Obadiah 8-14)? What did Yahweh promise Abraham and Jacob (Genesis 12:3; 25:23; 27:27-29)?

b.   What will Jacob (Israel) do to Esau (Obadiah 18-21)? What land will the many Israelite exiles possess (Obadiah 19-20)? Copy out the last line of Obadiah's prophecy (Obadiah 21).

c.   Whose laws does Jehoiachin break (2 Kings 24:9; see Daniel 3:29)? What all does Nebuchadnezzar carry away (2 Kings 24:12-16)? When did Yahweh declare that these things would happen (2 Kings 24:13)? Follow the first cross-reference for 24:13.

224.   Jeremiah 50:1-46

a.   Did Yahweh send Babylon (and Assyria) against Israel and Judah to judge them (50:6-7; see 25:8-9)? But are the Babylonians guilty also (50:7, 14, 24, 29, 33, 38; see 25:12-14)? Why did Yahweh punish the king of Assyria (50:18; see Isaiah 10:5-7, 12-15)?

b.   Who directs the attack against Babylon (Jeremiah 50:14-15, 21, 25-28)? Who will be put to shame and filled with terror when Babylon is captured (see 50:2 and study note)? What other nations' attack and defeat will Babylon's attack and defeat be like (50:41-46)? See the study notes for 50:41-43, 44-46.

c.   What will Israel and Judah do when Yahweh judges Babylon (50:4-5, 8)? What will Yahweh do for Israel (50:19-20, 34)? Which prophets foretold this great blessing (Deuteronomy 30:1-10; Isaiah 59:19-20)?

225.   Jeremiah 51:1-64

a.   How did Nebuchadnezzar and the Babylonians treat Yahweh's temple and his people (51:11, 24, 34-35)? So what will Yahweh do (51:5-6, 11, 36, 49, 56)? Who is Yahweh's new war club or hammer (50:23; 51:11, 20-23, 28-29)?

b.   How does Yahweh show that he is greater than the idols of Babylon (51:15-19)? How does Yahweh use the sea to punish Nebuchadnezzar the dragon and Bel (51:34, 36-37, 42-44, 54-56)? What will Babylon look like after Yahweh judges it (51:2-3, 25-26, 29, 37, 42-43, 58, 62)?

c.   What is Yahweh's purpose for Babylon (51:11-12, 29)? How does Jeremiah get Seraiah to prophesy before the Euphrates River against Babylon (51:59-64)? What is Babylon still like today (50:39-40)? Read the study note for 50:39 and follow it to the notes for Isaiah 13:20-22.

226.   Jeremiah 27:1-29:32; 24:1-10

a.   Why should Judah and the other nations serve Nebuchadnezzar (27:6-8, 11-13, 17)? What are Hananiah and other prophets saying (27:9-10, 14-16; 28:1-4)? What does Jeremiah wish were true (28:6)?

b.   How does Yahweh show that Jeremiah is the true prophet (28:9, 16-17)? How should Yahweh's people live while they are in exile (29:5-7)? Does Yahweh know what he's doing, or has he slipped up (27:5-6; 29:4, 11)?

c. Through which earlier prophet did Yahweh promise to bring his people back to the land (29:10-14)? See the study note for 29:14. Who will suffer more severe punishment: the people who are already in exile in Babylon or the people who remain in Jerusalem (29:4-7, 15-19; 24:5-6, 8-10)? When Yahweh brings the exiles back to Judah, what will their relationship with him be like (24:5-7)?

227.   Daniel 4:1-37

a.   Who gave Nebuchadnezzar authority to write to all the people he writes to (Daniel 4:1; see Jeremiah 27:4-7)? Which gods does Nebuchadnezzar honor (Daniel 4:8)? See Daniel 2:47; 3:26, 28-29 and the study note for 1:7. Has Nebuchadnezzar been a just king who honors the God who made him his servant (4:27, 29-30)?

b.   In Nebuchadnezzar's dream, what is the tall tree a picture of (4:10-15, 20-24)? Does Nebuchadnezzar heed Daniel's counsel (4:27-30)? What happens to Nebuchadnezzar while he is away from people (4:15-16, 23-25, 32-33)?

c.   What must Nebuchadnezzar learn (4:17, 25, 32)? Copy into your journal the words of praise Nebuchadnezzar writes to all peoples (4:34b-35, 37). Which prophet said that after the Babylonians conquered many nations and Yahweh judged them, the whole earth would know about Yahweh's glory (Habakkuk 1:5-6; 2:8, 10, 12-14)?

Ezekiel

228. Ezekiel – Introduction

Pray. Then Read, Think and Mark.

Read your study Bible's introduction to the book of Ezekiel. Think about the questions for each of the following sections. Mark the answers and other things that seem important.

for the ESV Study Bible

- Author and Title
    - o   Read the first paragraph. What class or family did Ezekiel belong to?
- Date
    - o   When did Ezekiel speak his first and his last oracles?
- Theme and Purpose
    - o   Read the first paragraph. What was the primary purpose of Ezekiel's message?
- Occasion and Background
    - o   Read the first paragraph. When did the Babylonians exile Judah's king and leading citizens, including Ezekiel?
- Key Themes
    - o   Read the first theme. With what two things was Ezekiel deeply concerned?
    - o   Read the second theme. Over what is God supreme?
    - o   Read the fourth theme. What hope did Ezekiel give people who accepted God's judgment?
- Style
    - o   Read the first paragraph. What formulaic statement in Ezekiel showed God's desire to restore his glory before Israel and the nations?
    - o   Read the second paragraph. What unusual or odd method did Ezekiel often use when he prophesied?

- History of Salvation Summary
    - How and why would God restore Israel?
    - What calling did God give Israel?
- Literary Features
    - Read the first two observations in the second paragraph. How did Ezekiel use visions and imagination to tell God's message?
- Outline
    - Read the first paragraph. When was Jerusalem destroyed?

for the NIV Study Bible

- Background
    - Read the third paragraph.
    - When did Nebuchadnezzar exile many Jews, including Ezekiel, to Babylon?
    - When was Jerusalem destroyed?
- Author
    - Read the second paragraph. What kind of family did Ezekiel belong to?
    - Read the third paragraph. What did Ezekiel use to explain large issues?
    - Read the last paragraph. How did God direct Ezekiel to involve himself personally in God's word?
- Dates
    - Read the third paragraph. When was Ezekiel called, and when did he receive his last prophecy?
- Themes
    - Read the first paragraph. What do Ezekiel and the prophets show that God is sovereign over?
    - Read the second paragraph. What clause in Ezekiel shows God's desire to be known and acknowledged?
    - Read the fourth paragraph ("God is free..."). How does God show Israel both judgment and grace?
- Theological significance
    - Read the second paragraph. What does Ezekiel focus uniquely on?

Write

Write your own introduction to the book of Ezekiel. In the first paragraph, tell the story of Ezekiel's life: what kind of family he was from; what happened in 597 BC, when God called him and gave him his first prophecy, what happened in 586 BC and when he spoke his last prophecy. In the second paragraph, state the purpose of Ezekiel's message or the things he focuses on. Connect that purpose or focus with the phrase Ezekiel often ends his prophecies with. Summarize how Ezekiel described what God is like. Explain how God showed Israel both judgment and grace, how he punished them but also restored them. In the third paragraph, discuss two methods God had Ezekiel use in his prophecies: visions and symbolic actions. Finally, outline the book of Ezekiel under three main headings:

A.   (1-24)
B.   (25-32)
C.   (33-48)

229.   Ezekiel 1:1-6:14

a.   Where is Ezekiel when he sees the vision of the appearance of the likeness of the glory of Yahweh (1:1-2, 28)? Ask someone else to read chapter one aloud to you. Close your eyes and imagine what Ezekiel saw. Now draw and color what you see.

b.   Who helps Ezekiel do what Yahweh tells him to do (2:1-2; 3:1-2, 8, 12, 22, 24)? What must Ezekiel do; what is his responsibility (2:4-7; 3:10-11, 16-21, 27)? How has Israel acted (2:3-4; 3:7, 27)?

c.   When Ezekiel lays siege to a brick, stares at an iron griddle, lies on his side and eats only a very little bit of food each day, what do his actions show (4:1-17)? Why will Yahweh judge Jerusalem and the mountains of Israel (5:5-6, 11; 6:3-6, 13)? Then what will everyone know (5:13; 6:7, 10, 13, 14)?

230.   Ezekiel 7:1-12:28

a.   How much longer will Yahweh wait before he destroys Israel (7:2-10)? If Ezekiel is sitting in his house in Babylon, how does he go and see what is happening in Jerusalem (8:1-4)? What detestable or abominable things does Ezekiel see the people doing in Jerusalem (8:5-6, 9-11, 13-17)?

b.   What does Yahweh tell the man clothed in linen to do to the people who are saddened by Jerusalem's sin (see 9:3-4 and the study note)? How have the people of Jerusalem made Yahweh feel about his house (9:6-9)? List step-by-step where Yahweh's glory goes (8:3; 10:4, 18-19; 11:22-23)?

c.   Where is Yahweh's sanctuary now (9:6; 11:16)? When Yahweh gathers his scattered people back into the land, what will he change inside them (11:17-20)? What are Ezekiel's actions a symbol of (12:3-20)?

---

(3) Think about and answer the questions. (4) Return to your bookmark.

231.   Ezekiel 13:1-16:63

a.   What have the false prophets and the daughters of the people done to the people (13:10, 19, 22)? Why will Lord Yahweh
cut off from his people those who have idols in their hearts
and yet still come to seek Yahweh (14:8-11)? What will Lord
Yahweh do to the land and the people of Jerusalem (15:1-8)?

b.   What all did Yahweh do for Jerusalem when she grew up
(16:4-14)? How did Jerusalem act like a prostitute (16:15-19,
23-26, 28-34)? What else did Jerusalem do (16:20-21, 36)?

c.   How will Yahweh judge Jerusalem's adultery and murder
(16:37-41)? What all will Yahweh do when he establishes an
everlasting covenant with Jerusalem (16:60, 62-63)? As the
story goes along, what does Jerusalem remember (16:22, 43,
52, 61-63)?

232.   Ezekiel 17:1-19:14

a.   Who are the great eagle, the topmost twig, the seed and the
other great eagle (17:3-7, 12-15)? Write their names in the
margin beside verses 3, 4, 5 and 7. With whom does the vine
(Zedekiah) break covenant (17:16, 18, 19)? What will the cedar
tree that Lord Yahweh plants be like (17:22-24)?

b.   How do righteous people live (18:9)? Whom does Lord Yahweh punish (18:4, 13, 18, 20, 24, 26)? What does Lord Yahweh
want (18:23, 30-32)?

c.   Who are the strong, young lion and the second strong, young
lion (19:3-4, 5-9)? See the study notes for 19:3, 5 or 19:1-9.
What kind of vine was Israel like, and what is it like now
(19:10-11, 12-14)? What is a lament (19:1, 14; see the study note
for 19:1)?

233.   Ezekiel 20:1-21:32

a.   Why will Yahweh not let the elders of Israel inquire of him,
ask him questions (20:3-4, 8, 13, 16, 21, 24, 30-31)? Why has
Yahweh not yet destroyed Israel (20:9, 14, 22; see Exodus
32:10-14)? What kind of decrees and laws (statutes and rules)
did Yahweh give Israel (Ezekiel 20:11-13, 19-21; see Exodus 13:2;
34:20)?

b.   What kind of rules did Yahweh let the Israelites come up
with (Ezekiel 20:18, 25-26, 30-31, 39)? See also 2 Kings 16:3;
21:6; Jeremiah 7:30-31. How will Lord Yahweh stop the Israelites from worshiping idols like the nations (Ezekiel 20:32-38)?

How will Yahweh treat the Israelites when he brings them back into the land (20:42-44)?

c. Whom all will Yahweh judge (20:45-48; 21:1-5)? Who leads the king of Babylon to come destroy Jerusalem (21:18-23)? Whom else will Yahweh judge (21:28-32)?

234. Ezekiel 22:1-24:27

a. What are the princes of Israel doing (22:6-12)? What will Yahweh put an end to (or consume) and melt (22:15, 18-22)? Is Lord Yahweh's judgment just (22:31)?

b. With which nations did Oholah and Oholibah engage in prostitution (or play the whore) (23:3, 5-8, 12, 14-17, 19-21)? What will Lord Yahweh use Oholibah's lovers to do (23:22-29)? Is Lord Yahweh's judgment just (23:29-30, 49; see 24:14)?

c. On January 15 of what year did the king of Babylon lay siege to Jerusalem (see the study note for 24:1)? Write down that very date in the margin beside 24:1. What all will Lord Yahweh burn in the "pot" (24:6-13)? How will the exiled Israelites feel when they hear that Yahweh's temple has been desecrated (or profaned) and the children they left behind have been killed (24:21-24)?

235.   2 Kings 24:18-25:2; Jeremiah 21:1-23:8

    a.   Who all are fighting against Jerusalem (2 Kings 25:1-2; Jeremiah 21:2, 4-7, 9-10)? If people in Jerusalem want to live, what should they do (Jeremiah 21:9; see 2 Kings 24:12, 15)? Righteousness is an important theme in these chapters. As you read along, <u>underline</u> all words related to right, righteousness etc. (Jeremiah 22:3, 13, 15 etc.).

    b.   Draw a family tree that shows how the last five kings of Judah are related to each other (Jeremiah 22:11, 18, 24; see 2 Kings 23:30, 34; 24:6, 17). Which of Josiah's offspring will come back to the land and rule Judah as king (Jeremiah 21:11-13; 22:5-7, 11-12, 18, 24-26, 30)? Will Jesus be born to one of Jehoiachin's (Coniah's) offspring (Jeremiah 23:30)? Look at how Matthew's genealogy (Matthew 1:12-16) is different from Luke's (Luke 3:23-31). See also the ESV study notes for Matthew 1:1-17, 12; Luke 3:23-38 or the NIV study notes for Matthew 1:16; Luke 3:23-38.

    c.   How will David's righteous Branch rule (Jeremiah 23:5-6)? Follow the cross-reference for "Branch" to Isaiah. How is the name of the Righteous Branch ("Yahweh is our Righteousness") a play-on-words with the name of the king to whom Jeremiah gives this message (Zedekiah) (see the study note for Jeremiah 23:6)? How great will it be when Yahweh rescues his people (Jeremiah 23:3-4, 7-8)?

236.   Jeremiah 23:9-40; 34:1-22; 37:1-38:13; 39:15-18

    a.   From where have the prophets of Samaria and Jerusalem gotten their prophecies (23:13-14, 16)? What all should prophets do (23:18, 22)? What two meanings can the one Hebrew word *massa'* have (see the study note for 23:33)? Read back through 23:33-39 and say both meanings each time you come to that word.

    b.   Who all are fighting against Jerusalem (34:1)? When people who are "cutting" a covenant walk between the halves of an animal they cut in two, what are they showing (see 34:15-20 and the study note for 34:18)? What does Yahweh say when the people of Jerusalem repent and then when they turn around (34:8-10, 11, 15, 16, 17-22)?

    c.   Why has the Babylonian army withdrawn from Jerusalem (34:21; 37:5)? What all do the king's grandsons and the other officials do to Jeremiah (37:13-16; 38:1-6)? Who all rescue whom (38:7-13; 39:15-18)?

237. Jeremiah 30:1-31:40

a. What does Yahweh promise to do (30:1-3, 8-10)? But what is happening right now (30:5-7, 11-15)? What will the buildings and the people be like when Yahweh restores Jacob (30:18-22)?

b. What do Yahweh and the people call each other (30:3, 9, 10, 22; 31:1, 6, 7, 9, 14, 18, 20, 22, 33)? What will life in Zion look like (31:11-14)? What does Yahweh say about Rachel's children (see 31:15, 16-17, 20 and the study note for 31:15)?

c. Which covenant is the new covenant not like (31:31-32)? Do the people in the new covenant have to keep God's laws (31:33)? Write out the new covenant (31:33-34).

238. Jeremiah 32:1-33:1-26

a. How does Jeremiah know it is the word of Yahweh that has come to him (32:6-9)? Why does Yahweh tell Jeremiah to buy his cousin's field (32:8, 14-15)? How does Jeremiah pray when he doesn't understand what Yahweh is doing (32:16-25)?

b. Who will gather Israel, bring them back, establish them safely in the land and do them good (32:37-38, 41)? How will he make Israel become the sort of people to whom he does good (32:39-40)? How long will Yahweh's covenants with Israel, David and the Levites last (32:39-40; 33:20-22)?

c. How will Yahweh turn Jerusalem into a city that makes him joyful instead of angry (33:5-9)? Which son of David is sitting on the throne of the house of Israel (see 33:15-17 and your notes for lesson 232, question c)? Who are the Levitical priests that are offering sacrifices to Yahweh (33:18)? Read Isaiah 66:18-23 and follow the cross-reference for Isaiah 66:21 to 1 Peter.

239. Jeremiah 38:14-39:14; 52:1-30; 2 Kings 25:3-26

a. In what months and years did Nebuchadnezzar besiege Jerusalem and enter Jerusalem (see the study notes for Jeremiah 39:1, 2)? Write those dates in the margins beside Jeremiah 39:1, 2; 52:4, 6; 2 Kings 25:1, 3. Did Zedekiah's sons and the nobles of Israel listen to Yahweh and honor his prophet (Jeremiah 39:6; 52:10; see 37:15; 38:1-6)? Through which prophet did Yahweh foretell that Zedekiah would lose his sight (follow the cross-reference for Jeremiah 39:7; 52:11; or 2 Kings 25:7)?

b. What does Nebuzaradan do to Yahweh's house (Jeremiah 52:13, 17-23; 2 Kings 25:9, 13-17)? What do Nebuchadnezzar and his army do to Jerusalem's houses, walls and leaders (Jeremiah 52:13-14, 24-27; 2 Kings 25:9-10, 18-21)? Now who all is left in the land of Judah (Jeremiah 52:16; 2 Kings 25:12)?

c. Whom does Nebuchadnezzar choose to take care of Jeremiah and the other people left in the land (Jeremiah 39:11-14; 2 Kings 25:22)? What kind of men are Gedaliah, his father and his grandfather (2 Kings 25:24; see 22:3, 8-12, 14, 20; Jeremiah 26:24; 36:10-12)? Where does everyone, small and great, go after Gedaliah is killed (2 Kings 25:26)?

Lamentations

240. Lamentations – Introduction

Pray. Then Read, Think and Mark.

When people lament, they mourn or grieve a loss. In a lament (or lamentation) they sing or write about how sad or hurt they are about what has happened.

Read your study Bible's introduction to Lamentations. Think about the questions for each of the following sections. Mark the answers and other things that seem important.

for the ESV Study Bible

- Author and Title
    - ○ Read the first three sentences of the second paragraph.
    - ○ Does the book of Lamentations say who wrote it?
    - ○ Who do many people think wrote Lamentations?
    - ○ Read the last paragraph.
- Date
    - ○ When was Lamentations written?
- Theme
    - ○ Read the first paragraph.
    - ○ What is the key passage in Lamentations?
    - ○ What does the speaker affirm there?
- Key Themes
    - ○ Read the first theme. What do the prayers in Lamentations do?
    - ○ Read the fourth theme. What does Lamentations say are the reasons Jerusalem fell?
    - ○ Read the fifth theme. What is God's mercy like?
    - ○ Read the sixth theme. In what three ways is Lamentations like the Psalms?
- Literary Features
    - ○ Read about acrostic forms in paragraphs 4-8.

- What is an acrostic poem?
- How many lines are in the first two chapters and how many in the fourth?
- What is the acrostic in chapter 3 like?
- What is required to compose acrostics?
- Read about the basic movement within Lamentations in paragraphs 10-13.
- What are the prayers in chapters 1 and 2 like?
- What is chapter 3 about?
- What are the prayers in chapters 4 and 5 like?

for the NIV Study Bible

- Author and Date
  - Read the first paragraph.
  - Does the book of Lamentations say who wrote it?
  - Who did ancient Jewish and early Christian traditions say wrote Lamentations?
  - What does Lamentations express poignantly (that is, with sadness that is almost sharp)?
  - Read the second paragraph. When was Lamentations written?
- Literary Features
  - How many verses are in the first, second, fourth and fifth laments?
  - What is an alphabetic acrostic?
  - What makes the middle lament distinct or different?
  - How were these laments composed?
- Themes and Theology
  - Read the fourth paragraph ("But this recital ..."). What does the poet wrestle with?
  - Read the fifth paragraph ("The author ...").
  - What does the author understand about the destruction of the city and the temple?
  - What is the proper response to judgment?
  - What does the author trust in?
  - What does the book begin with, and what does it end with?
  - Read the sixth paragraph ("In the middle ..."). At its apex (highest point), what does Lamentations focus on?
  - Read the last paragraph. What does the end of the book acknowledge?

Write

Write your own introduction to the book of Lamentations. In the first paragraph, explain what a lamentation is and what the lamentations in Lamentations are lamenting. Suggest who may have written Lamentations. In the second paragraph, show how the prayers in Lamentations change from the beginning to the end. Describe the prayers at the beginning. Summarize the reasons Jerusalem and the temple were destroyed. State what the high point of the book, in the middle of the middle chapter, is like. Tell what the proper response to judgment is. Describe the prayers at the end of the book. In the third paragraph, explain how an alphabetic acrostic poem works. Tell how many lines and verses are in each of the chapters.

241.   Lamentations 1:1-2:22

   a.   What has happened to Jerusalem (1:1-4)? Why have these things happened (1:5, 8-9)? Who is there to comfort Jerusalem (1:9, 11, 12, 16, 17)?

   b.   What does Zion tell Yahweh (1:18, 20)? How has the Lord treated Zion (2:1-5)? How has he treated his own house (1:10; 2:6-7)?

   c.   What have the prophets failed to do (2:14)? When long ago did Yahweh say he would overthrow his people (2:17)? Follow the cross-reference to Deuteronomy. What distresses the poet and the city (2:11-12, 20-22)?

242.   Lamentations 3:1-66

   a.   Who speaks in chapter 3 (3:1)? What all has Yahweh done to him (3:1-16)? How does the young man feel (3:17-21)?

   b.   What gives the young man hope (3:18, 21-24)? What three things are good (3:25-30)? How does the Lord show his steadfast, unfailing love (3:31-33)?

   c.   What does the man call on the people to do (3:34-42)? What has Yahweh done for the man (3:55-58)? What will Yahweh do (3:34-36, 59-66)?

243.   Lamentations 4:1-5:22

   a.   What has happened to the gold and the stones from the temple (4:1)? Even after the fall of the city, how severe is the famine (4:3-4, see 9-10)? Who made all this misery happen (4:11)?

b. What did Yahweh and the people think of the priests and the prophets (4:13-16)? What happened to the king (4:20; see 5:16)? What does the poet warn Edom about (4:21-22)?
c. What do the people tell Yahweh (5:1, 7, 16)? What do they still believe about him (5:19)? What do they ask him to do (5:21)?

244. Jeremiah 40:1-44:30

a. How does Yahweh keep his promise to look after Jeremiah and deliver him (40:1-6; see 1:19)? Who all are living in the land of Judah now (40:7, 11-12)? Why does Ishmael kill Gedaliah (40:14, 15; 41:1-2, 10)?

b. What do the people do when they are afraid (42:1-6)? Then what does Yahweh say about the disaster and say he will do (42:10-12)? But what do the people show they are really like (43:1-4, 7)?

c. When else has Yahweh said Nebuchadnezzar would attack Egypt (43:10-13)? See the cross-reference for 43:11. How is the people's explanation of all that has happened different from Jeremiah's explanation (44:15-18, 20-23)? What will the people know when only a few of them are still alive and able to return to Judah (44:27-28)?

This reading guide studies the Psalms separately. If you would like to read each part of the Old Testament when it was written, this is a good place to read Psalms, Book III (see lessons 338-346).

---

245. Ezekiel 25:1-27:36

a. Why will Yahweh punish Ammon, Edom and Philistia (25:3, 6, 12, 15)? What will Ammon, Moab, Seir and Philistia know (25:5, 7, 11, 17)? What will Edom know (25:14)?

b. Why is Yahweh against Tyre (26:2-3)? What will happen to Tyre (see 26:3-14, 19-21 and the study note for 26:14)? How many laments are there in chapters 26 and 27 (26:17-18; 27:3-31, 32-36)?

c. What do they sing about first (26:17; 27:3-25, 32-33)? Then what do they sing about (26:17; 27:26-27, 33)? How do they end their laments (26:18; 27:28-31, 35-36)?

246. Ezekiel 28:1-30:26

a. For what reasons does Lord Yahweh say he will judge Tyre (28:1, 5-6)? What was the "king" of Tyre, and where was he (28:12-14)? What wickedness was found in the guardian cherub (28:15-17)?

b. On which of Israel's neighbors has Yahweh said he will execute judgment (28:26; see 25:2, 8, 12, 15; 26:2; 28:21)? Find them on Map 5 in the back of your study Bible. What will Lord Yahweh treat Pharaoh like (29:3-5)? How has Egypt been like a staff of reed for the house of Israel (see 29:6-7 and the study note)?

c. What will Egypt be like after the forty years (29:13-15)? Does Lord Yahweh use Nebuchadnezzar and pay his soldiers because they are good and kind (28:7; 29:18-20; 30:10-11)? Who all will know what (28:22, 23, 24, 26; 29:6, 9, 16, 21; 30:8, 19, 25, 26)?

247. Ezekiel 31:1-32:32

a. Why does Yahweh talk to Pharaoh king of Egypt about Assyria (31:1-3, 9, 18)? Why did Yahweh have the tree (Assyria) cut down (31:10-14)? What words does Yahweh use to describe death (31:14-15)? See the NIV translation note for 31:15.

b. What was Egypt like (32:2; see 29:3)? What happened the last time Yahweh fought the dragon Egypt (Psalm 74:13-14; Isaiah 51:9-10)? How does Yahweh explain this allegory? Compare Ezekiel 32:2-8 with 32:9-15?

c. What will everyone know (32:15)? What did those in the pit do while they were in the land of the living (32:23, 24, 25, 26, 30)? What does Lord Yahweh say he will do to Pharaoh and all his army (32:31-32)?

248. Ezekiel 33:1-36:38

a. What does Lord Yahweh take pleasure in (33:11)? How does the Lord judge (33:12-20)? What will the people know when Yahweh makes the land a desolate waste (33:23-33)?

b. Why will Yahweh judge the shepherds and the sheep (34:2-6, 8-10, 17-22)? What will Yahweh himself do for his sheep (34:11-16)? Who will be their shepherd (34:23-24)? Follow the cross-reference to John (ESV, 23; NIV, 24).

c. Why will Yahweh gather his people and change them (Ezekiel 36:19-23, 32)? How will Yahweh change his people (36:25-28)? What will the land look like (36:9-11, 29-30, 33-35)?

249. Ezekiel 37:1-39:29

a. What does Lord Yahweh tell Ezekiel the bones and the breath mean (37:11-14)? What does Lord Yahweh say he will do for Israel (37:21-28)? When does God make peace with Israel, make David their prince and set his sanctuary in their midst (37:24-27; see Ephesians 1:20-23; 2:13-14, 17-22)?

b. Who and where are Magog, Meshech and Tubal (Ezekiel 38:2)? See the study note for 38:2, follow the cross-reference for Magog to Genesis and look at the map there. How does Gog decide to attack Israel (38:8, 10-12, 16; 39:2)? Who will defeat Gog and his many armies (38:18-19, 21-22; 39:2-6)?

c. Why does Yahweh fight this battle (38:16, 23; 39:7, 13)? What will the nations and Israel know (39:21-28)? When does this battle happen? See Revelation 20:7-9.

250. Ezekiel 40:1-43:12

a. How is the temple Ezekiel sees similar to and different from the temple Solomon built? Compare Ezekiel 41:2, 4, 16-19 with 1 Kings 6:14-22, 29-30. What does Ezekiel not see in the Most Holy Place? Read 1 Kings 8:6-8; Ezekiel 41:1-4; and Jeremiah 3:16-17. Later on, who will build a temple the same size but with an outer courtyard around it (Ezekiel 40:17)? Compare the chart of Ezekiel's Temple with the chart of Herod's Temple Complex in the Time of Jesus (in the *ESV Study Bible* at Luke 2) or the charts of Herod's Temple and Jerusalem During the Ministry of Jesus (in the *NIV Study Bible* at Matthew 4 and Mark 4).

b. What does Yahweh's glory do (Ezekiel 43:1-4; see 10:18-19)? Why does Lord Yahweh show Ezekiel the design of the temple (43:10-11)? What is the law of the temple (43:12)?

(3) Think about and answer the questions. (4) Return to your bookmark.

c.   When does God's glory return to the temple (John 1:14; Luke 2:22-38)? What does Jesus think of Herod's temple (John 2:13-22)? Which temple's design does Paul make known (Ephesians 1:22-23; 2:19-22; 3:16-21)?

251.   Ezekiel 43:13-46:24

a.   Why must the priests offer sacrifices for seven days before they use the altar for other offerings (43:18-25, 26-27)? What does Ezekiel do when Yahweh brings him again to the front of the temple (44:4)? Who may not enter Lord Yahweh's sanctuary (44:6-7, 9)?

b.   What should the priests' lives show (44:15-24; see 22:26)? What all is in the holy portion of the land (45:1-5; see the map with chapter 48)? How should the prince lead the people (45:9-17; see 22:6-12, 27)?

c.   On the Sabbath day, where and how does the prince worship (46:1-2, 8)? Where and how do the people worship (46:3, 9-10)? Why do the priests have kitchens separate from the Levites' and the people's kitchens (46:19-20)?

252.   Ezekiel 47:1-48:35

a.   Where does the trickle of water that becomes a river flow from (47:1-6, 12)? As the water flows, what does it do to the land and plants all around (47:7-12)? What earlier scripture do the river, the trees and fruit, and the fish in the sea remind you of? Follow the cross-reference for 47:12 to Genesis.

b.   Why does Joseph get a double portion (Ezekiel 47:13; see Genesis 48:3-5)? How does Lord Yahweh tell the Israelites to treat the foreigners who live among them (47:22-23)? Compare the map of Ezekiel's vision with map 4 in the back of your study Bible. Which tribes have been moved to new territories?

c.   Who all live in and work around the city (48:15, 18-19)? Find some blank space in your Bible near chapter 48. Draw a square (the city) and then label the city's twelve gates (48:30-34). Compare this chart with the chart of the camp of Israel's tribes at Numbers 2. In Hebrew, the new name of the city is *Yahweh-shammah*. What does it mean (48:35)?

253.   Ezekiel – Review

Pray. Think through the following points.

You've now read all of Ezekiel. Well done! Today you will think back over the book.

    a.   Reread your own introduction to the book (lesson 225).

    b.   What was the purpose or focus of Ezekiel? How did Ezekiel show God's glory to Israel and the nations?

    c.   What hope does Ezekiel give his listeners, who are now captives in Babylon? What does Lord Yahweh promise to do for them?

    d.   Look back through the book. Note the words and verses you marked. What are the main things God was showing and teaching Ezekiel?

    e.   What things seemed important to you?

    f.   Look back at your answers to question *d* each day (lessons 226-231, 242-249). What were some things you discovered on your own?

    g.   Think back through your answers to question *f* each day. What are some key ways God is telling you to change the way you love, think or live?

    h.   Jesus told his disciples, "Everything must be fulfilled that is written about me in the Law of Moses, the Prophets and the Psalms" (Luke 24:44). What parts of Ezekiel made you think about the Messiah? You may think about Ezekiel's visions of God's glory, "David" the prince who will shepherd Yahweh's human sheep, the return of Yahweh's glory to the new temple or something else.

Write

Write a review of Ezekiel. In the first paragraph, state the purpose or focus of Ezekiel. Describe some ways Ezekiel focused on that purpose in the book. In the second paragraph, write about some of the things you discovered or that seemed important to you. Describe how God is changing the way you love, think or live. In the third paragraph, explain one of Jesus' "shadows" in Ezekiel. Finally, end your review with a prayer to Jesus, Lord Yahweh. Tell him how you felt when you read about his glory. Praise him for his judgment and his grace. Thank him for making you one of his sheep and part of his temple.

254.   2 Kings 25:27-30; Kings – Review

Pray. Then Read, Think and Mark.

Read 2 Kings 25:27-30. Mark any words that seem important to you. In what year does Awel-Marduk king of Babylon release Jeremiah from prison (see the study note for 25:27)? Write that date in the margin beside 25:27. Which promise seems like it may still be true (25:27-30)? See 2 Samuel 7:14-16.

You've now read all of 1-2 Kings, and you've finished reading the Former Prophets. Today you will think back over Kings.

a.   Reread your own introduction to Kings (lesson 131) and your orientation to Old Testament 2 (lesson 151).

b.   What was the purpose of Kings? What reasons does Kings give for why Israel and Judah have been exiled from the land?

c.   By what standard (of from what perspective) did the authors assess the lives of the kings? Which kings led the people faithfully?

d.   Look back through the book. Note the words and verses you marked. What are the main things God was showing and teaching Israel and Judah?

e.   What things seemed important to you?

f.   Look back at your answers to question *d* each day (lessons 132-149, 158, 162, 173, 181-183, 196, 205, 214, 220, 232, 236). What were some things you discovered on your own?

g.   Think back through your answers to question *f* each day. What are some key ways God is telling you to change the way you love, think or live?

h.   Jesus told his disciples, "Everything must be fulfilled that is written about me in the Law of Moses, the Prophets and the Psalms" (Luke 24:44). What parts of Kings made you think about the Messiah? You may think about Solomon's glorious kingdom and temple, Elijah and Elisha's miraculous ministries or the faithfulness of some of the kings.

Write

Write a review of Kings. In the first paragraph, state the purpose of Kings. Describe how the authors assessed the kings. Summarize the ups and downs of Israel (and Judah) from Solomon to Jehoiachin. Explain how the book of Kings shows the reason why Yahweh scattered Israel and Judah out of the land. In the second paragraph, write about some of the things you discovered or that seemed important to you. Describe how God is changing the way you love, think or live. In the third paragraph, explain one of Jesus' "shadows" in the book of Kings. Finally, end your review with a prayer to King Jesus. Tell him what kind of king he is. Thank him for gathering you from the nations and making you part of his kingdom.

255.   Jeremiah 52:31-34; Jeremiah – Review

Pray. Then Read, Think and <u>Mark</u>.

Read Jeremiah 52:31-34. <u>Mark</u> any words that seem important to you. How is today's reading like yesterday's? Which promise seems like it is coming true (29:1-7, 11)?

You've now read all of Jeremiah. Today you will think back over the book.

   a.   Reread your own introduction to Jeremiah (lesson 201).
   b.   How did it feel as you read about Jeremiah's life, the things that happened around him and to him, and people's responses to his message?
   c.   What hope does this book give to a faithful Jew living in exile in Babylon? What all does God promise to do when he gathers his people again?
   d.   Look back through the book. Note the words and verses you marked. What are the main things God was showing and teaching Jeremiah and Judah?
   e.   What things seemed important to you?
   f.   Look back at your answers to question *d* each day (lessons 202-211, 214, 217-218, 221-223, 232-236, 241). What were some things you discovered on your own?
   g.   Think back through your answers to question *f* each day. What are some key ways God is telling you to change the way you love, think or live?
   h.   Jesus told his disciples, "Everything must be fulfilled that is written about me in the Law of Moses, the Prophets and the Psalms" (Luke 24:44). What parts of Jeremiah made you think about the Messiah? You may think about Jeremiah as the servant who suffers; David's son, the righteous Branch who will be king; or how Yahweh will be God to his people in the new covenant.

Write

Write a review of Jeremiah. In the first paragraph describe Jeremiah's life and ministry. Tell how God used him and how people responded to him. Summarize what God promises he will do for his people after the exile. In the second paragraph, write about some of the things you discovered or that seemed important to you. Describe how God is changing the way you love, think or live. In the third paragraph, explain one of Jesus' "shadows" in the book of Jeremiah. Finally, end your review with a prayer to Jesus. Praise him for who he is. Thank him for what he is teaching you. Ask him to help you become what he wants you to be.

This reading guide studies the Psalms separately. If you would like to read each part of the Old Testament when it was written, this is a good place to read Psalms, Book IV (see lessons 347-355).

256. Daniel 5:1-6:28

a. Who is King Belshazzar (5:1-2)? See the study note for 5:1 or 5:1-4 and read Jeremiah 27:6-7. What did Nebuchadnezzar learn (5:21)? What has God found wanting (or missing) in the way Belshazzar reigns (5:22-23, 27)?

b. What do the Aramaic words *mene, tekel* and *parsin* mean (5:25-28)? See the translation notes and study notes for 5:25-28. How might Daniel know how to interpret the message (Daniel 5:26-28; see Isaiah 13:17-19; Jeremiah 50:1-2; 51:7, 11, 24, 28, 49-62)? In what year do these events happen? See the study notes for 5:30-31. Write that year in the margin beside 5:1, 31.

c. Who is "Darius the Mede" (5:31)? See the study notes for 5:30-31 (and the NIV translation note for 6:28). See also 11:1-2 and the study note for 11:2. How does God show Darius that he is the living God (6:16-23, 27)? How do Darius's words and deeds fulfill Habakkuk's prophecies (Daniel 5:30-31; 6:25-27; Habakkuk 1:5-6; 2:12, 14, 16-19)?

257. Daniel 7:1-9:26

a. Which four kings (and kingdoms) do the four great beasts represent (7:3-8, 17)? In the ESV, see the study note for 7:3 and the chart under chapter 2 ("The Traditional View of Daniel's Visions"). In the NIV, see the study note for 7:4-7 and the chart under chapter 7 ("Visions in Daniel"). What does the Ancient of Days do (7:9-14, 22, 26)? Who is the "one like a son of man" (7:13-14, 18, 22, 27)?

b. What do the little horns do (7:8, 11, 20-21, 24-25; 8:9-11, 23-25)? Who do most scholars think the horn in chapter 8 is? See the study notes for 8:23-25. What all did he do? See the study notes for 8:9-14.

c. In the letter Jeremiah sent to Babylon, what did Yahweh tell the exiles (Jeremiah 29:1-4, 10-14; Daniel 9:1-2)? What is Yahweh like, and what does he do (9:4, 7, 9, 11-14, 16-18)? Who decrees the things that will happen (9:24-27)?

Ezra-Nehemiah

258.   Ezra-Nehemiah – Introduction

Pray. Then Read, Think and <u>Mark</u>.

Read your study Bible's introductions to the books of Ezra and Nehemiah. Think about the questions for each of the following sections.
<u>Mark</u> the answers and other things that seem important.

for the ESV Study Bible

Ezra

- Author and Title
    - ○ A memoir is a story that someone remembers from
      his own life and writes down.
    - ○ Why do we read Ezra and Nehemiah as one book?
    - ○ Who probably wrote Ezra and Nehemiah?
    - ○ What material did he probably use to put the books
      together?

- Date
    - ○ Read the second paragraph. About when was the
      book of Ezra-Nehemiah actually written?

- Theme
    - ○ What is the theme of Ezra?

- Purpose, Occasion, and Background
    - ○ Read the first paragraph. What pressures made it
      hard for the Jewish community to hold onto their
      identity as the Lord's people?
    - ○ Read the fifth paragraph ("The author of Ezra ...").
      What is the community like even after they are back
      in the land?
    - ○ Read the last paragraph. What does the book aim to
      do?

- Key Themes
  - Read the first two themes. What is the Lord like, and how does he work?

Nehemiah

- Theme
  - What is the theme of Nehemiah?
- Key Themes
  - Read the second theme. How does the Lord work?

for the NIV Study Bible

- Ezra and Nehemiah
  - Read the first paragraph. Why do we read Ezra and Nehemiah as one book?
- Literary Form and Authorship
  - Read the last paragraph. Who do most scholars think wrote (or compiled) Ezra and Nehemiah?
- Date
  - Memoirs are stories that someone remembers from his own life and writes down.
  - About when was the book of Ezra-Nehemiah put together?
- Major Theological Themes
  - Read the first paragraph. What do the books of Ezra and Nehemiah relate?
  - Read the first theme. What all did God do to restore Israel?
  - Read the third theme. Whom did God use to restore his people?
  - Read the fourth theme. What happened while Israel was being restored?
  - Read the fifth theme. What was the community of Israel like even after they were restored to the land?

Write

Write your own introduction to the books of Ezra and Nehemiah. Say who wrote Ezra and Nehemiah. Explain why we read them as one book. Tell the story of what happens in Ezra-Nehemiah. Point out what God is like and what he does in the story. Describe the opposition that the Israelites face, and explain why the author wrote these books.

259. Ezra 1:1-4:24

a. What word did Yahweh speak through Jeremiah (Ezra 1:1)? Follow the cross-reference for verse 1. When did Yahweh appoint Cyrus to build a house for him at Jerusalem (Ezra 1:2)? Follow the cross-references for Isaiah 44-45. When did Yahweh's prophets begin to promise that the people of Israel would return to the land (Ezra 1:3-5; see Deuteronomy 30:1-10)?

b. Who are Zerubbabel and Joshua (see the study note for 2:2)? Which types of people return to Jerusalem (Ezra 2:2, 3-35, 36-39, 40-42, 43-54, 55-58)? What are the people careful to do (3:2, 4, 5)?

c. Why might the older people be weeping (3:12)? Compare the offerings in Ezra 2:68-69 with the offerings for the first temple in 1 Chronicles 29:3-9. What else are the leaders and people careful to do (Ezra 2:59-62; 4:1-4)? How long do the people around Judah oppose them (4:4-5, 24)?

260.   Daniel 10:1-12:13

a.   What two things take 21 days to happen (10:2-3, 12-14)? How
does the man dressed in linen strengthen Daniel (10:10-11, 16-
19)? Who are the prince of Persia, the prince of Greece and
Michael (see 10:13, 20-21 and the study notes)?

b.   Who are the kings of the north and the kings of the south
(11:5, 6 etc.)?)? In the ESV, read the box "Rulers Foretold in
Daniel 11." In the NIV, read the box "Ptolemies and Seleucids."
As you read Daniel 11, the study notes will help you understand the details of who does what to whom when. You may
want to get important names and dates from the notes and
write them in the margins beside the verses.

c.   What will happen after Michael arises (12:1)? What similar
things does Jesus teach (Matthew 24:9-13, 15, 21-22, 30-31, 34)?
How long must the blessed people wait (Daniel 12:11-12)?

261.   Daniel – Review

Pray. Then Read, Think and Mark.

You've now read all of the book of Daniel. Today you will think back
over the book.

a.   Reread your own introduction to Daniel (lesson 215).

b.   Now that you've read things written in an apocalyptic style,
can you explain what apocalyptic writing is like? Why might
God have revealed things to Daniel in this style rather than
simply in a plain style?

c.   What do the stories about Daniel and his friends in Babylon
and the apocalyptic visions about the future show you about
how to be faithful when times are hard?

d.   Look back through the book. Note the words and verses you
marked. What are the main things God was showing and
teaching Daniel?

e.   What things seemed important to you?

f.   Look back at your answers to question *d* each day (lessons
216, 224, 253-254, 257). What were some things you discovered on your own?

g.   Think back through your answers to question *f* each day.
What are some key ways God is telling you to change the way
you love, think or live?

h.   Jesus told his disciples, "Everything must be fulfilled that is
written about me in the Law of Moses, the Prophets and the
Psalms" (Luke 24:44). What parts of Daniel made you think
about the Messiah? You may think about the big stone

mountain in Nebuchadnezzar's dream, the Ancient of Days and the kingdom of the son of man or something else.

Write

Write a review of Daniel. In the first paragraph, tell the story of Daniel's life, what happened to him and the kings he served. Explain how Daniel wrote. Summarize the history he foretells. State how he was trying to encourage his people (who lived then and long after) to live. In the second paragraph, write about some of the things you discovered or that seemed important to you. Describe how God is changing the way you love, think or live. In the third paragraph, explain one of Jesus' "shadows" in the book of Daniel. Finally, end your review with a prayer to Jesus the King. Talk with him about what it's like to read apocalyptic and how you feel as one of his followers when times are hard. Then praise him for being the kind of king he is.

Haggai

262.   Haggai – Introduction

Pray. Then Read, Think and <u>Mark</u>.

Read your study Bible's introduction to the book of Haggai. Think about the questions for each of the following sections. <u>Mark</u> the answers and other things that seem important.

for the ESV Study Bible

- Author and Title
  - o   Who was Haggai?
- Date
  - o   In what year did the word of the Lord come to Haggai?
- Theme
  - o   What will happen when the people restore the Lord's house?
- Purpose, Occasion, and Background
  - o   Read the first paragraph. What did Haggai do?
  - o   Read the second paragraph. What all happened to the temple after Cyrus allowed Jews to return to Jerusalem in 538 BC?
- Key Themes
  - o   Read the fourth theme. What will the restored (or rebuilt) house convey? That is, what will it bring to the people?

for the NIV Study Bible

- Author
  - o   Who was Haggai, and what did he do?
- Background
  - o   Read the first paragraph. What all happened to the temple after Cyrus allowed Jews to return to Jerusalem in 538 BC?

- Date
  - o In what year did Yahweh's words come through the prophet Haggai?
- Themes and Theological Teaching
  - o Read the first paragraph.
  - o What will happen when the people give priority to God and his house?
  - o What will obedience bring?

Write

Write your own introduction to the book of Haggai. Describe the background of the book, the things that happened in Jerusalem after Cyrus allowed the Jews to return in 538 BC. Tell when the Lord's word came to Haggai and what that word was. Describe how the Lord will bless the people when they rebuild his house.

263. Haggai 1:1-2:23

a. Which houses have the people built and not built (1:2-4, 9)? What has Yahweh been doing to the people (1:5-6, 9-11)? Why do the people fear Yahweh (1:10-12)?

b. How is Yahweh keeping the covenant he made with the people when he brought them out of Egypt (Haggai 1:12; 2:5; see Deuteronomy 30:1-4, 8)? Why should the people not fear Yahweh (Haggai 1:13; 2:4-5)? What will the glory of this second temple be like (2:3, 7-9)? Follow the first cross-reference for 2:3.

c. How does Yahweh encourage the people (1:14; 2:4)? Why had Yahweh not been receiving the people's offerings or blessing their work (2:13-19)? What does Yahweh mean when he calls Zerubbabel a "signet ring" (see 2:23 and the study note)?

Zechariah

264. Zechariah – Introduction

Pray. Then Read, Think and <u>Mark</u>.

Read your study Bible's introduction to the book of Zechariah. Think about the questions for each of the following sections. <u>Mark</u> the answers and other things that seem important.

for the ESV Study Bible

- Author and Date
  - ○ Into what kind of family was Zechariah born?
  - ○ Where was he born?
  - ○ When did Zechariah prophesy?
  - ○ Who else prophesied at the beginning of this time?
  - ○ What need do they address?

- Theme, Purpose, and Occasion
  - ○ Read the second paragraph.
  - ○ What would the people discover if they turned to the Lord?
  - ○ How was the Lord showing his commitment to his people?
  - ○ How would he show his commitment?
  - ○ Read the third paragraph. What will the Messiah do?

- Key Themes
  - ○ Read through the themes to review the main points.

- History of Salvation Summary
  - ○ In the end, what will God do?
  - ○ What will the Messiah do?

- Literary Features
  - ○ Read the first paragraph. What sort of literature are the visions?

for the NIV Study Bible

- Background
  - In what period did Zechariah prophesy?
- Author and Unity
  - Read the first paragraph.
  - Into what kind of family was Zechariah born?
  - Where was he born?
  - Read the second paragraph.
  - When did Zechariah prophesy?
  - Who else prophesied at the beginning of this time?
- Occasion and Purpose
  - What was the purpose of Zechariah (and Haggai)?
  - What was the purpose of Zechariah's night visions?
- Theological Teaching
  - Read the first paragraph.
  - What did God's promised deliverance from exile in Babylon include?
  - What grand pictures does the book of Zechariah show?
  - Read the second paragraph. What is God sovereign over?
- Literary Forms and Themes
  - Read the first paragraph.
  - What sort of literature are the prophetic visions?
  - Read the second paragraph.
  - What is the central theme of the book of Zechariah?
  - What will the Messiah do?
  - Read the third paragraph.
  - What will be purged and removed from Israel?

Write

Write your own introduction to the book of Zechariah. In the first paragraph, tell Zechariah's story: where he was born, what kind of family he had, what was going on at the time and when he prophesied. Tell who else prophesied along with Zechariah and what they encouraged the people to do. In the second paragraph, state what the Lord would do if the people returned to him. Say who would come later and describe what he would do for Israel and to all nations. Explain what sort of literature Zechariah's visions are and how that kind of literature works. Finally, outline the book of Zechariah under two main headings:

A.   (1-8)

B.   (9-14)

265. Zechariah 1:1-6:15

a. What does Yahweh promise the people (1:3)? Now that the horse patrol has seen that the earth is at rest, what is going to happen in Jerusalem (1:11, 16-17)? Why are the four crafts-men coming to terrify and throw down the four horns of the nations (1:18-21; see 1:14-15)?

b. What does Yahweh's angel promise Daughter Zion (2:9-12)? What does Yahweh's angel do to make Joshua ready to be the high priest (3:1-5)? Who will help Zerubbabel finish building Yahweh's house (4:2-3, 6-7, 9-10, 12, 14)?

c. What do the scroll and the two women do to the people's in-iquity (5:3-4, 6-10)? How is the work of the four chariots like the work of the horse patrol and the four craftsmen (1:10-11, 20-21; 6:5-8)? Who are the branches (3:8; 4:12-14; 6:11-13)? See the study note for 3:8, and check Isaiah 11:1; Jeremiah 23:5-6; 33:15-16, 17-22; Revelation 5:5; 22:16.

266. Zechariah 7:1-8:23; Ezra 5:1-6:22

a. Why have the people of Bethel been weeping and fasting in the fifth month (Zechariah 7:2-3; see the study notes for 7:3 and 8:19)? What does Yahweh promise to do for his people (Zechariah 8:7-8, 13)? Follow the first cross-reference for "blessing" (Zechariah 8:13). What does Yahweh want more: fasting or true justice (Zechariah 7:5, 8-10; 8:16-17)?

b. So what should the people do with their fasts (Zechariah 8:19)? How are the prophets Haggai and Zechariah sup-porting Zerubbabel the governor and Joshua the priest (Ezra 5:1-2; Haggai 2:1-4; Zechariah 4:6-10; 6:11-13)? What does Darius want to happen in the house of the God of heaven (Ezra 6:8-10)?

c. How many years after it was destroyed is the temple rebuilt (see Ezra 6:15 and the study note)? Are the people listening to Yahweh and his prophets now (Zechariah 7:11-14; Ezra 5:11-12; 6:16-20)? Which other prophecies are already coming true (Zechariah 8:15, 20-23; Ezra 6:21-22)?

267. Zechariah 9:1-14:21

a. When Yahweh comes to save Jerusalem, how will the king come to Zion (9:8-10)? Follow the cross-references to Mat-thew and John. What will Yahweh do for his sheep (Zechariah 10:3, 5-6, 8-10, 12)? What do the sheep think of Yahweh's shepherd (11:4, 7-8, 12-13)?

b.   How does Yahweh feel about the way the sheep have treated him (11:12-13)? Follow the cross-references to Matthew. What will Yahweh do for Jerusalem (Zechariah 12:6, 9, 10)? Then how will the people of Jerusalem feel about Yahweh (12:10)? Follow the cross-reference to John; see also Acts 2:36-37.

c.   What will Yahweh do for the sheep after he strikes his shepherd (Zechariah 13:7-9)? Follow the cross-references to Matthew and Mark. In the end, what will Yahweh be (Zechariah 14:9)? And what will the people and the things in Jerusalem be like (14:16, 20-21)?

Esther

268.　Esther – Introduction

Pray. Then Read, Think and <u>Mark</u>.

Read your study Bible's introduction to the book of Esther. Think about the questions for each of the following sections. <u>Mark</u> the answers and other things that seem important.

for the ESV Study Bible
- Theme
    - o   What story does the book of Esther tell?
- Purpose, Occasion, and Background
    - o   Read the first paragraph. Why was Esther written?
    - o   Read the third paragraph ("In terms of biblical history ..."). When and where is the story of Esther set?
- Key Themes
    - o   Read the second paragraph ("1. *Divine providence*"). How do fortuitous events (just the right things) keep happening at just the right time?
    - o   Read the third paragraph.
    - o   Who is not mentioned in the book of Esther?
    - o   But is he there?
    - o   Read the fourth and fifth paragraphs ("2. *Human responsibility*"). What do Esther and Mordecai show?
    - o   Read the last paragraph ("3. *The absurdity of wickedness*"). What does God do about wicked, arrogant people?
- Relevance for Christians Today
    - o   Read the first paragraph. What would have happened if Haman had succeeded?

for the NIV Study Bible
- Author and Date
    - o   When and where is the book of Esther set?

- Purpose, Themes and Literary Features
  - o Read the first paragraph. What was the author's central purpose?
  - o Read the second paragraph. When did Israel's conflict with the Amalekites begin?
  - o Read the fourth paragraph. What all did Haman's edict jeopardize (put in danger)?
  - o Read the last paragraph.
  - o What words are completely absent from the book of Esther?
  - o But what does the story assume at every point? That is, what does the author believe to be true even though he doesn't write about it?
  - o So are the events in the story just coincidences?

Write

Write your own introduction to the book of Esther. In the first paragraph, state the purpose of the book. Then tell the story: describe Haman's plan; explain how the Jews were saved; and say what they did afterwards. List a few important things that would not have happened if Haman's plan had worked. In the second paragraph, explain where God is (or isn't) in (or behind) the story. Suggest why the author may have written the story this way.

269. Esther 1:1-4:17

a. Which of the king's many commands, edicts, orders, laws and instructions seem wise (1:8, 10-12, 15, 19-20, 22)? Is this a good way to get a wife (2:2-4, 14)? Whom is Esther obeying, and whom is she disobeying (Esther 2:9-10; see Daniel 1:8)?

b. After you read Esther 2:23, how did you feel when you read 3:1? What happened many years before between Mordecai's people and Haman's people (see the study notes for 2:5 and 3:1)? When you read that the lot tells Haman to set the date for day "13" of the twelfth month, what do you begin to wonder about what may be going on behind the scenes (Esther 3:7, 13; see Proverbs 18:18)?

c. Who all respond the right way (and who the wrong way) when they learn about the edict? Compare Esther 4:1, 3, 16 with Joel 2:12-13? Why might Esther be willing to risk her life (Esther 4:14, 17)? Who obeys whom (2:10; 4:8, 16-17)?

270.   Esther 5:1-10:3

   a.   How does Esther show her faith (5:1)? What kind of man is
         Haman (5:10-14)? List the many coincidences that all hap-
         pened at just the right time on one night (6:1-9).

   b.   Who all rise, who won't rise and who falls (5:9, 11, 14; 6:10-13;
         7:7-8, 10; 8:2)? What does the king's second edict allow the
         Jews to do (8:11; see 3:13)? In what different ways do the tables
         turn or does the reverse occur (6:6-11; 7:9-10; 9:1-10)?

   c.   What did Moses tell the Israelites to do when God gave them
         rest from their enemies (Deuteronomy 25:17-19; Esther 9:22)?
         Why might the Jews have laid no hand on the plunder (Es-
         ther 9:10, 15, 16; see Deuteronomy 20:16-18; 1 Samuel 15:1-3, 9,
         18-22)? What do Jews remember when they celebrate Purim
         (9:20-22, 26-28)?

Malachi

271.   Malachi – Introduction

Pray. Then Read, Think and <u>Mark</u>.

Read your study Bible's introduction to the book of Malachi. Think about the questions for each of the following sections. <u>Mark</u> the answers and other things that seem important.

for the ESV Study Bible

- Author and Title
    - o   What does the name "Malachi" mean?
- Date
    - o   When did Ezra and Nehemiah, and probably Malachi as well, live?
- Theme
    - o   What were the people too ready to do?
    - o   What does Malachi's prophecy come as?
- Purpose, Occasion, and Background
    - o   Read the first paragraph. When the people thought about the prophecies and then looked at the way things really were all around them, what made them feel disillusioned or disappointed?
- Key Themes: Malachi's Sixfold Wake-up Call to Renewed Covenant Fidelity
    - o   How many disputations or arguments are there?
    - o   What is the focus of the first three disputations?
    - o   What is the focus of the last three disputations?

- Literary Features
    - o   What were some ways in which the people were halfhearted or negligent about serving God?
    - o   What does the book picture the people of Judah and God doing?

for the NIV Study Bible

- Author
  - What does the name "Malachi" mean?
- Background
  - Read the third paragraph. When Nehemiah came back to Jerusalem, what did he discover?
- Date
  - When may Malachi have been written?
- Themes and Theology
  - Read the first paragraph. What is the theological message of the book of Malachi?
  - Read the second paragraph.
  - What things discouraged the Jews and made them feel not so good about religion?
  - How did they feel about God?
  - Read the third paragraph ("Malachi rebukes ...").
  - What did Malachi rebuke?
  - What did Malachi warn them about?
  - Read the fourth paragraph ("Because the Lord ..."). What must the people do if they want God to spare them and bless them?
- Literary Features
  - Read the first paragraph. What does the text of Malachi feature?

Write

Write your own introduction to the book of Malachi. Say when Malachi probably prophesied. Explain why the Jews felt the way they did about God. Describe the way they were living. Say what "Malachi" means. State the theme of the book of Malachi. Tell what Malachi warns the people about and how he calls them to live. Finally, describe what the text of Malachi features the people and God doing.

272. Malachi 1:1-4:6

a. In the first dispute (or argument), how does Yahweh show Israel that he really does love them (1:2-5)? In the second dispute, how does Yahweh say the priests are showing contempt for his name (1:6-8, 13-14)? And how have the priests turned from Yahweh's covenant with Levi and corrupted it (2:4-9)?

b. In the third dispute, for what two reasons does Yahweh say he no longer accepts the people's offerings (2:11-12, 13, 14-16)? In the fourth dispute, how will the Lord show he really is just

(2:17-3:5)? In the fifth dispute, how are the people robbing God (3:8-10)?

c. In the sixth dispute, what does Yahweh promise those who fear his name (3:16-18; 4:2-3)? In sum, what does Yahweh tell the people to do (4:4)? How will the prophet Elijah prepare the people for the Lord (4:5-6)? Follow the first cross-reference for 4:6.

273.   Ezra 7:1-10:43

   a.   What kind of person is Ezra (7:6, 10-11)? What does King Artaxerxes want to make sure happens in Jerusalem (7:17-21, 25-26)? Why does he want to make sure it happens (7:23)?

   b.   Which prophecies does Artaxerxes's decree begin to fulfill (Ezra 7:27; see Isaiah 60:1-7)? Why does everything keep going well for Ezra (Ezra 7:6, 14, 28)? Why doesn't Ezra ask the king to send soldiers to protect them as they travel to Judah (Ezra 8:21-23, 31; see Isaiah 52:9-12)?

   c.   What did Yahweh command the people of Israel about marrying people from other nations (Ezra 9:1-4, 10, 14; 10:3; see Deuteronomy 7:1-4)? What does Ezra lead the people to do (Ezra 10:1-5, 10-11, 44)? In the new covenant, what should a believer do if he or she is already married to an unbeliever (1 Corinthians 7:10-16)?

274.   Nehemiah1:1-4:23

   a.   Which of Moses' words does Nehemiah remind Yahweh of (Nehemiah 1:8-9)? Follow the cross-reference in 1:9 to Deuteronomy 30. To whom does Nehemiah talk about the great trouble in Jerusalem (Nehemiah 1:4-6, 11; 2:3-8)? Why are the survivors in Jerusalem in great trouble and disgrace (1:3; 2:17)? Follow the cross-reference in 2:17 to Ezekiel.

   b.   What do Nehemiah and the people call themselves (Nehemiah 1:6, 10-11; 2:20)? What did Yahweh promise to do about Jerusalem's ruins (Nehemiah 1:3; 2:5, 18, 20; see Ezekiel 36:33-36)? What kinds of people work on the wall (Nehemiah 3:1, 8, 9, 12, 14-19, 22, 26, 28, 29, 31-32)?

   c.   How do Sanballat and the others oppose the Jews (2:10, 19; 4:1-3, 7-8, 11)? What all does Nehemiah lead the people to do to protect the city (4:4-5, 9, 12-23)? In these chapters, what does Nehemiah's faith in God's grace lead him to do (1:4-6, 11; 2:4-5, 8, 12, 18, 20; 4:4-6, 9, 14-15, 20)?

275.   Nehemiah 5:1-7:73

   a.   What have the people had to do just to get food (5:1-5)? Now, to whom do the people's fields and vineyards and even the people themselves belong (5:1, 5)? What does Yahweh's law say about taking interest from poor people (see Exodus 22:25-27; Deuteronomy 23:19-20)?

   b.   What does Nehemiah tell the nobles and officials they should do (Nehemiah 5:9-11, 14, 18)? What all do Sanballat,

Tobiah and Geshem do to try to stop Nehemiah (6:1-14)? What does Nehemiah ask God to remember (5:19; 6:14)?

c. Are all the people of Judah on Nehemiah's side (6:17-19)? How was the wall finished so quickly (6:9, 15-16)? How does Nehemiah know how many people came up to Judah in the first return (7:5; see the study note for 7:6-73)?

276. Nehemiah 8:1-10:39

a. What do the people want (8:1-3, 5-6)? What should a holy day feel like (8:9-12, 17)? What does Yahweh do because he is righteous (9:8, 32-33)?

b. What events do the Levites recall as they confess their sins, worship Yahweh their God and tell of all he has done? Write a phrase to summarize each of the following verses: 10:6, 7-8, 9-12, 13-14, 15-17a, 17b-21, 22-25, 26-29, 30-31, 32-35. Now read several times over your list of ten phrases and see if you can tell the story of God and his people in the Old Testament.

c. In the covenant the people make with Yahweh their God, what kind things do they say he has done (9:5-35)? What stipulations or requirements do they swear to keep (10:238-31, 39)? What blessing do they probably want God to give them if they keep this covenant (9:36-38)?

277. Nehemiah 11:1-13:31

a. What does 11:3-24 list (11:1-2; see 7:4)? Where do the rest of the people live (11:3, 20)? What is 12:1-26 about (12:1, 8, 10-11, 22)?

b. When the leaders are ready to dedicate the wall, what do they call the Levites to come and do (12:27, 30)? What do the choirs, the priests and the people do (12:31, 38, 40-43)? What does all Israel do for the Levites: the priests, musicians and gatekeepers (12:44-47)?

c. When Nehemiah comes back from Babylon to Jerusalem, what problems does he find (13:6-7, 10, 15-16, 23-24, 28)? What does Nehemiah remind the people (13:18, 26)? What does Nehemiah want God to remember (13:14, 22, 30-31)?

278. Ezra-Nehemiah – Review

Pray. Then Read, Think and <u>Mark</u>.

You've now read all of Ezra-Nehemiah. Today you will think back over the book.

    a.   Reread your own introduction to Ezra-Nehemiah (lesson 255).

    b.   What were the main things Ezra and Nehemiah wanted to lead the people to do? What challenges did they have to overcome to do that?

    c.   By the end of the book of Nehemiah, what are the people, the city and the temple like (Ezra 6:14-18; 9:8-9; Nehemiah 9:34-37; 12:27, 40-43)? Now think about what Yahweh promised he would do for his people after the exile. See, for example, Ezekiel 34:23-24; 36:24-30, 33-36; 43:1-5; Haggai 2:3, 6-9. Has Yahweh fulfilled all his promises, or does it seem like there must be more to come?

    d.   Look back through the book. Note the words and verses you marked. What are the main things God was showing and teaching Ezra and Nehemiah?

    e.   What things seemed important to you?

    f.   Look back at your answers to question *d* each day (lessons 256, 263, 273-277). What were some things you discovered on your own?

    g.   Think back through your answers to question *f* each day. What are some key ways God is telling you to change the way you love, think or live?

    h.   Jesus told his disciples, "Everything must be fulfilled that is written about me in the Law of Moses, the Prophets and the Psalms" (Luke 24:44). What parts of Ezra-Nehemiah made you think about the Messiah? You may think about the king who rules all the kingdoms of the earth, a high priest named "Joshua," leaders who love God and lead his people faithfully or something else.

Write

Write a review of Ezra-Nehemiah. In the first paragraph, tell the story of the people returning to the land. Describe the challenges the people faced and what the prophets, the priests and the governors led them to do. In the second paragraph, explain how Yahweh has fulfilled his promises to his people. Then identify a couple promises that are not yet fulfilled. In the third paragraph, describe how God is changing the way you love, think or live. In the fourth paragraph, explain one of Jesus' "shadows" in the book of Ezra-Nehemiah. Finally, end your review with a prayer to Jesus the King and Priest. Praise him for keeping his promises to his people. Thank him for coming later to keep his other promises. Then talk with him about the challenges you face and tell him what you want to be like.

This reading guide studies the Psalms separately. If you would like to read each part of the Old Testament when it was written, this is a good place to read Psalms, Book V (see lessons 356-377).

Chronicles

279.   1-2 Chronicles – Introduction

Pray. Then Read, Think and <u>Mark</u>.

Read your study Bible's introduction to Chronicles. Think about the questions for each of the following sections. <u>Mark</u> the answers and other things that seem important.

for the ESV Study Bible

- Author and Title
    - o Read the first paragraph. What kind of person probably wrote Chronicles?
- Date
    - o When was Chronicles probably written?
- Theme
    - o What is the central theme of Chronicles?
    - o What two institutions derive (or come) from Yahweh's covenant with David?
    - o What do those two institutions together represent?
- Purpose, Occasion, and Background
    - o Read the first two paragraphs. At this time in Israel's history, what two questions were pressing ones?
    - o Read the third paragraph ("With such questions ..."). Circle the word "to" every time it occurs in this paragraph. What were the Chronicler's four purposes for writing Chronicles?
    - o Read the fourth paragraph ("The Chronicler's ..."). According to the Chronicler, what do people who seek God experience?
    - o Read the fifth paragraph ("The converse ..."). How does God punish those who forsake him?
    - o Read the sixth paragraph ("Just as important ..."). What is the connection between the temple, David, repentance and forgiveness?

o   Read the seventh paragraph ("The destruction ..."). Now that many Israelites have returned to the land after the exile, what should Israel do for God to bless them and restore them?

for the NIV Study Bible
- Author, Date and Sources
  o   Read the first paragraph. When was Chronicles probably written?
- Purpose and Themes
  o   Read the first paragraph.
  o   What was the burning issue for the community of Israelites that had come back to the land?
  o   What sort of questions may they have been asking?
  o   Read the first theme. What were the supreme gifts God gave Israel through the Davidic dynasty?
  o   Read the second theme. What two things assure Israel that they are still God's people, the ones he chose?
  o   Read the third theme. What did faithful Davidic kings do?
  o   Read the fourth theme. What does sin bring?
  o   What do repentance, obedience and trust bring?

Write

Write your own introduction to Chronicles. Describe what was going on in Israel when Chronicles was written. State the "pressing questions" or "burning issue" that concerned the people. Explain why the Chronicler thinks Yahweh's covenant with David, the Davidic dynasty and the temple were so important. List a couple questions the people may have been asking about Yahweh's promises. Summarize the Chronicler's purpose for writing the Chronicles. Compare the way the Chronicler writes about people who are faithful and people who are unfaithful. Finally, outline Chronicles under three or four headings.

280.   I Chronicles 1:1-2:55

a.   Turn to the map at Genesis 10: "Table of Nations." Trace over the outline of the lands and seas. Then label at least the following nations: Gomer, Magog, Javan, Tiras; Cush, Egypt (Mizraim), Canaan; Ashur, Aram. Use markers or colored pencils to show whether the nations are descended from Shem, Ham or Japheth (1 Chronicles 1:4-23).

b.   On the next page make a family tree "From Adam to Israel" (1:1-54). Include at least the following names: Adam, Seth,

Enosh, Kenan, Mahalalel, Jared, Enoch, Methuselah, Lamech, Noah (1-4); Shem, Ham, Japheth (4); Nahor, Terah, Abram, Isaac, Ishmael (26-28); Midian (32); Israel, Esau (Edom), Eliphaz, Amalek (34-36).

c. Now make a family tree "From Israel to David" (2:1-17). Include at least the following names: Israel, Reuben, Simeon, Levi, Judah, Issachar, Zebulun, Dan, Joseph, Benjamin, Naphtali, Gad, Asher (1-2); Tamar, Perez (4); Hezron, Ram (5, 9-10); Boaz, Obed, Jesse, David (12-13, 15); Zeruiah, Joab (16).

281. I Chronicles 3:1-5:26

a. Make a family tree "From David to Elioenai" (3:1-24). Include at least the following names: David, Amnon, Absalom, Adonijah, Nathan, Solomon, Tamar (1-9); Solomon, Rehoboam, Abijah, Asa, Jehoshaphat, Jehoram, Ahaziah, Joash, Amaziah, Azariah, Jotham, Ahaz, Hezekiah, Manasseh, Amon, Josiah, Johanan, Jehoiakim, Zedekiah, Jehoiachin (10-16); Shealtiel, Pedaiah, Zerubbabel, Hananiah, Shekaniah, Elioenai (17-24).

b. As the Chronicler records the people who lived in the south, what line of people does he put in the center of all his lists (2:9-15; 3:1-24)? See the ESV study note for 2:3-4:23 or the NIV study note for 4:1-23. Why might the Chronicler tell us something extra about Jabez (4:10)? See the ESV study note or the NIV translation note for 4:10. Where are some of the people of Simeon still living at the time of the Chronicler (4:43)?

c. How did Joseph get the rights of the firstborn (5:1-2)? How did the people of Gad get and hold their land (5:19-22)? How did the two and a half tribes end up in exile (5:24-26)?

282. I Chronicles 6:1-7:40

a. As he records the people who lived in the east and north, which tribe does the Chronicler put in the center of his lists (6:1-81)? And which line of people does he record at the beginning and middle of that chapter (6:1-15, 49-60)? What important service did these men do (6:49)?

b. Through which two men did Yahweh say who should do what in the house of Yahweh (6:31-32, 48, 49)? What were the Levites Heman and Asaph in charge of (6:31-33, 39)? Who was Heman's grandfather (6:33)?

c. Which cities did the sons of Aaron live in (6:57)? In which tribe did no Levites live (6:62-66)? In these lists, do some people share the same name? For example, look at "Uzzi" in 6:5-6, 51; 7:2-3, 7.

283.   I Chronicles 8:1-9:44

a. By what other names are Esh-Baal and Merib-Baal called (8:33-34)? See the ESV study note for 8:29-40, the NIV translation notes for 8:33, 34 and the study note for 2 Samuel 4:4. What kind of men were the people of Benjamin (1 Chronicles 7:6-7, 11; 8:40)? So how were the southern tribes taken into exile (9:1)?

b. Who were the first tribes to return (9:2-3)? What kind of men were the priests (9:13)? What did the gatekeepers used to do (9:17-19)?

c. What other responsibilities did the Levites have (9:28-32)? When were the singers on duty (9:33)? Why might the Chronicler give us Saul's genealogy again (7:6-12; 8:1-40; 9:35-44; 10:1-14)?

284.   I Chronicles 10:1-12:40

a. Why does Saul die (10:13-14)? How does Saul die (10:3-5, 14)? Why might the Chronicler begin this part of Chronicles with this story about Saul (10:13-14)?

b. What do David and the elders do at Hebron (11:3)? How does David become more and more powerful (11:9; 12:18, 22)? Which groups of people support David (11:10; 12:1-2, 8, 16, 19, 22, 23)?

c. What does all Israel say about David (11:2; 12:18)? What does all Israel want to do (11:1-3; 12:23, 38)? What part of the story from 2 Samuel does the Chronicler leave out (2 Samuel 2-4)?

285.   I Chronicles 13:1-16:43

a. What does David say the people didn't do while Saul was king (13:3)? What happens when David doesn't inquire of Yahweh and when he does? Compare 13:1, 4, 10-12 with 14:10-11, 14-17. When David inquires of Yahweh about how to bring the ark, how does Yahweh tell him what to do (15:13-15)?

b. What would this procession have looked and sounded like (15:16, 19-21, 24-28)? Whom is David acting like (see the study note for 16:1-3)? Which psalms does the Chronicler put together in chapter 16 (see the study note for 16:8-36)?

c. What do these psalms tell the people to do (16:8-13, 23-24, 28-30, 34)? Why should Israel, the nations and all creation worship Yahweh (16:8-9, 14, 23-27, 29-34)? Why might David's prayer "gather us and deliver us from the nations" be especially meaningful to the Chronicler (16:35)? See the ESV study note for 16:34-36 or the NIV study note for 16:8-36.

286. I Chronicles 17:1-22:1

a. What all does Yahweh promise David (17:8-14)? Which earlier promises do these promises sound like? Compare 1 Chronicles 17:8-10 with Genesis 12:2-3; 15:18; 22:17-18. Which of David's offspring will fully fulfill these promises? Follow the cross-reference for 1 Chronicles 17:13 to Hebrews 1.

b. How does David feel (1 Chronicles 17:16-27)? What does David do (18:1-3, 11, 14, 17; 19:17-19; 20:8)? What is Yahweh doing (17:8-10, 23-24; 18:6, 13)?

c. To understand 1 Chronicles 21, look back at lesson 129 and your answers to question c. Who incites David to take a census of Israel (21:1)? After the plague against Israel begins, what kind of shepherd does David show he is (21:17; see 17:6)? Why do you think the Chronicler tells these stories together (17:1, 11-12; 18:7-8, 10-11; 22:1)?

287. I Chronicles 22:2-24:31

a. What does David say the house to be built for Yahweh must be like (22:5)? Why did Yahweh not let David build a house for Yahweh's name (22:8)? But what kind of man will David's son be (see 22:9 and the study note)?

b. What all does David do to help Solomon be ready to build Yahweh's house (22:11-12, 14, 15)? What did Moses tell the Israelites to do once Yahweh had given them rest from all their enemies around them (1 Chronicles 22:18; see Deuteronomy 12:10-11)? So what does David tell all the leaders of Israel to do (1 Chronicles 22:19)?

c. What did Yahweh set apart Aaron and his sons to do (23:13)? Why does David give the Levites new duties (23:25-26)? Follow the cross-reference for 23:26. What kinds of duties does David give the Levites (1 Chronicles 23:4-5, 28-32)?

Every day: (1) Follow your bookmark and pray. (2) Read and <u>mark</u> the passage.

288. **I Chronicles 25:1-27:34**

   a. What do Asaph, Jeduthun and Heman do (25:1-3, 5)? What does that make you think about the psalms written by David, Asaph, Jeduthun and Heman? What all do David, Asaph, Jeduthun and Heman do to prepare the musicians to sing to Yahweh (25:6-8)?

   b. What kind of people does David choose to be leaders (26:6, 31)? From where did the dedicated gifts in the treasuries come (26:26-28)? What are the officials and judges responsible for (26:29-30, 32)?

   c. Who are the men who lead the divisions of the army (27:1-15; see 11:24-31)? To whom did Yahweh promise that the Israelites would be as many as the stars in the sky (23:23)? Follow the cross-reference to Genesis. When David tried to count the Israelites, what did it show that he was thinking about Yahweh's promise (1 Chronicles 23:23-24)?

289. **I Chronicles 28:1 – 2 Chronicles 1:17**

   a. Before David dies, what does he make sure Israel knows that God has chosen (1 Chronicles 28:3-7)? How does David know what the temple and all its contents should look like (28:11-19)? What all does David twice tell Solomon to do (28:9-10, 20)?

   b. What kind of building will Yahweh's house be (29:1)? How did Israel have so much to give (29:12-16)? What does David ask Yahweh to do for his people (29:17-18)?

   c. Why do Solomon and the whole assembly of Israel go to Gibeon (2 Chronicles 1:2-6)? How does God feel about Solomon and his request (1:7-12)? Which of David's prayers for Solomon are answered, and which are not? Compare 1 Chronicles 22:12-13; 28:9; 29:19 with 2 Chronicles 1:1-3, 6, 10-12, 14, 16, and see Deuteronomy 17:16.

290. **2 Chronicles 2:1-6:11**

   a. For what purpose does Solomon build a house for Yahweh (2:4-6)? Which earlier worker's mother was also from Dan (2 Chronicles 2:13-14; see Exodus 31:6)? What earlier sacrifice happened on Mount Moriah (see the study note for 2 Chronicles 3:1)?

   b. What happened when David offered a sacrifice on Araunah's threshing floor (3:1)? See 1 Chronicles 21:14-22:1. Do you think the temple Solomon built for Yahweh was great and magnifi-

(3) Think about and answer the questions. (4) Return to your bookmark.   191

cent (2 Chronicles 2:9; 3:3-4:22)? What things finally come back together again (2 Chronicles 5:5; see 1 Samuel 4:3-4)?

c. Copy out the words that the musicians use to sing praise to Yahweh (2 Chronicles 5:13). What does Solomon say Yahweh has done (6:4, 8-10)? And what should Israel do (5:10; 6:11)?

291. 2 Chronicles 6:12-9:31

a. How is Yahweh different from the other gods (6:14)? What does Solomon think most people will ask for when they pray toward Yahweh's house (6:24-25, 26-27, 29-30, 36-39)? What do you think the Chronicler wants the people who read about Solomon's prayer to do (6:36-39)?

b. How does Yahweh show that he hears and accepts Solomon's prayer (7:1-2)? What does Yahweh tell Solomon he has done and will do (7:12-16)? But what will Yahweh do to his house if his people forsake him and serve other gods (7:19-22)?

c. What does Solomon know about Pharaoh's daughter, the woman he married (8:11)? How glorious does Yahweh make the king who sits on his throne (8:1-10, 18; 9:2-6, 8, 10-11, 13-27)? What do the kings and queens of other nations think about Solomon and his God (2:11-12; 9:8, 22-23, 26)?

292. 2 Chronicles 10:1-14:1

a. Who caused events to turn out this way (10:15; 11:1-4)? Does that mean King Rehoboam didn't make the choices he wanted to (10:6-14)? Why do some people from all the tribes of Israel move to Judah (11:13-16)?

b. Who all abandon whom (12:1-5)? Whose prayer does Yahweh answer (12:6-7, 12; see 6:24-25; 7:14)? What made Rehoboam do evil (12:14)?

c. Why does Abijah think Judah will defeat Israel (13:5, 8)? What does Abijah say is the other main difference between Israel and Judah (13:9-12)? How do the men of Judah win over the men of Israel (13:14-18)?

293. 2 Chronicles 14:2-18:37

a. How does Asa show what he thinks of Yahweh his God (14:2-7)? Why does Yahweh strike down Zerah's enormous army (14:9-12)? What does Yahweh promise Asa, Judah and Benjamin (15:1-2, 7)?

Every day: (1) Follow your bookmark and pray. (2) Read and mark the passage.

b. What does Asa lead the people to do (15:8-14)? But what does Asa do later on (16:1-4, 7-9)? Are the people in the Scriptures simply all bad or all good; that is, do good people only ever do right, and do bad people only ever do wrong (15:17-18; 16:9-10, 12)?

c. How does Jehoshaphat act like his father David (17:3-4)? What does Jehoshaphat do for the people of Judah (17:7-9; see 14:4; 15:3)? When Jehoshaphat and Ahab seek Yahweh's counsel, which of the people there really think that Yahweh ("the LORD") is God (18:4, 5, 6, 7, 10-11, 13, 27, 31)?

294.   2 Chronicles 19:1-23:21

a. When Jehu corrects Jehoshaphat, what does Jehoshaphat do (19:4, 5-9)? In what different ways do Jehoshaphat and Judah show that they are seeking Yahweh (20:3-4, 5-12, 13, 18-19, 20-21)? How does Yahweh defeat the Ammonites, Moabites and Edomites without the Israelites fighting (20:22-23)?

b. Why does Jehoram do evil (21:6)? What two things does Elijah rebuke Jehoram for doing (21:12-13)? What all do the Edomites, Philistines and Arabs do (21:8-10, 16-17)?

c. In what ways does Athaliah do evil (21:6; 22:2-5, 10)? How does Yahweh punish Jehoram (22:7-9)? How do Jehoiada, the people and the new king Joash show that they are Yahweh's people (23:16-21)?

295.   2 Chronicles 24:1-26:23

a. How do the priest, the king and the people all encourage each other to seek Yahweh and restore his house (24:4-14)? When Joash abandons Yahweh, how does he treat Yahweh's prophets and priests (24:17-22, 25)? How does Yahweh punish Joash (24:20, 22-25)?

b. How much does Amaziah trust Yahweh (25:5-11)? Why does Amaziah insist on fighting against Joash king of Israel, even though Joash advises him not to (26:16-22)? How does the Chronicler show that Amaziah did right with part of his heart but not all of it (25:2)?

c. What do the priest, the king and God do (26:5, 7, 15)? How is Uzziah unfaithful to Yahweh his God (26:16-20)? How is Uzziah's reign like the reigns of his father Amaziah and his grandfather Joash (see 26:4 and the study note for 26:1-23)?

(3) Think about and answer the questions. (4) Return to your bookmark.

296.   2 Chronicles 27:1-30:27

a. Why does Jotham become a powerful king (27:2-6)? What evil things does Ahaz do (28:1-4, 22-25)? Whom all does Yahweh allow to defeat Ahaz and Judah (28:5-8, 17-23)?

b. What is the very first thing Hezekiah does when he becomes king (29:3-5, 17)? In what different ways does Hezekiah act like David (29:2, 2-5, 25-29)? How does Hezekiah restore the service of Yahweh's house (29:3-5, 18, 20-24, 25, 30, 31-36)?

c. From which tribes do people turn to Yahweh (30:6, 9, 11-13, 18)? Why does Yahweh pardon and heal the people who eat the Passover without first cleansing themselves (30:16-20)? How do the people and Yahweh feel about all that happens in these seven weeks (29:9-10, 24, 30, 36; 30:9, 11-12, 21-23, 25-27)?

297.   2 Chronicles 31:1-33:25

a. Where all do the people put a stop to false worship (31:1)? Who is living in Ephraim and Manasseh at this time (see 31:1 and the study note for 30:1)? When the king and the priests and the people seek Yahweh and keep his law, what promise does God keep (2 Chronicles 31:3-10, 20-21; see Deuteronomy 28:1-14)?

b. How does Sennacherib ridicule Yahweh God (2 Chronicles 32:13-17, 19)? Why does Yahweh save Hezekiah and the people of Jerusalem (32:6-8, 17, 20, 22)? What happens to Hezekiah and Jerusalem when he is proud and what happens when he is humble (32:24-26)?

c. What happens to Manasseh (33:2-6, 10, 11, 12-13, 16)? How might the Chronicler be using Manasseh as an example to show his readers what they should do? Does Amon act like his father Manasseh in Manasseh's early years or his later years (33:22-23)?

298.   2 Chronicles 34:1-36:23

a. Where all does Josiah purge (34:3-7)? While Manasseh and Amon were king, how much had the priests and the people forgotten about worshiping Yahweh in the temple (34:8, 14-15)? How does Josiah inquire of Yahweh (34:21-28)?

b. How does Josiah lead everyone in Israel to follow Yahweh (34:29-33)? How do the king, the leaders and the Levites make sure everyone gets to be part of the Passover (35:7-15)?

What about Josiah made him such a good king (34:2-3, 19-20, 27, 29-33; 35:18, 26)?

c. What are the kings and people like in the twenty years after Josiah (36:5, 9, 12-14, 16)? So what does Yahweh do (36:12, 15, 17-21)? Why do you think the Chronicler closes the book with Cyrus' proclamation (36:22-23)?

299. Chronicles – Review

Pray. Then Read, Think and Mark.

You've now read all of Chronicles. Today you will think back over the book.

a. Reread your own introduction to Chronicles (lesson 279).
b. For what reasons did the Chronicler write Chronicles? How did he show that the Davidic dynasty (that is King David and his descendants who were kings after him) and the temple are important?
c. How does the Chronicler encourage his readers to seek Yahweh faithfully? As the book closes, what do you think the Chronicler wants his readers (1) to think about who they are and (2) to do?
d. Look back through the book. Note the words and verses you marked. What are the main things God was showing and teaching the kings and people of Judah?
e. What things seemed important to you?
f. Look back at your answers to question *d* each day. What were some things you discovered on your own?
g. Think back through your answers to question *f* each day. What are some key ways God is telling you to change the way you love, think or live?
h. Jesus told his disciples, "Everything must be fulfilled that is written about me in the Law of Moses, the Prophets and the Psalms" (Luke 24:44). What parts of Chronicles made you think about the Messiah? You may think about David or Solomon, the temple, any of the faithful kings who cleansed the temple or something else.

Write

Write a review of Chronicles. In the first paragraph, describe the Chronicler's context. Then state his purpose for writing the book. In the second paragraph, explain how the Chronicler writes the book to encourage his readers to think about the temple in Jerusalem and to seek Yahweh faithfully. In the third paragraph, describe how God is changing the way you love, think or live. In the fourth paragraph, explain one of Jesus' "shadows" in the book of Chronicles. Finally, end your review with a prayer to King Jesus. Praise him for being the sort of king he is. Thank him for cleansing the temple and making you part of it. Then tell him how you want to seek him.

300. Old Testament 2 Review

You've now read the whole story of God and his people from Adam to Nehemiah. Well done! Today you will think back over the Prophets.

Pray. Think through the following points.

a. Reread your orientation to the Prophets (lesson 151).
b. Reread your own introduction and review for each book in Old Testament 2 (lessons 152, 154, 159, 165, 170, 173, 198, 200, 202, 204, 215, 218, 222, 228, 240, 253, 254, 255, 258, 261, 262, 264, 268, 271, 278, 279, 299).
c. How does Isaiah describe who Yahweh is and what he is like?
d. How does Deuteronomy set the perspective for the prophets and Israel's history right through the exile and the return (Deuteronomy 28:58-68; 30:1-10)?
e. What does Yahweh send his prophets to do? For example, what does Joel tell the people to do?
f. What does Yahweh want most from his people? For example, see Micah 6:6-8.
g. What are the main sins the prophets keep confronting? Consider Hosea and Amos.
h. What does Yahweh tell his people he will do if they do not repent? See Isaiah 1-39.
i. What does Yahweh promise to do when they repent? See Isaiah 40-66; Jeremiah 31; Ezekiel 36.
j. What will Yahweh do if his people respond the right way to the prophet's message? For example, what does Yahweh do when the people of Nineveh hear Jonah's message and repent?
k. How do the people usually respond to the prophets? For example, how do the king and the people treat Jeremiah?
l. What horrible idea does Habakkuk have to struggle with?
m. What all do the Babylonians do to Jerusalem, the temple and the people? See 2 Kings 25; Jeremiah 38-39; Lamentations.
n. According to Ezekiel, what does Yahweh want Israel and the nations to know?
o. How does Yahweh take care of his people in exile? Consider Daniel and his friends and Esther.
p. What special style of writing do Ezekiel, Daniel and Zechariah use for some of their prophecies? What do these prophets help God's people to see, believe and hope in?
q. After the exile, when the people return to the land, what do the leaders (Zerubbabel and Joshua, Ezra and Nehemiah) and the prophets (Haggai and Zechariah) encourage the people to do?

r.   But which promises are still unfulfilled? For example, what questions are the people in Malachi's day struggling with?

s.   What are some of the most important lessons you have learned as you've read 2 Kings – Malachi?

t.   What are some key ways God has changed the way you love, think or live?

u.   Jesus told his disciples, "Everything must be fulfilled that is written about me in the Law of Moses, the Prophets and the Psalms" (Luke 24:44). If you were living in Jerusalem during the days of Nehemiah, and you read carefully through the Law and the Prophets, what kind of Messiah would you be expecting? Consider Isaiah 2:1-4; 4:1-6; 9:1-7; 42:1-9; 49:1-13; 52:13-53:12; 61:1-4.

Write

Write a review of the Prophets. In the first paragraph, summarize the story of Yahweh God's plans for humans and how he used his covenants with Abraham, Israel and David to prepare his people to live faithfully in his kingdom. In the second paragraph, tell the story of Judah's unfaithful kings, rebellious people and faithful prophets. Explain how Yahweh uses the prophets to call his people to turn back to him and keep the covenant faithfully. State what Yahweh says he will do if the people do not repent. In the third paragraph, summarize the promises Yahweh gave his people through Moses, Isaiah, Jeremiah, Ezekiel and other prophets about what he would do for them when they turn to him. In the fourth paragraph, tell the story of what has happened after the exile, what the people have done, which promises have been fulfilled and which have not. Describe the sort of Messiah the people may have been hoping for. Finally, end your review with a prayer to King Jesus. Explain something he's taught you. Tell him how he's changing you. And thank him for something he has done for you as your king.

PART THREE

OLD TESTAMENT WRITINGS
Worship and Wisdom

Psalms

301. Psalms – Introduction

Pray. Then Read, Think and <u>Mark</u>.

An introduction gets you ready to read a book. It usually tells you who wrote the book, when and for whom. It points out the important themes you should look out for and summarizes the book's message.

Read your study Bible's introduction to Psalms. Think about the questions for each of the following sections. <u>Mark</u> the answers and other things that seem important.

for the ESV Study Bible

- Title
    - o Read the second paragraph. <u>Mark</u> the Hebrew and Greek titles for this book. What does each title mean?
- Authorship, Occasion, and Date
    - o Read the seventh paragraph ("The individual psalms ..."). When were the individual psalms written?
    - o Read the last paragraph. What did the Psalter serve as?
- Key Themes
    - o Read the first two paragraphs. Who is God and what will he do?
- The Psalms as Scripture
    - o Read the first paragraph. What did some of the authors of the psalms do?
    - o Read the second paragraph. What do the psalms give God's people?
    - o What do the psalms do to the emotions of godly people?
    - o Read the third paragraph. What do the psalms show?
    - o Read the fourth paragraph.

- What was the king supposed to be for the people?
- How could the people (and how can you) use the psalms the king wrote?
- Literary Features
  - Follow the note in the third paragraph to the article "Introduction to the Poetic and Wisdom Literature."
    - Read the second paragraph in the section "What is Hebrew 'Poetry'?" It starts with "One prominent feature of biblical poetry...."
    - What is that prominent feature?
    - How many parts does a line of Hebrew poetry usually have?
    - In poetic parallelism, what three things can the second part of a line of poetry do with the first part of the line?
  - Go back to the introduction to Psalms and read the fourth paragraph ("Scholars have tended ...") in "Literary Features." What are the basic categories of psalms?
- Structure
  - Read through the table. What is each of the five books like?

for the NIV Study Bible
- Title
  - Mark the Hebrew and Greek titles for this book. What does each title mean?
- Collection, Arrangement and Date
  - Read the first paragraph.
  - What are the Psalms often called?
  - How did the final editors of the Psalms view the book?
  - Read the last paragraph. What does each of the five books of the psalms end with?
  - Which psalms introduce the Psalter? Which psalms conclude it?
- Psalm Types
  - Read the second paragraph. What are the main types of psalms?
- Literary Features
  - Read the first paragraph. What type of writing does the Psalter use?
  - Read the second paragraph. Mark the "most distinctive feature" of Hebrew poetry.

- o In Hebrew poetry, what are the three things the second segment (or part) of a line can do with the first segment?
- o Read the last four lines of the last paragraph ("The authors of the psalms..."). Mark how the psalms are best appreciated.
- Theology: Summary, Messianic Import and Conclusion
  - o Read the first paragraph. What is "the most basic metaphor and most pervasive theological concept in the Psalter"?
  - o Read the second paragraph. What will God's kingdom do?
  - o Read the fourth paragraph. Who truly fulfills the psalms about the king?
  - o Read the sixth paragraph ("These cries became ..."). What words did Christ pray when he suffered?
  - o Read the last paragraph. How should you use the psalms?

Write

Write your own introduction to the book of Psalms. Tell what the book is and how God's people have used it. Mention the first key theme or main theological concept of the Psalter. In the second paragraph, state what the distinctive or prominent feature of Hebrew poetry is. Explain how the two parts of a line of poetry work together. In the third paragraph, list the main types or categories of psalms. Give one example of each type. Finally, outline the Psalms in five books.

302. Psalms 1-2

Follow your bookmark. Then answer these questions:

a. What two basic types of people are there (1:5-6)? What is each type of person like (1:3, 4)? What does the blessed person do (1:1-2)?

b. In your notebook, sketch a comic strip with five frames to show what is happening in 2:1-3, 4-6, 7, 8-9, 10-12.

c. What several things does Psalm 2 say about Yahweh's Anointed (3, 6, 7, 8, 9, 12)? (The Hebrew word is *mashiyakh* or Messiah.) When Yahweh made a covenant with David, to whom did Yahweh say he would be a father (see the study note for 2:7)? Follow the cross-reference for 2:7 to Acts. Who do Paul and the apostles say the "son" is?

Return to your bookmark and do d through g.

(3) Think about and answer the questions. (4) Return to your bookmark.

303. Psalms 3-5

Follow your bookmark. Then answer these questions:

    a. Look back in your introduction at your list of types or categories of psalms. What type of psalm is Psalm 3? What does David do night and day (3:5; see 1:2)? What will Yahweh do for David (3:7-8; see 1:1, 4-6)?

    b. In the middle of his distress or trouble, what does David do (4:1-2, 5)? Then what does Yahweh do (4:1, 3, 7-8)? Now how does David feel (4:7-8)?

    c. What does David call Yahweh (5:2)? How does Yahweh treat David and the righteous (5:7-8, 12)? How does Yahweh treat people who do evil (5:4-7, 10)?

Return to your bookmark and do d through g.

304. Psalms 6-8

Follow your bookmark. Then answer these questions:

    a. What has David done (6:1-2)? See the study notes for Psalm 6 and 6:1-3/5. How bad is David's trouble (6:2-3, 5-7)? What is David's hope (6:4, 9)?

    b. In Psalm 7, has David done wrong (7:3-4, 8)? How does David describe Yahweh (7:6, 8, 11-13)? What does Yahweh do to the righteous and to the wicked (7:9-16)?

    c. What does David marvel at (8:3-4)? How did God make man (the human race) and you special (8:5-8)? Write out the sentence that David uses like bookends at the beginning and end of Psalm 8.

Return to your bookmark and do d through g.

305. Psalms 9-10

Follow your bookmark. Then answer these questions:

    a. Who is Yahweh (9:2, 4, 7, 11)? Over whom does he reign (9:4-8, 19)? How does Yahweh rule and judge (9:4, 7-8)?

    b. What is the wicked person like (10:2-11)? Are the wicked supposed to prosper or not? Compare Psalm 1:3-6 with Psalm 10:5, 10. How does the psalmist hope things will be set right (10:12, 15, 17-18)?

    c. When wicked people or nations grow strong, whom do they oppress (9:9, 18; 10:2, 8-10, 14, 17-18)? What does Yahweh do for those who are oppressed (9:7-10, 12, 19-20; 10:14, 17-18)? Is

Yahweh big enough to save the helpless from the strong, even whole nations (9:2, 7-8, 20; 10:16)?

Return to your bookmark and do d *through* g.

306. Psalms 11-14

Follow your bookmark. Then answer these questions:

a. What does Yahweh love, and whom does he hate (11:5, 7)? Why does David feel safe (11:1, 4)? What is everyone around David like (12:1-2)?

b. What does Yahweh promise at last (12:5)? Does Yahweh act right away (13:1-2)? How strong is David's trust (13:5-6)?

c. What are the children of man (the human race) like (14:2-3)? Who cares for the righteous and the poor (14:5-6)? Explain how the two parts at the end of 14:7 are parallel: "let Jacob rejoice / let Israel be glad."

Return to your bookmark and do d *through* g.

307. Psalms 15-17

Follow your bookmark. Then answer these questions:

a. What kind of person does Yahweh welcome in his tent or sanctuary (15:1-2)? How does that kind of person treat others (15:2-5)? Who will never be shaken or moved (15:5; 16:8; see 10:6)?

b. What is David's lot in life like (16:2, 5-6)? When he dies, where does David hope to be (16:10-11; 17:15)? What is David seeing and speaking about (16:8-11)? Follow the study note for 16:9-11 to Acts 2.

c. Has David done wrong (17:1-5)? What is David's trouble (17:10-12)? What is David's hope (17:6-7, 15)?

Return to your bookmark and do d *through* g.

308. Psalm 18

Follow your bookmark. Then answer these questions:

a. What did it look like when Yahweh came to help David (18:7-15)? How did Yahweh rescue David (18:17, 28-29, 32-36, 39-40)? What different things does David call Yahweh (18:1-2)?

b. Whose cry did Yahweh answer (18:3, 6, 41)? Why did Yahweh rescue him (18:19-27)? How is David's life like the man in Psalm 1 (18:20, 22, 24; see 1:2, 5-6)?

c. What has Yahweh made David (18:43, 50)? How does Psalm 18 begin to fulfill Psalm 2 (2:2, 6, 8-9, 11)? Which of David's descendants will really fulfill this psalm (18:43, 50)?

309. Psalm 19

a. What does David call God in the first half of the psalm (19:1)? How does God show himself in these verses (19:1-6)? Who all hear what the heavens declare (19:3-4)?

b. What does David call God in the second part of this psalm (19:7-9)? How does God reveal himself in these verses (19:7-11)? What is Yahweh's law like (19:7-11)?

c. What is David's delight in (19:10; see 1:2)? What does Yahweh's law do (19:7-11)? What does David ask God to do so that David will be innocent (19:12-13)?

310. Psalms 20-21

a. In Psalm 20, who speaks to whom (see 20:1-5 and the study note)? As the king leads the army into battle, what do the people trust in (20:7)? What kind of parallelism do you see in the two parts of verse 8?

b. What phrase sits like bookends at the beginning and at the end of Psalm 21 (21:1, 13)? What has Yahweh done for the king (21:2-6; 20:4)? What is the desire of the king's heart (21:6-7)?

c. Who saves the king and establishes his kingdom (21:1, 3, 5, 7)? What will Yahweh do for the king (21:8-12)? What would it be like to live in a kingdom ruled by a king like this (21:2-7)?

311. Psalm 22

a. What is happening to the man (22:6-8, 12-18)? Who is attacking him (22:12-13, 16)? So what does the man do (22:1-2, 11, 19-20)?

b. But what does Yahweh do (22:1-11, 19)? Then what does Yahweh do (22:21, 24)? And what do all nations and future generations do (22:26-31)?

c. As Matthew writes his gospel, how does Psalm 22 help him understand Jesus' death (Psalm 22:1, 7, 8, 18; see Matthew 27:35, 39, 43, 46)? In the Letter to the Hebrews, who does it say is the man who speaks in Psalm 22 (Hebrews 2:10-12)? What has the Lord done (Psalm 22:31; see John 19:30)?

312. Psalms 23-24

a. How does Yahweh give his "sheep" everything he needs (23:1-4)? What does Yahweh do to David (23:5)? What is chasing David now (23:6)?

b. What does Psalm 24 seem to be about? See the study note for Psalm 24. Who is Yahweh (24:1-2, 10)? Where is Yahweh coming (24:3, 7-10)?

c. Which earlier psalm is Psalm 24 like? Follow the cross-reference for 24:3. What do clean-handed, pure-hearted worshipers receive (24:5)? Whom does Jacob (Israel) get to be close to (24:1-2, 6, 10)?

313. Psalms 25-26

a. What kind of poem is Psalm 25? See the translation note for Psalm 25. What does David want Yahweh to remember, and what does he want him not to remember (25:6, 7)? What does David ask Yahweh to do (25:1-2, 20)?

b. Whom does Yahweh teach and lead (25:8-9)? Is David that kind of person 25:4-5, 7, 11, 18)? What kind of God is Yahweh (25:6, 10)?

c. How did David become blameless, a person of integrity (26:1, 3)? Whom does David stay away from (26:4-5; see 1:1-2)? How does David enter Yahweh's house (26:6-8; see 24:3-4)?

314. Psalms 27-28

a. What might David fear (27:2-3, 12)? Where does David want to be (27:1, 4)? What will Yahweh do for him there (27:5, 9-11)?

b. What will David do there (27:6, 8)? When does David believe he will see Yahweh's goodness (27:13)? What does David tell himself to do till then (27:14)?

c. Who all does what kind of work (or deeds) (28:3-5)? Can a rock hear and speak (28:1-2, 6)? Whom all does Yahweh help (28:7-9)?

315. Psalms 29-30

a. How many times does David use the name "Yahweh" ("the LORD") in the opening stanza and in the closing stanza (29:1-2, 10-11)? Whom does David tell to praise Yahweh (29:1; see the study note)? Why should heavenly beings and humans worship Yahweh (29:1-2, 10)?

b. How many times does David use the phrase "the voice of Yahweh" ("the voice of the LORD") (29:3-9)? What is the voice of Yahweh (29:3, 7)? Whom do Canaanites and many Israelites praise as the god of the thunderstorm? See the study note for Psalm 29.

c. Why was David going down to the pit (30:3, 5, 7, 9; see 28:1)? When did David call to Yahweh for help and mercy (30:2, 8, 10; see 28:2)? What does David do when Yahweh shows him favor (30:4, 11-12)?

316. Psalms 31-32

a. What did Yahweh do when David was in trouble before (31:4, 7-8)? What are the two reasons David is in distress again (31:9-10, 11-13)? Why does David call on Yahweh (31:14, 16)?

b. Who loves whom (31:14, 21, 23)? Which son of David also trusted Yahweh (see the cross-reference in 31:5)? Which psalm ends like Psalm 31 (see the cross-reference for 31:24)?

c. How did David feel when he tried to cover his iniquity (32:3-4)? When David revealed his transgression and confessed it to Yahweh, what did Yahweh do (32:1, 5)? Does Yahweh count David as a sinner or as righteous now (32:1, 11)?

317. Psalms 33-34

a. What is Yahweh's word like (33:4-5, 11)? When Yahweh looks down from heaven on all people, whom is his eye on (33:13-19)? What should Yahweh's nation do (33:1-3, 12, 20-22)?

b. Why does David praise Yahweh (34:1-6)? What does Yahweh do for those who fear him (34:9-10)? How do people live when they fear Yahweh (34:11-14)?

c. What do three parts of Yahweh's body do (34:15-16)? Does Yahweh keep troubles away from the righteous (34:6, 17, 19)? Whose bones did Yahweh keep from being broken (follow the cross-reference for 34:20)?

318. Psalms 35-36

a. What is happening to David (35:4, 7, 11-12, 15-16, 19-21, 26)? Did David do them wrong (35:12-14, 24)? What does David call himself (35:27)?

b. What does David ask Yahweh to do for him (35:1-3, 17, 22-24)? What does David hope will happen to those who fight against him (35:4-6, 26)? In the end, what will David and others do (35:9-10, 18, 27-28)?

c. When people do not fear God, what do they think and speak about (36:1-4)? What does David think and speak about (36:5-9)? In the end, what happens to evildoers (36:12)?

319. Psalm 37

a. What are the wicked like (37:7, 21, 32-33, 35)? How do they try to get the land (37:12, 14)? Why should the righteous not fear the wicked (37:1-2, 8-10, 13, 15, 17, 20, 22, 36, 38)?

b. Who will inherit the land (37:9, 11, 29)? Do they have to try to get it (37:22, 34)? How should they live as they wait for the land (37:3-7)?

c. If Yahweh is your delight, what will your heart desire (37:4)? What will Yahweh do for the righteous (37:18-19, 23-24, 28, 33, 37, 39-40)? In what ways does Psalm 37 make you think about Jesus' Sermon on the Mount (37:11; see Matthew 5:1-11; 6:25-34)?

320. Psalms 38-39

a. Why does Yahweh rebuke David (38:1, 3-5)? How does Yahweh discipline David (38:1-3, 5-10, 17)? What do David's enemies do while he is weak (38:12, 19-20)?

b. Does Yahweh's rebuke mean that he has forsaken David (38:1, 9, 21-22)? Whom does David call on to stop Yahweh from hurting him (38:1, 15, 21-22)? Since the two parts of verse 18 are parallel, how does that help you understand what it means to confess your sin (38:18)?

c. When Yahweh disciplines someone for sin, how does he do it (39:11)? When you are in distress or anguish, does God want you to be quiet about it (39:1-3) or to talk to him about it (39:3-10)? Even though Yahweh is the one who is rebuking him for his sin, whom does David call on to deliver him from his transgressions (39:8)?

321. Psalms 40-41

a. What has Yahweh done for David before (40:1-3)? In which scroll is it written that David would tell the great assembly about Yahweh's saving acts (40:7-12)? Follow the cross-reference for "the great assembly" or "congregation" (40:9).

When David sins against God again, whom does he call on for help (40:11-13)?

b. What is happening to David (41:3-5, 8)? How is it possible for David both to sin and to have integrity (41:4, 12)? Which close friend shared bread with one of David's descendants and then lifted up his heel against him? Follow the cross-reference for 41:9 to John.

c. What is verse 13 (see the study note)? In your introduction to Psalms, look at the list of the types of psalms. What type of psalm are most of the psalms in Book I? Whatever your trouble, who is always your best hope (41:13)?

322. Psalms 42-43

a. Who wrote this psalm? You can read about them in the NIV's footnote or in the ESV's Introduction to the Psalms (in the third paragraph of the section "Authorship, Occasion, and Date"). What does the psalmist's soul want (42:1-2)? Where is his God (42:3-4, 10; 43:3-4)?

b. Where is the psalmist (42:6 and study note)? So why is the psalmist's soul downcast? How many times does the refrain occur in these psalms (42:5, 11; 43:5)?

c. What verse is in the middle of the middle stanza (42:5-10) just before the middle refrain (42:11)? Look carefully at how the first two parts of that verse are parallel. Now, can you figure out what Yahweh's song is (42:8)? The last two lines are parallel also. What does Yahweh's song become for the psalmist (42:8)?

323. Psalms 44-45

a. What is happening to the psalmist and the rest of Israel's army (44:9-16, 19)? Is God cursing Israel because they have not kept his covenant (44:4-8, 17-18, 20-21; see Deuteronomy 28:15, 25)? What is the psalmist's hope and the hope of God's children in the new covenant (44:22, 26; see Romans 8:35-39)?

b. For what does the king fight (45:3-5)? What does God do for the king (45:2, 6-7)? What is the tone of the psalm: what is its main feeling (45:1-2, 7-9, 11-13, 15, 17)?

c. To whom did God promise a kingdom forever (45:6-7; see 2 Samuel 7:12-16)? Which of David's sons will fulfill this blessing (Psalm 45:6-7)? Follow the cross-reference to Hebrews.

Who is that king's bride (see Ephesians 5:23, 25-27, 31-32; Revelation 21:2-3, 9-11)?

324. Psalms 46-48

a. What are the nations like (46:2-3, 6)? What do God's desolations bring about (46:8-10)? What does God do for his people in his city (46:1, 4-5, 7, 11)?

b. What did God promise Abraham (47:9; see Genesis 12:2-3; 17:4-6; 22:17-18)? Who is king of all the earth (Psalm 47:2, 5-7; see Matthew 28:18; Acts 2:32-37)? Is it really true that the nations of the earth will fear, praise and exalt Yahweh Most High (Psalm 46:10; 47:1-2, 6-7, 9)?

c. What is Yahweh's city (48:1-3, 8, 11-13; 46:4-5)? How far did Yahweh go to defend his city (48:2, 4-7, 10, 12-13)? How, where and when will Yahweh be praised (48:1, 10, 13-14)?

325. Psalms 49-50

a. What kind of psalm is Psalm 49 (49:3)? In the end, what does it benefit people to have wealth if they have no understanding (49:7-9, 11-12, 17, 19-20)? What do wise and upright people take with them when they die (49:10, 14-15)?

b. What does it look like when El God Yahweh summons his people to judge them (50:1-4)? Why do animal sacrifices not glorify God (50:8-13)? What kind of sacrifice does God want (50:14-15, 23)?

c. From where does God shine forth (50:2)? Since the Israelites are God's people, do they have the right to live as they please (50:7, 16-17, 21)? How must God's people live (50:5, 23)?

326. Psalm 51

a. What evil has David done (51:3-4)? What does David want God to do (51:1-2, 7-12)? Which books of the Bible instruct the Israelites about washing, cleansing and purging with hyssop (see the study notes for 51:2, 7, 10)?

b. What does David appeal to; that is, what reasons does he give God to cleanse him (51:1)? After God forgives David, what does David do (51:14-15)? What kind of sacrifice pleases God (51:16-17; see 50:8, 13-14)?

c. What does David do with the very personal story of his sin and forgiveness (51:13)? When sinners learn and return to God, what happens in God's city (51:18-19)? If you are a transgressor or sinner, what should reading Psalm 51 do for you (51:13)?

327. Psalms 52-54

a. What is the story behind Psalm 52? Follow the cross-reference for "Doeg the Edomite" in the title. How does this mighty man do evil (52:1-4)? What happens when you trust in your wealth, and what happens when you trust in God's love (52:1, 5, 7-8)?

b. Which earlier psalm is Psalm 53 very much like (see the study note for Psalm 53)? Which fool did David no good (53:1; see 1 Samuel 25:25)? How did God put him to shame (Psalm 53:5; 1 Samuel 25:37-38)?

c. What is the story behind Psalm 54? Follow the cross-reference for "when the Ziphites" in the title. What does David make his focus and the center of this psalm (54:4)? Just before and after the center, what does David say about his enemies and about God (54:3, 5)?

328. Psalms 55-56

a. What is happening in the city (55:3, 9-11)? How does David feel (55:2, 4-5)? Who is troubling David (55:12-14, 20-21)? Also follow the cross-reference for 55:13 to 2 Samuel.

b. What does David ask God to do to them (Psalm 55:15)? What might God do if the enemy feared God and changed (55:19)? What does God do for David (55:17-18, 22)?

c. What story is behind Psalm 56 (see 1 Samuel 21:10-15)? What are humans trying to do to David (Psalm 56:1-2, 4, 5-6, 11)? Why can humans not do that to David (56:4, 9-11, 13)?

329. Psalms 57-58

a. What is the refrain at the end of each half of Psalm 57 (57:5, 11)? In each half of the psalm, what does David hope in (57:3, 10)? In the first half, what does David do at night, and in the second half, what does he do in the morning (57:4, 8)?

b. When God Most High divided the children of Adam (humans), how did he set up their borders (Deuteronomy 32:8-9)? (For the NIV, see the translation note for 32:8.) Who does David say judge the children of Adam unjustly (see Psalm 58:1 and the study note)? When did a serpent lead Adam astray (Psalm 58:3-5; see Genesis 3:1-13)?

c. What hope did God give the man Adam and the woman (Genesis 3:15, 20)? How will Yahweh God judge the unjust judges (Psalm 58:6-10)? Then what will Adam (humanity) say (58:11)?

330. Psalms 59-60

a. What is the story behind Psalm 59? What do the dogs do with their mouths (59:6-7, 12, 14-15)? What will David do with his mouth (59:16-17)?

b. How has God made Israel feel (60:1-3)? Why does David think God will help Israel now (60:4-5)? Turn to Map 4 in the back of your study Bible and find the lands God claims: Shechem, Sukkoth, Gilead, Manasseh, Ephraim, Judah, Moab, Edom, and Philistia (60:6-8).

c. How does God say he will treat Moab, Edom and Philistia (60:8)? What makes David confident as he leads the army into battle (60:11-12)? What was the outcome of the battle? See the title of the psalm.

331. Psalms 61-63

a. Where is David (61:1-2)? Where does David want God to take him (61:2-4)? What pair of things does David ask God to appoint to watch over him (61:7)?

b. What is God like, and what is David like (62:2, 3)? What are highborn people like (62:9-10)? What two things are true of God (62:11-12)?

c. What story is probably behind Psalm 63? See the ESV note for Psalm 63 or the NIV note for 63 title. Why will David's lips praise God (63:3)? How satisfying is God (63:5)?

332. Psalms 64-65

a. Is it okay to complain to God (64:1)? Who all use arrows (64:3-4, 7)? By the end of the psalm, is David still complaining (64:10)?

b. How does God show his goodness to his people (65:3-4)? How awesome is God's power (65:6-7)? Look carefully at how the three parts of 65:7 are parallel to each other. What is the turmoil of the nations like?

c. How do the people far away at the ends of the earth feel about God (65:5, 8)? What is the whole land like (65:9-13)?

(3) Think about and answer the questions. (4) Return to your bookmark.   213

Which promise is God keeping (see Deuteronomy 7:12-13; 11:11-15)?

333. Psalms 66-67

a. How should all the earth praise God (66:1-4)? What awesome works did God do in the past (66:5-6)? Who laid burdens on the psalmist and others and let men ride over their heads (66:11-12)?

b. Why did he do that (66:10)? In the middle of his trouble, what did the psalmist do (66:13-14, 17)? Now what is the psalmist doing (66:1-5, 8, 13, 15-16, 19-20)?

c. Why does the psalmist ask God to bless Israel (67:1-2, 7)? How does God judge and rule the peoples of the earth (67:4)? What does the psalmist really want to see happen (67:3, 5)?

334. Psalm 68

a. When did God lead prisoners through the wilderness (68:4-8)? What did the Israelites say when the ark of Yahweh's covenant would set out (see the study note for 68:1-3)? Which earlier song also talks about God's stormy march (see the study note for 68:7-10)?

b. At Sinai, why did Yahweh God receive gifts from men (68:18; see Exodus 35:20-36:7)? Where is God's sanctuary now (Psalm 68:24, 29)? When Christ the Anointed ascends on high, what will the men build up with the gifts he gives them? Follow the study note for 68:18 to Ephesians 4:8-13.

c. What will God the King do now (Psalm 68:1-2, 21, 28, 30)? What will the leaders of the nations do (68:29, 31-32)? How does God show his majestic power (68:32-35)?

335. Psalm 69

a. Do David's enemies have a reason to hate him (69:4)? What reason did Jesus' enemies have for hating him? Follow the cross-reference for 69:4 to John 15. When others scorned David or Jesus, for whose sake did they bear the insults (Psalm 69:7, 19)?

b. Did David's or Jesus' own brothers understand them and accept them (Psalm 69:8; see 1 Samuel 17:26-37; Matthew 13:54-58)? When Jesus was consumed with zeal for God's house, what did he do? Follow the first cross-reference for Psalm 69:9. As Jesus was dying, what was the final reproach that fulfilled Scripture and finished everything (Psalm 69:21; John 19:28-30)?

   c.   What did Psalm 69:25 tell Jesus' disciples to do about someone who had reproached Jesus? Follow the cross-reference to Acts. After Jesus' affliction, how did God save him and set him in a high place (Psalm 69:29)? See the NIV study note and Philippians 2:8-9. Now who will praise God the Father and the Son (Psalm 69:34; see Philippians 2:10-11)?

336.   Psalms 70-71

   a.   Which earlier psalm is Psalm 70 very much like (see the study note for Psalm 70)? How does David open and close his prayer (70:1, 5)? In what ways are the three pairs of lines in 70:2-3 parallel?

   b.   Why is the psalmist weak (71:9, 18)? How do the psalmist's enemies trouble him (71:4, 10-11)? Yet who is the very one who planned the troubles (71:20)?

   c.   To whom does the psalmist cry for help (71:4, 12, 21)? What does the psalmist appeal to (71:2, 16, 19, 24)? What does the psalmist do with his mouth (71:8, 15, 23, 24)?

337.   Psalm 72

   a.   How should the king rule (72:1-3)? When a king reigns like that, what does he do (72:4, 12-14)? What will life in the kingdom be like (72:5-7, 16)?

   b.   How big will the king's kingdom be (72:8-11)? How long will his kingdom last (72:5, 15, 17)? Who is this royal son of David (72:1)? See the study notes for Psalm 72 and title. See also Matthew 28:18-20; Acts 2:36.

   c.   What are verses 18-19 (see the study note for 72:18-19)? Who wrote most of the psalms in Books I and II (72:20)? What do both Psalm 2 (at the beginning of Book I) and Psalm 72 (at the end of Book II) talk about?

338.   Psalms 73-74

   a.   Who wrote this psalm (73 title; see also 1 Chronicles 16:4-7; 25:2)? What are the lives of wicked people like (73:3-12)? How did that make Asaph feel (73:3, 13-14, 21-22)?

   b.   What did Asaph come to understand when he was in the sanctuary (73:16-20, 27)? What does God do for faithful people in this life and after it (73:23-24, 28)? What does Asaph want most of all (73:25-26)?

c.   What have God's enemies done (74:3-8)? What great things did God the King do before (74:12-17)? What does Asaph tell God to remember (74:10, 18, 22-23)?

339.   Psalms 75-77

a.   What does God say he will do (75:2-5)? What is God's judgment like (75:7-8)? What is *horn* a symbol or metaphor for (75:4-5, 10; see the study not for 75:4)?

b.   What does God defend (76:1-2, 9)? Which event might Psalm 76 be singing about? See the ESV study note for 76:3-9 or the NIV study note for Ps 76. What should God's people do (76:11-12)?

c.   What does Asaph wonder (77:7-9; see Exodus 34:6)? How did El the Wonderworker show his might (Psalm 77:14-16, 19; see Exodus 7:2-6)? When did Israel see his awesome holiness (Psalm 77:13, 17-18; see Exodus 15:11)?

340.   Psalm 78:1-39

a.   What does Asaph do in this psalm (78:1-4)? Why did Yahweh command the Israelites to teach their children (78:5-8)? Who else sang a song to the Israelites for this same reason (Deuteronomy 32:1, 7, 44-47)?

b.   Why did the men of Ephraim turn back on the day of battle (Psalm 78:9-11)? How did their ancestors sin against God (78:12, 17-20)? How did Yahweh feel when they did not trust him (78:21-22)?

c.   What phrase in the second part of verse 32 is parallel to the phrase "they kept on sinning" in the first part of the verse (78:32)? What did God do before Israel repented at last (78:32-34)? How did God treat them even though they were not faithful to his covenant (78:37-39)?

341.   Psalm 78:40-72

a.   What words in 78:40-42 are parallel to "rebelled" in verse 40? What signs did God display in Egypt (78:43-51)? What wonders did he do in his holy land (78:54-55)?

b.   In which tribe is Shiloh (78:9, 60, 67)? When did God abandon his tent and give his people over to the sword (78:60-64)? Follow the first cross-reference for 78:64. After that battle, how did the Lord put his enemies to shame (78:61, 65-66; see 1 Samuel 5:1-7; 17:41-51)?

c. How special is Mount Zion (78:67-69)? Who are the shepherds of Israel (77:20; 78:52, 70-71)? How did David shepherd them (78:72)?

342. Psalms 79-80

a. What is the story behind Psalm 79? Follow the cross-reference for *Jerusalem* (79:1). Why did these horrible things happen to Jerusalem (79:5, 8)? What reason does Asaph give God to save his people and judge the nations (79:9-10)?

b. Who is the Shepherd of Israel (80:1; see 79:13)? What is the refrain that occurs several times (80:3, 7, 19)? How do verses 14-15 explain what it means for God to restore Israel, let his face shine and save them (80:14-15)?

c. What has God done with his vine (80:8-13)? Who is God's son (80:8, 14-15; see the study note for 80:15)? Who is the son of God's right hand (80:2, 15, 17)?

343. Psalms 81-83

a. When were the Israelites to sing Psalm 81 (see 81:3 and the study note)? What does God really want (81:8, 13)? What would he do then (81:14-16)?

b. How should the gods judge (82:2-4)? See lesson 329 for your notes on Psalm 58. How will God inherit the nations (82:6-8)? Who is son of God, son of man, son of the Most High and God himself (80:15, 17; 82:6)? Follow the cross-reference for 82:6.

c. How dangerous is this attack on Israel (83:2-8)? Which stories from Israel's history encourage Asaph (83:9-12; see the cross-references for 83:9, 11)? Why does Asaph want Yahweh to shame Israel's enemies (83:16-18)?

344. Psalms 84-85

a. Where does this son of Korah want to be (84:1-4)? What does Yahweh give people who seek him and trust him (84:5-7, 12)? Why is it better to serve in God's house than to live with wicked people (84:10-11)?

b. What has Yahweh done for his people before (85:1-3)? Why is God Yahweh angry with them again (85:4-5, 8)? What do his people ask him to do again (85:4-7)?

c. What must they do (84:12; 85:9)? How will Yahweh treat his people and their land (85:10-13)? When did Yahweh teach his people to trust his abounding love and faithfulness (Exodus 34:5-7)?

345. Psalms 86-88

a. What trouble is happening to David (86:1-3, 7, 14)? Why will all the nations worship the Lord instead of the gods (86:8-10)? How does the Lord help David (86:15-17)?

b. Who are the peoples Yahweh says acknowledge him (see 87:4 and the study note)? What does Yahweh write down as their birthplace; that is, what does he say their nationality or citizenship is (87:5-6)? Which prayers does this psalm fulfill (83:16, 18; 86:9)?

c. How is Yahweh treating the psalmist (88:6-8, 14-18)? To whom does the psalmist cry (88:1-2, 9, 13)? From the beginning of the psalm to the end, does the psalmist have any hope or relief (88:1, 7, 14, 18)?

346. Psalm 89

a. How has Yahweh shown his love and faithfulness (89:1-2, 5-18)? What did Yahweh promise David (89:3-4, 19-37)? What is the tone or feeling of verses 1-37?

b. What is the tone of verses 38-51? What has Yahweh done (89:38-45; see also 89:33-36)? What themes or key words from verses 1-37 does verse 49 bring up again?

c. Does the psalm end with any hope or relief (89:38, 46, 49)? Is this doxology at the end of Book III as glorious as the doxologies at the ends of Books I and II (89:52; see 41:13; 72:18-19)? What was the tone of most of the psalms in Book III?

347. Psalms 90-91

a. In Book III, which place and which leader made the people of Israel feel safe (78:68-72; 84:1-5; 89:20-36)? But what has happened to that place and those leaders (74:1-7; 79:1-4; 89:38-45)? Now at the beginning of Book IV, which leader's prayer teaches them wisdom (see the title for Psalm 90; see also 77:20)?

b. What dwelling "place" does that man say will still keep them safe (90:1)? What does the Lord make their lives like (90:7-10)? But who can make their days glad (90:12-17)?

    c.   When the people live in tents, in which fortress can they find refuge (91:1-2, 9-10)? What will Yahweh God do for them (91:3-4, 11, 14-16)? What will they do with their feet (91:12-13)?

348.   Psalms 92-93

    a.   How does Yahweh show his love and faithfulness (92:2-4; see 90:14-17)? When does the psalmist thank and praise Yahweh Most High (see the title for Psalm 92 and 92:2)? What does Yahweh do to his enemies and the psalmist's enemies (92:7, 9, 11)?

    b.   What kind of wood did Solomon use to cover the inside walls of the temple, and what trees did he carve into the walls (92:12-13; see 1 Kings 6:15-18, 29)? What happens when the righteous spend time worshipping Yahweh in his house (92:1-2, 12-15)? Which earlier psalm does the flourishing tree remind you of? See the cross-reference for 92:12 or 14.

    c.   Who is the king (93:1)? What thunders against him (93:3-4)? See your notes from lesson 332 on Psalm 65. How secure is his reign (93:1-2, 4)?

349.   Psalms 94-95

    a.   What are wicked people doing (94:3-7, 20-21)? What will El of Vengeance do about the situation (94:1-2, 14-15, 23)? What does Yahweh do for the psalmist's heart and soul (94:17-19)?

    b.   Why should the people praise Yahweh (95:1-3)? Why else should they praise Yahweh (95:6-7)? What should the people not do (95:8)?

    c.   What did the people do at Meribah and Massah (95:8-9)? Follow the cross-reference for Meribah (95:8). What did Yahweh do when they kept going astray (95:10-11)? Follow the first cross-reference for 95:11. How can we enter God's rest (95:11; see Hebrews 3:7-15, 19; 4:3, 5-7, 11)?

350.   Psalms 96-98

    a.   What is Yahweh like (96:4-6)? Who should praise him (96:1, 7-8)? Why will all creation rejoice (96:11-13)?

    b.   What does King Yahweh's reign look like (97:1-5)? Who should worship whom (97:7, 9)? What does Yahweh do for the righteous (97:10-11)?

c. What have the nations seen (98:2-3)? Who should praise King Yahweh (98:4-6)? What is Yahweh coming to do (98:9)?

351. Psalms 99-101

a. Since Yahweh is the great king, what should the peoples and the earth do (99:1-3, 5, 9)? What does the king do (99:4)? What did Yahweh do through the prophets and priest (99:6-8)?

b. Whom did Yahweh make, and who all belong to him (100:1, 3)? Why should all people thank and praise him (100:4-5)? In what ways is Psalm 100 like Psalm 95 (100:1-4; see 95:1-2, 6-7)?

c. About whom and to whom does David sing (101:1-2)? What will David do to evildoers (101:3-5, 7-8)? What will David do for the faithful (101:6)?

352. Psalms 102-103

a. What are the psalmist's days like (102:3-4, 11, 23-24)? What are Yahweh's years like (102:12, 24, 27)? What did Yahweh build a very long time ago (102:25)?

b. What does the psalmist want Yahweh to build now (102:14, 16, 20-21)? Where will the nations worship Yahweh (102:15, 20-22)? A long time from now, who will praise Yahweh (102:12, 18, 28)?

c. How does Yahweh forgive us (103:3, 8-12)? To whom does Yahweh show compassion, love and righteousness (103:13, 17-18)? Who all should bless Yahweh (103:1-2, 19-22)?

353. Psalm 104

a. What clothing does Yahweh wrap himself in (104:2)? In Genesis 1 does Moses talk about Yahweh laying the beams for his chambers or setting the earth on its foundations (Psalm 104:3, 5)? Why might the psalmist sing the song of creation a little differently from the way Moses tells the story of creation?

b. Does the psalmist sing about what Yahweh did with the water or what he does with the water (104:6-9, 10, 13)? Why does Yahweh give humans wine, oil and bread (104:14-15)? How do the sun and the moon mark the times for animals and humans (104:19-23)?

c. How many of God's creative works does the psalmist sing about: creatures, plants, places, times (104:24)? What will happen to the creatures if God stops helping them (104:27-30)? What Hebrew phrase do the English words "Praise the LORD" translate (see the translation or study note for 104:35)?

354. Psalm 105

a. Where are the Israelites now (105:1)? How did Yahweh treat them when they were there before (105:12-15)? What does the psalmist tell Abraham's offspring to remember (105:5)?

b. In verses 8-10 what other words or phrases are parallel to "covenant" and have much the same meaning (105:8-10)? How are the things that happened to Joseph like the things that have happened to Israel (105:17-19; see 2 Kings 25:11, 21)? How did Yahweh take care of Israel when he brought them out of Egypt (105:37-41)?

c. Why did Yahweh care for them that way (105:42)? What does the psalmist call the Israelites (105:6, 15, 23)? What should Israel be doing already (105:1-6, 43)?

355. Psalm 106

a. Compare the following verses in Psalms 105 and 106: 105:40 and 106:14-15; 105:44 and 106:34-35. As Psalm 105 tells the story of Israel, what does it sing about (105:5)? As Psalm 106 tells the story of Israel, what does it sing about (106:6)?

b. What did Israel not remember (106:7, 13, 21-22; see 105:5)? How did Israel sin in the wilderness (106:14, 16, 19, 24-25, 28)? How did Israel sin in the pleasant land (106:34-39)?

c. Which prophet's words taught Israel to hope that Yahweh would gather them again (Psalm 106:47; see Deuteronomy 30:1-6)? Who taught the Israelites to sing the words at the beginning and end of this psalm (Psalm 106:1, 47-48; see 1 Chronicles 16:1-2, 34-36, 41)? Compare this doxology at the end of Book IV with the doxology at the end of Book III (Psalm 106:48; see 89:52).

356. Psalm 107

a. How does the beginning of Psalm 107 (at the beginning of Book IV) answer the prayer from the end of Psalm 106 (at the end of Book III) (106:47; 107:1, 3)? From how many directions did Yahweh gather his people, and how many stanzas describe what happened to them (107:3, 4-9, 10-16, 17-22, 23-32)?

---

(3) Think about and answer the questions. (4) Return to your bookmark.   221

What does the psalmist describe at the beginning of each of these stanzas (107:4-5, 10-12, 17-18, 23-27)?

b. What does the psalmist sing next (107:6, 13, 19, 28)? What other verse does the psalmist echo in each stanza (107:8, 15, 21, 31)? What is the psalmist remembering (107:8, 15, 21,31; see 105:5; 106:7, 21-22)?

c. How does Yahweh treat a land (107:33-34, 35-38)? How does Yahweh treat oppressors and the people they oppress (107:39-40, 41)? What should wise people ponder (107:43)?

357. Psalms 108-109

a. Which two of David's psalms are put together to make Psalm 108 (see the study note for Psalm 108)? What did David do when he was among the nations (108:3-4; see 57:9-10)? After David sang Psalm 60, did God trample down David's enemies and save God's beloved people (60:5, 12; 108:6, 13; see the title for Psalm 60)?

b. What have the wicked done (109:2-5, 16)? What does David ask God to do to them (109:17-20)? Who stands at the wicked person's right hand, and who stands at the needy person's right hand (109:6, 31)?

c. Does David take vengeance himself (109:4, 26-27)? Which enemy of the Son of David does Peter say David is talking about (Psalm 109:8; see Acts 1:15-20)? What did Jesus say about that enemy (see Matthew 26:24; John 17:12)?

358. Psalms 110-111

a. What two things does Yahweh make David's Lord (110:1-2, 4)? Who else was both king and priest (110:4; see Genesis 14:18-20; Hebrews 7:1-3, 15-17, 21-22)? When did Yahweh make David's Lord king and priest and tell him to sit at his right hand (Psalm 110:1, 4; see Acts 2:32-36; Ephesians 1:20-22; Hebrews 1:3, 13; 5:19-20)?

b. If David calls the Messiah "Lord," how can the Messiah be David's son (Psalm 110:1; see Matthew 22:41-45; Luke 1:26-35)? What did Jesus teach his followers to do (Matthew 6:9-10; 28:18-20)? Will Jesus Christ really rule all the nations (1 Corinthians 15:24-25)?

c. What are Yahweh's works like (111:2-4, 6-7)? What has Yahweh done for his people (111:9)? How should Yahweh's people live and work (111:1-2, 4, 7-8, 10)?

359. Psalms 112-114

a. Who is the person who fears Yahweh like (112:1, 3, 4; see 111:3, 4)? What do righteous people do (112:5, 9)? What happens to the wicked (112:10)?

b. What are Psalms 113-118 called? See the study note for Psalm 113 or Ps 113-118. What does Yahweh our God do for the poor and needy (113:7-8)? Who sang words very like these (113:7-9)? Follow the cross-reference for 113:9 to 1 Samuel.

c. What might Jews think about as they sang Psalm 114 at Passover? When did the sea and the Jordan River flee and turn back (114:3)? What is the Lord able to do (114:8)?

360. Psalms 115-116

a. What are the gods of the nations like (115:2, 4-8)? What is Yahweh like (115:1-3, 15-16)? How are verses 9-11 and 12-13 like and unlike each other?

b. What was happening to the psalmist (116:3)? Then what did he do (116:4)? When the psalmist called out, "I am greatly afflicted!", did that show that he was not trusting God (116:10)?

c. Why did Yahweh save him (116:5-6)? What does the psalmist tell himself (116:7)? How does the psalmist pay Yahweh back for the good benefits Yahweh gave him (116:12-14, 17-19)?

361. Psalms 117-118

a. Whom does the psalmist tell to praise Yahweh (117:1)? To whom does Yahweh show love and faithfulness (117:2)? How does Paul use Psalm 117 when he writes to Jews and Gentiles in the church in Rome (Romans 15:5-11)?

b. How did Yahweh help the psalmist when all the nations surrounded him (118:7, 10-13)? What do the psalmist and the righteous people sing after Yahweh saves him (118:14-16)? As the psalmist enters the city, what do the people shout to Yahweh about him (118:25-26)?

c. When will the people of Jerusalem shout these words about the Son of David (118:25-26)? Follow the cross-references for 118:26. How is Yahweh's saving the psalmist like choosing a rejected stone and setting it in the most important part of the building (Psalm 118:21-23)? Which rejected stone will Yahweh set as the cornerstone in his temple (118:22)? Follow the cross-references for 118:22.

362. Psalm 119:1-32

a. How does the psalmist shape the structure of Psalm 119? See the translation note for Psalm 119. How many letters are in the Hebrew alphabet, and how many verses are in each stanza? Use the study note for Psalm 119 to fill in the following table of eight Hebrew words.

English translation	Hebrew word
	torah
Statutes, testimonies	*'edot*
	piqqudim
Decrees, statutes	*khuqqim*
	mitswot
Laws, rules	*mishpatim*
Word (promise)	*'imrah*
Word	*dabar*

b. What kind of people is blessed or happy (119:1-3)? What does the psalmist want his way to be like (119:2, 5, 9, 10, 15, 30)? How does the psalmist feel about Yahweh's precepts (119:14-16, 20, 24)?

c. What does the psalmist do, even when he is in danger (119:15, 23, 27)? How do these verses fit with the beginning of the Psalter (see 1:1-2)? Whom does the psalmist ask to teach him (119:12, 18, 26, 27, 29)?

363. Psalm 119:33-72

a. What does the psalmist want to be sure that his way not be like (119:9-11)? What has the psalmist done (119:67)? And what did Yahweh do to the psalmist (119:67)?

b. How did affliction change the psalmist (119:71)? So what does the psalmist think about the way Yahweh has treated him (119:65, 68, 71)? What does the psalmist do when he thinks about his ways (119:58-59)?

c. What does the psalmist ask Yahweh for (119:36-37)? How does he feel about Yahweh's commandments (119:35, 47-48, 70, 72)? When he might be put to shame, what makes the psalmist confident (119:39, 42, 46, 51, 61)?

364.   Psalm 119:73-104

a.   Had Yahweh stopped caring for the psalmist when he afflict-ed him (119:75)? When Yahweh afflicts him, what does the psalmist ask him for (119:76-77)? When arrogant people hurt him, what does the psalmist do (119:78, 83, 85, 87, 95)?

b.   How does the psalmist feel (119:81-84)? What is Yahweh's word like (119:86, 89-91, 96)? What has Yahweh's law done for the psalmist (119:92-93)?

c.   What do Yahweh's commandments give the psalmist (119:98-100)? How does the psalmist feel about Yahweh's law (119:97, 103)? How does the psalmist feel about other ways of living (119:101, 104)?

365.   Psalm 119:105-144

a.   What are wicked people doing to the psalmist (119:107, 109-110, 115, 121, 134)? What does the psalmist love, and whom does he hate (119:113, 127-128)? What will God do to evildoers (119:118, 119)?

b.   What does the psalmist ask Yahweh to do (119:114, 116-117, 121-123)? What does the psalmist ask Yahweh to help him live like (119:106, 108, 112, 124-125, 133)? How does Yahweh treat those who love his name (119:132)?

c.   How does the psalmist feel when people refuse to keep Yah-weh's law (119:126, 136, 139)? What is Yahweh like (119:137, 142)? What is Yahweh's law like (119:137-138, 142, 144)?

366.   Psalm 119:145-176

a.   How much is the psalmist crying to Yahweh (119:145-147)? Who is near, and who is far (119:150-151)? What is Yahweh's word like (119:152, 160)?

b.   Even when they are persecuted, what does Yahweh give those who love his law (119:156, 159, 165)? Who teaches the psalmist (119:171)? What does the psalmist do because he has Yahweh's word (119:162, 164, 171-172)?

c.   What does the psalmist ask Yahweh to do (119:173, 175)? De-spite his great love for Yahweh and Yahweh's word, does the psalmist still go astray (119:175)? Then what does he ask Yah-weh to do (119:2, 176)?

367. Psalms 120-124

a. What are Psalms 120-134 called? See the study note for
Psalms 120 or 120-137. As the people sang these songs, what
were they ascending or going up to (122:1-4)? Where is the
person who sings Psalm 120? See the study note for 120:5.

b. What does Yahweh do (121:3, 4, 5, 7, 8)? Where do Yahweh's
people find peace (120:6-7; 122:3, 6-8)? How do we pray for
the peace of the New Jerusalem (122:6-8; see Ephesians 2:13-
22; 4:1-3; Revelation 21:2, 10, 12)?

c. How do proud people treat Yahweh's servants (123:3-4)? To
whom do the psalmists lift up their eyes (121:1-2; 123:1)? How
great is his help (121:2; 124:1-5, 8)?

368. Psalms 125-129

a. What makes Mount Zion secure, and what makes those who
trust in Yahweh secure (125:1-2)? When did Yahweh restore
the fortunes of Zion (126:1)? What would it look like if
streams ran in the Negev (see the study note for 126:4)?

b. How do people feel when they go out to sow seed in the field
(126:5-6)? How do they feel later at the harvest when they
reap (126:5-6)? Do you get good things in life only by toiling
anxiously (127:1-3)?

c. Besides laboring with his hands, what else does the blessed
man do (128:1-2, 4)? What happened to Israel (129:2-3)? What
do they ask Yahweh to keep doing to their enemies (129:5-6)?

369. Psalms 130-134

a. If the Lord kept a record of sins instead of forgiving them,
who could stand before him (130:3-4)? Why should Israel
hope in Yahweh (130:7-8)? If a child is still nursing and not
yet weaned, is he calm and quiet with his mother (131:2)?

b. When was Yahweh's ark in Jaar (follow the last cross-
reference for 132:6)? Which son of David called Yahweh to
arise and come to his resting place in Zion (Psalm 132:8-10;
see 1 Chronicles 6:41-7:1)? After Israel came back from exile,
what would singing Psalm 132 make them long for (Psalm
132:10-12, 17)? See the end of the first paragraph of the study
note for Psalm 132.

c. What did the oil do to Aaron (see the study note for 133:2)? If
dew as heavy as the dew that falls on Hermon fell on the
mountains of Zion, what would happen on Zion (see the

study note for 133:3)? Where have the people who sing the Songs of Ascents reached now (134:2-3; see 120:5)?

370. Psalms 135-136

a. How great is Yahweh (135:5-6)? How has Yahweh shown his greatness to Israel (135:4, 8-14)? Who all should praise and bless Yahweh (135:1-3, 19-21)?

b. Why should you give thanks to Yahweh (136:1, 26)? Who is Yahweh (136:2-3, 26)? What great wonders does the psalmist praise Yahweh for in 136:4-9?

c. What great wonders does the psalmist praise Yahweh for in 136:10-16? What has Yahweh done for the Israelites who sing Psalm 136 (136:23-25; see 135:5-12)? When you sing Psalm 136, how does the way the psalmist wrote the words make you feel that Yahweh's love really does endure forever?

371. Psalms 137-138

a. When Babylon first attacked Jerusalem, what did Yahweh tell Jeremiah to say about Jerusalem (Jeremiah 25:1-11)? After taking them away to Babylon, how did the Israelites' captors torment them even more (Psalm 137:1-3)? In his message to Jeremiah, what did Yahweh say about Babylon's doom (Jeremiah 25:12-13)?

b. Who will pay Babylon back for what they did to Jerusalem (Psalm 137:8; Jeremiah 25:14; 51:24)? Do the Israelites try to get even with the Edomites and the people of Babylon (Psalm 137:7-9; see Romans 12:19)? What does the Lord do to those who do not love him and who kill his people (Psalm 137:8-9; see 1 Corinthians 16:22; Revelation 18:1-2, 19-20, 24)?

c. What does Yahweh do for David (Psalm 138:6-8)? Why does David praise and thank Yahweh (138:1-3)? Why will all the kings of the earth praise and thank Yahweh (138:4-5)?

372. Psalms 139-140

a. How well does Yahweh know David (139:1-6)? Where can David go to get away from Yahweh's Spirit (139:7-12)? Who formed David's body part by part (139:13-16)?

b. How do you feel about the way Yahweh knows you? Whose enemies does David hate (139:19-22)? How does Yahweh feel about wicked people (139:19; see 5:5-6; 11:5)?

(3) Think about and answer the questions. (4) Return to your bookmark.

c. What are evil and arrogant people doing to David (140:1-5)? What does David know Yahweh will do (140:12)? What does David do to be protected from violent people (140:1, 4, 6-11)?

373. Psalms 141-143

a. What does David ask Yahweh to make sure he doesn't do (141:3-4)? What is it like when a righteous person rebukes you (141:5)? What deeds will David do to protect himself (141:4, 8)?

b. When was David in the cave? See the title for Psalm 142; see also 1 Samuel 22:1; 24:3; and the title for Psalm 57. Who is David's only refuge (Psalm 142:4-5)? When Yahweh rescues him, will David still be alone (142:6-7)?

c. What has David done (143:2)? But what does he still want most of all (143:6-8)? When David asks Yahweh to help him, what does he appeal to (143:11-12)?

374. Psalms 144-145

a. What does Yahweh do for David (144:1-2)? How does Yahweh do this for Jesus, the Son of David (144:2)? See your notes on Psalm 110 (lesson 358). What do the people ask Yahweh to do for them (144:12-14)?

b. What does David call God (145:1)? How does David describe Yahweh's goodness (145:7-9)? How does David describe Yahweh's greatness (145:3, 5-6, 10-13)?

c. How is Yahweh faithful and trustworthy in all he says (145:13-16)? How is Yahweh righteous in all he does (145:17-20)? How does David open and close Psalm 145 (145:1, 21)?

375. Psalms 146-147

a. Why is it better to trust in Yahweh God than to trust in princes or leaders (146:3-7)? What does Yahweh do for the helpless (146:7-9)? What will Yahweh do (146:10)?

b. What Hebrew phrase is the first and last phrase of Psalms 146-150? See the study note for Psalm 146 or 146-150. How many different things can Yahweh think about and take care of at the same time (147:4-5)? And how does he care for the many outcasts of Israel (147:2-3, 6)?

c. How does Yahweh feed his creatures and his people (147:8-9, 14-18)? When he sends out his word, what other blessing does it bring to his people (147:15, 18, 19)? What is parallel to fearing Yahweh (147:11)?

376. Psalms 148-150

a. Why should the creatures and creation of heaven praise Yahweh (148:1-6)? Why should the creatures and creation on earth praise Yahweh (148:7-13)? Why should Yahweh's people praise him (148:14)?

b. What words in 149:2, 6-9 remind you of Psalm 2? What will Yahweh's Son the King do (2:6-9)? What honor does Yahweh give his faithful and godly people as well (149:6-9; see 1 Corinthians 6:2)?

c. Why should all Yah's creatures praise him (150:1-2, 6)? How should Yah's people praise him (150:3-5)? How does this doxology at the end of the whole Psalter compare with the doxologies of the other four books (150:1-6; see 41:13; 72:18-19; 89:52; 106:48)?

377. Psalms – Review

Pray. Think through the following points.

You've now read all the Psalms. Well done! Today you will think back over the book.

a. Reread your own introduction to the book. What is the Psalter, and how have God's people used it? What was the first key theme or main theological concept of the Psalter?

b. Look back through the Psalter. Which psalms were your favorites? Then look in your introduction at the list of the main types or categories of psalms. Which types of psalms were your favorites?

c. Note the words and verses you marked. What things seemed important to you?

d. How has reading through the psalms changed the way you think about God, trust him and talk to him?

e. Look back at your answers to question *d* each day. What were some things you discovered on your own?

f. Think back through your answers to question *f* each day. What are some key ways God is teaching you to change the way you love, think or live?

g. Jesus told his disciples that everything written about him in the Psalms had to be fulfilled (Luke 24:44). Which psalms made you think about the Messiah? How did those psalms

(3) Think about and answer the questions. (4) Return to your bookmark.   229

change the way you think about God's king (Jesus) and his kingdom?

Write

Write a review of the Psalms. In the first paragraph say what the Psalter is and how God's people have used it. List a few different types of psalms and explain what they are like. Then say what your favorite psalms were. In the second paragraph, state the key theme or main theological concept of the Psalter. Describe how reading through the psalms changed the way you think about God, trust him and talk to him. Finally, end your review with a prayer of praise to King Jesus, God's Messiah. Praise him for his greatness. Talk to him about what's going on in your life right now and how you feel; ask him for help, or thank him for the help he has given you. Then praise him for his goodness and tell him how you trust in him.

Job

378.   Job – Introduction

Pray. Then Read, Think and <u>Mark</u>.

Read your study Bible's introduction to the book of Job. Think about the questions for each of the following sections. <u>Mark</u> the answers and other things that seem important.

for the ESV Study Bible

- Author
    - o Read the second paragraph. What can we know about the author of Job?

- Theological Themes
    - o Read the first paragraph. With what question does the book of Job concern itself?
    - o Read the second paragraph.
    - o What does the book of Job show about the reasons for human suffering?
    - o Why do Job's sufferings come upon him?
    - o Read the third paragraph. What do Job's friends think that all troubles are?
    - o Read the fourth paragraph. What is not required before people can trust God and live faithfully in the middle of terrible suffering?

- Purpose, Occasion, and Background
    - o Read the first paragraph. To whom is the book of Job written?
    - o Read the second paragraph.
    - o Are Job's friends able to resolve the dilemma: If God is just and almighty, why is the world filled with suffering?
    - o   What does Job do through the whole book?

- Job and His Setting
  - When does it seem the events of the book of Job happened?
- Literary Features
  - Read the first paragraph. What appears to be the leading concern of the prose sections at the beginning and end of Job?

for the NIV Study Bible

- Author
  - Read the first paragraph. What can we know about the author of Job?
- Date
  - When did Job probably live?
- Theological Theme and Message
  - Read the first three sentences. What question have humans struggled to understand?
  - Read the fifth paragraph ("In his story ..."). What does Satan attempt to do?
  - Read the seventh paragraph ("The accusation ..."). Why does God let Satan (the adversary) have his way with Job?
  - Read the eighth paragraph ("So the adversary ...").
  - How is God's delight in godly people vindicated (shown to be right)?
  - How does Job pass the test?
  - Read the ninth paragraph ("The first test ...").
  - What does human wisdom want to know?
  - Does Job's friends' wisdom help Job understand why he is suffering?
  - What is chapter 28 about?
  - What is supreme wisdom?
  - Whose life is marked by this wisdom?

Write

Write your own introduction to the book of Job. Describe the author and setting of Job. State the main questions of Job. Tell how Job's friends and Job cannot answer these questions with words. But then show how the events of Job's life (what happens to him and what he does) answer the questions. Finally, outline Job under five headings.

A.	(1-2)
B.	(3-27)
C.	(28)
D.	(29:1-42:6)
E.	(42:7-17)

379. Job 1:1-2:13

a. Who are the "sons of God" (see 1:6 and study note)? What is the meaning of *Satan* (see the translation note for 1:6)? To whom do the sons of God present themselves and submit (1:6-7, 10-12; 2:1-2, 6-7)?

b. What sort of man does Yahweh say Job is (1:1, 8)? Which of the main questions in the book of Job does Satan ask (1:9)? How does Job respond to his suffering (1:20-22; 2:3)?

c. What is Job willing to receive from God (2:10)? How does Job's response answer Satan's question (1:9, 21; 2:3, 10)? How do Job's three friends respond to Job's great suffering (2:11-13)?

380. Job 3:1-26

a. What words does Job use to describe (or paint the picture) of what he wishes would have happened on the day of his birth (3:3, 4-6)? How do some people at that time curse a day (see 3:8-9 and the study note)? Why does Job curse the day of his birth (3:10)?

b. What does Job wish for next (3:11-12, 16)? How does Job describe what happens after people die (3:13)? What question does Job ask over and over again (3:11, 12, 16, 20)?

c. Look carefully at the parallelism in verse 20: What word is parallel to *life* (3:20)? How much does Job long for death (3:21)? Does Job like being hedged in by God (see 3:23 and the study note)?

381. Job 4:1-5:27

a. What does Eliphaz think happens to the innocent and to sinners (4:7-9)? But what has Job said he actually wants to happen to him (3:21-22)? What does Eliphaz think is true of all people (4:17)?

b. Whom does Eliphaz warn Job not to be like (5:2-7)? What does Eliphaz think is happening to Job (5:17)? Why does Eliphaz think Job should seek God (5:8, 17-26; see 1:9-11)?

c. Who does Eliphaz think has true wisdom (4:2, 21; 5:27)? Which of Eliphaz's ideas are often true? Which of them are wrong? Read 4:6, 17; 5:8 and then read 1:8, 20-22; 2:9-10.

382.   Job 6:1-7:21

a.   Who does Job say is terrorizing him (6:4)? What does Job request of God (see 6:8-10 and 4:7)? How are Job's friends like intermittent streams that dry up when the torrent of rain stops (6:15-21)?

b.   How does Job describe his words (6:3, 10, 26, 30)? What does Job want his friends to do (6:24-25, 28-30)? Why does Job go ahead and complain bitterly to God (7:7-11)?

c.   What all does Job say God does to him (7:8, 12, 14, 17-20)? What can Job not understand (7:17-20)? What does Job want God to do (7:21)?

383.   Job 8:1-9:20

a.   In what three or four ways does Bildad agree with Eliphaz? Compare 8:3, 5, 6-7 with 4:7-9; 5:8, 18-26. Whom does Bildad warn Job not to be like (8:13, 14-19)? How does Bildad try to encourage Job (8:20-22)?

b.   What does Job say in response to Bildad (9:2a)? What is Job's main question (9:2; see 4:17)? How do God's earlier words, which Job and his friends did not hear, help you answer Job's question (see 1:8; 2:3)?

c.   What does Job say about himself (9:15, 20-21)? But why does Job think he would not be able to prove to God that he is right (9:4, 12-20)? How does God show his wisdom and power (9:4, 5-10)?

384.   Job 9:21-10:22

a.   How does Job say God treats the blameless (9:22-24)? Who does Job say is behind everything that is happening to him (9:24)? What does Job feel like God is determined to do (9:28-31)?

b.   How does Job think an arbiter (a judge who settles disputes between people) would help him (9:32-33)? What would Job say to God (10:2)? What does Job say God knows (10:7)?

c.   What all did God do for Job before this (10:8-12)? But how is God treating him now (10:6-7, 13-17)? What does Job wish would have happened or would happen now (10:18-22)?

385.   Job 11:1-12:25

a.   Why does Zophar wish that God would speak (11:5-9)? Why does Zophar think Job is suffering (11:6, 11-12)? How is Zophar's advice much like Eliphaz's and Bildad's? Compare 11:13-19 with 5:8, 18-26 and 8:5-7.

b. Does Job need to follow Zophar's advice (1:8; 2:3; 12:4)? As Job and his friends speak back and forth, what is happening to the length of their speeches? Compare 4:1-5:27; 8:1-22; 11:1-20 and 6:1-7:21; 9:1-10:22; 12:1-14:22. How does Job say people whose lives are easy treat others whose lives are misfortunate and hard (12:5)?

c. Who does Job say has done this (12:9-10)? Where does Job say wisdom is (12:13, 16)? But what does he say God does with his wisdom (12:17-25)?

386. Job 13:1-28

a. What does Job think of his friends' wisdom (13:1-2, 4-5)? What does Job say his friends are doing for God (13:7-8)? What does Job warn them will happen when God searches them out and examines them (13:9-11)?

b. What will Job do regardless of what happens (13:14-15)? How do Job's words answer Satan's question about him and Satan's charge against God (see 1:9, 10-11; 2:4-5)? Why does Job want to argue his case with God Almighty (13:3, 15-16)?

c. What does Job ask God to do before the case begins (13:20-22)? What questions has Job prepared for his case (13:18, 23-25)? Why does Job think God may be making him suffer bitter things (13:26)?

387. Job 14:1-22

a. What is Job's life like (14:1-2)? What does Job wish God would do (14:5-6)? What hope does a tree have (14:7-9)?

b. But what happens to a human (14:10-12)? What does Job wish God would do (14:13)? How long would Job be willing to wait (14:14)?

c. Then what does Job imagine his life would be like again (14:15-17)? But how is God treating Job (14:18-20)? How severe is Job's misery (14:21-22)?

388. Job 15:1-35

a. What does Eliphaz say Job's words are doing (15:4-6)? What does Eliphaz think of Job's wisdom (15:2-3, 8-10)? Why does Eliphaz think Job is suffering (15:14-16)?

   b.   Has Eliphaz said this before (see 4:17-19)? In his first speech, what did Eliphaz say happens after death to people who plow evil and sow trouble (4:8-9)? In his second speech, what does Eliphaz say happens to the wicked man in this life (15:20-21)?

   c.   Whose life looks just like the life of the wicked man that Eliphaz describes (15:20-30)? What comfort or counsel does Eliphaz offer Job (15:20-35)? Has Job turned against God Almighty and defied him (15:12-13, 25-26)?

389. Job 16:1-17:16

   a.   If Job were comforting his friends, how could he and would he speak (16:2-4, 5)? What all does Job say God has done to him (16:7-9, 11-14)? Who has done what to Job? Compare 16:7-9, 11-14 with 1:8, 9-11, 12, 13-19, 21-22; 2:3, 4-5, 6, 7, 10.

   b.   Which witnesses does Job say testify against him (see 16:8, 9 and 1:6, 9-11; 2:4-5)? Who might Job's witness in heaven be (see the study note for 16:19)? How does Job want this witness to help him (16:20-21)?

   c.   How does Job feel (17:1)? What does Job ask his friends to do (17:3, 10)? Does Job still hope to die (17:13-15)?

390. Job 18:1-19:29

   a.   How does Bildad respond to Job (18:1-4)? What does Bildad say happens to the wicked (18:5-7, 12-13, 16-19)? What does Bildad accuse Job of (18:5, 21)?

   b.   What does Job say God has done to him (19:6-7, 8-12; see 1:22)? What have Job's family and friends done (19:14, 17, 19)? What does Job want from his friends (19:2, 21, 22)?

   c.   What does Job want his Redeemer to do (see the study note for 19:25)? Who is his Redeemer (19:25-26)? How do these words come true in the end of the story? Compare 19:25-29 with 42:5-8.

391. Job 20:1-21:34

   a.   How does Job's warning make Zophar feel (19:28-29; 20:2-3)? Why does Zophar (still) think that Job is suffering (20:5, 29; see 11:6)? How does Zophar think God judges the wicked (20:10, 14-15, 18, 26)?

   b.   What does Zophar think about Job's hope that he will see God and God will redeem him (19:25-27; 20:6-9, 23, 27-29)?

How are Job and his friends talking to each other (21:2-3)? What simple thing does Job wish they would do (21:5)?

c. How does Job think God treats the wicked (21:7-9, 13, 16-21)? Who is the only one who can explain what is happening (21:22)? What happens to the rich and the poor when they die (21:23-26)?

392. Job 22:1-30

a. What does Eliphaz think about God and people (22:2-3, 12)? What did he say about this in his first two speeches (4:17-19; 15:14-16)? What does Yahweh think about Job's conduct and God's pleasure (2:3)?

b. What did Eliphaz think about Job's character at first (4:6)? What does he think about Job's behavior now (22:4-9; see 15:4-5)? Which wicked person's counsel does Eliphaz stay far from (see 22:17-18 and the cross-references)?

c. Does Eliphaz's advice to Job sound wrong or bad (22:21-28)? But is it the advice Job needs to hear (13:15-16; 16:19-21; 19:25-27)? Does God use Job's clean hands to deliver people who are not innocent (22:29-30; see 1:5; 42:7-9)?

393. Job 23:1-24:25

a. Have Job and his friends been talking for just a couple hours (23:2)? What does Job want to do (23:3-4; see 13:3, 15, 18)? How does Job think God will treat him when he hears Job's case (23:5-6)?

b. Why does Job think God will deliver him and say he is not guilty (23:7, 10-12)? What does Job think God is doing to him (23:10, 13-16)? How does Job feel about God (23:6, 8, 15-16, 17)?

c. What all happens in the dark (24:13-17)? How do some people treat the fatherless, the widow and the poor (24:2-12, 14, 21)? Then what does God do for them (24:12, 21-24)?

394. Job 25:1-27:23

a. Why does Bildad think that neither Job nor any human can be right before God (25:2-6)? Which of Job's other friends has said this all along? Follow the cross-references for verse 4. Which of Job's three friends does not speak in this third round (see 22:1; 25:1; 32:1)?

b. What does Job think of his friends (26:2-4)? Does Job agree or disagree with Bildad about God's greatness (25:2-3, 5; 26:5-

14)? But how are Bildad's and Job's conclusions different (25:4, 6; 26:14)?

c. Does Job agree or disagree with his friends about the way God treats the wicked (27:13-23)? But does Job think he has done wrong (27:5-6)? Whom else does Job want God to treat like the wicked (27:7-10)?

395. Job 28:1-28

a. Where does chapter 28 fit in the structure of Job? See the study note for 28:1-28. How far have humans searched to find and see and get precious things (28:1-11)? Underline the words "hidden," "search," "find," "see" and "eyes" wherever you find them in this chapter.

b. What can humans neither know nor find (28:12)? Have humans been to places where they could find wisdom or have they found precious stones that they could trade for wisdom (28:13-19)? Do even hidden things like Abaddon (Destruction) and Death know where wisdom and understanding are (28:22; see 26:5-6)?

c. What does God see and where does he work (28:24-27; see 26:5-14)? How does God answer the main question of chapter 28 and one of the main questions of the book of Job (28:12, 20, 28)? Which character in the book understands more and more of God's wisdom (1:1, 8; 2:3; 4:6; 23:13-16; 26:5-14; see 15:4; 22:4; 25:2)?

396. Job 29:1-30:31

a. What made Job's life in the past so good (29:2-5)? How did Job put on righteousness like clothing (29:12-17)? What did Job think about his life (29:18-20)?

b. How did the nobles and other people treat Job (29:7-12, 21-25)? But now what kind of people mock Job and try to destroy him (30:1-15)? Why do they feel free to treat Job this way (30:11)?

c. How is God treating Job (30:19-22)? Now what does Job think about his life (30:23)? In what different ways is Job suffering (30:15-18, 26-31)?

397. Job 31:1-40

a. What does Job still want (31:6, 35-37; see 10:2; 13:22-23; 23:3-7)? Since God does not accuse Job in court, what does Job do in this chapter (31:5, 7, 9 etc.)? What specific sins did Eliphaz accuse Job of (22:6-9)?

b. How has Job treated the poor and weak (31:13, 16-21, 31-32)? Why does he treat them this way (31:15)? In what other ways has Job lived righteously (31:1, 5, 7, 9, 24-27, 29-30, 33-34)?

c. Why has Job lived righteously (31:3, 14, 23)? In what ways does Job's life set an example for yours? What does Job do at the end of his speech (31:35)?

398. Job 32:1-33:33

a. Why does Elihu wait so long to speak (32:4-7, 11-12)? Why is Elihu angry with Job's three friends (32:3, 12)? Why does Elihu think he too should say something about Job (32:8-10, 16-20; 33:2-4)?

b. How does Elihu think he will be able to help Job (33:3-7; see 9:32-35; 13:3, 18-27)? Is Job righteous in his own eyes (32:1-2; 33:9)? Follow the cross-references for *pure* in 33:9. In which other person's eyes is Job righteous (1:8; 2:3)?

c. Why does God speak to humans (33:14-22, 29-30)? Has one of Job's friends already said something like this about why Job is suffering (5:17)? How is Elihu trying to help Job (33:23-26, 32-33)?

399. Job 34:1-37

a. Whom does Elihu address in this second speech (34:2? Does Elihu quote Job accurately (34:5-6, 9)? Look at your answer to question *b* in the last lesson. Then check Job 19:6; 27:2 and follow the cross-references for 34:9. Is Elihu's accusation against Job true (34:7-8)?

b. How does Elihu think God always treats everybody (34:10-12)? Why does Elihu think God does not need to investigate people or examine them before he punishes them (34:21-25)? For what reasons does Elihu think God punishes people (34:22, 26-28)?

c. What does Elihu think Job has no right to do (34:31-32)? How does Elihu think Job has sinned (34:7-9, 26-28)? How does Elihu think Job has added rebellion to his sin (34:35-37)?

400. Job 35:1-36:21

a. What is it about the way Job has claimed to be righteous that, Elihu says, shows that Job is not righteous (35:2-3, 6-8)?

What do oppressed people want more: God's help and relief, or to know God and learn from him (35:9-11)? Why does God listen neither to these people when they cry for help nor to Job (35:12-13, 14-15)?

b. What does Elihu think of his own knowledge (36:3-4; see 33:3-4, 33)? According to Elihu, why does God afflict righteous people and make them suffer (see 36:8-10 and follow the first cross-reference for 36:10)? But what has Job wanted all along (see 10:2; 13:22-23; 31:6, 35-37; 35:14)?

c. Who else said that if people listened to God and turned from their sin God would bless them with prosperity (36:10-11; see 5:8-27; 22:21-30 and 1:9-11; 2:4-5)? How does Elihu think Job is responding to his affliction (36:16-21)? Which parts of Elihu's speech are true and which are not?

401. Job 36:22-37:24

a. What seems to be happening as Elihu talks (36:27-37:13)? Where does Elihu see God's power and greatness (36:22, 26-33; 37:2-13)? What can humans understand about the weather or do with the skies (36:29; 37:5, 7, 14-18)?

b. Does Elihu need to tell Job to think about God's wonderful works (36:14; see 26:7-14)? How does the thunderstorm make Elihu feel (37:1-2, 24)? At the very end of his last speech, what does Elihu say about wisdom (37:24; see 28:12, 20, 23-28)?

c. Of the five men who speak, which one thought he was the wisest (37:24; see 33:3-4; 36:3-4)? What do you think: Has Elihu been able to show how Job is wrong or explain why Job is suffering (32:2-3, 10-12)? Now whose turn is it to speak (37:22-23)?

402. Job 38:1-38

a. If you had been there with Job and his friends, what would it have looked, sounded and felt like (38:1; see 36:30-37:5)? What does Yahweh say Job (or any other human) does when he tries to explain God's plans (38:2)? Does Yahweh answer Job's questions about why Job suffered in the first place (38:1-3; see 10:2; 31:35-37)?

b. What has neither Job nor any human ever seen, where have they never been, and what can they not do (38:4, 12, 16-17, 19-20, 22, 24, 31-32, 34-35, 37)? What can neither Job nor any human know or understand (38:4-5, 18, 33)? What is God making Job learn (see 28:12, 20, 23-28)?

Every day: (1) Follow your bookmark and pray. (2) Read and <u>mark</u> the passage.

c. Did Job say something similar to this earlier on (see 26:7-14)? But what did Job do anyway (38:2; see 15:3)? Is God's conversation with Job turning out the way Job hoped it would (38:3; see 13:3, 20-24; 23:3-7, 14-16)?

403. Job 38:39-40:5

a. Which animals does Yahweh know about and care for (38:29, 41; 39:1, 5, 9, 13, 19, 26-27)? Who gets more food than the lion and the raven, is freer than the wild animals, much more loving than the ostrich, stronger than the horse, and sees and knows more than the hawk or the eagle (38:39-41; 39:5, 9, 13-16, 19, 26-29)? Why does the ostrich have no fear (38:16-17)?

b. Did Job think he or anyone else could contend with God (40:2; see 9:3)? Did Job argue with God and accuse him anyway (40:2; see 13:3, 15; 19:6; 23:7)? Why did Job want to argue: what did he want to know (see 10:2; 31:35)?

c. Does Job answer God the way he thought he would (40:3-5; see 13:15; 23:14-17)? Now who is correcting, accusing and disciplining whom (40:2; see 5:17; 22:4; 33:19; 36:10)? Does Yahweh also say that Job is wicked or that Job suffered because he was wicked (see 34:35-37)?

404. Job 40:6-41:34

a. Who is the only one Yahweh speaks to (40:6; see 38:1)? How does the phrase "like a man" sound different when Yahweh says it than when humans say it (40:7; see 38:3)? Was it more important to Job to show that he was right or to show that God was right (40:8; see 9:22-24; 10:3; 19:6-7; 27:2)?

b. What about Behemoth does Yahweh point out (40:16-18, 23)? Have you seen pictures in books of animals that looked like Behemoth or Leviathan (40:15-24; 41:1-34)? Who made Behemoth and Leviathan (40:15, 19; see Genesis 1:21; Psalms 74:13-14; 104:26)?

c. Why does Yahweh tell Job to think about Leviathan (41:10-11)? Has God done something wrong so that Job has the right to condemn him (40:8, 11)? Is Job strong enough to judge God (40:9, 14; 41:10)?

405. Job 42:1-17

a. What does Job know and feel about Yahweh (42:2-6; see 23:13-17)? Will Job fear God for nothing (42:2-5; see 1:9; 2:3;

23:15; 26:14; 28:23-28; 40:4-5)? What does Job think about the things he has said (42:3; see 23:16-17)?

b. Of all the men in the book, who is the only one who wanted to speak *to* God and actually did speak with him (42:8; see 7:12-21; 10:2-22; 12:4; 13:3, 15-28; 14:13-22; 16:20; 23:3-17; 30:20-23; 40:3-5; 42:1-6)? What does Yahweh think about how Job spoke (42:7-8; see 26:14; 28:23-28)? How does Yahweh feel about Job's friends (42:7-8; see 13:7-12; 19:28-29)?

c. How does God comfort his servant Job (42:5-10; see 19:25-27)? Does God ever say why Job suffered? Who else comfort Job (42:11)?

406. Job – Review

Pray. Think through the following points.

You've now read the whole book of Job. Well done! Today you will think back over the book.

a. Reread your own introduction to the book. What were the main questions in the book of Job? How does the story of Job answer those questions?

b. What has Job's example taught you about what you should think and feel and say and do when you suffer? What has the example of Job's friends taught you about what you should and should not say to your friends when they suffer (see 2:12-13; 6:14; 19:2, 21-22; 21:5; 26:2-4)?

c. Look back through the book. Note the words and verses you marked. What things seemed important to the author of Job?

d. What things seemed important to you?

e. How has reading through Job changed the way you love or fear God, think about him or talk to him?

f. Look back at your answers to question *d* each day. What were some things you discovered on your own?

g. Think back through your answers to question *f* each day. What are some key ways God is teaching you to change the way you love, think or live?

h. Jesus told his disciples that everything written about him in the Scriptures had to be fulfilled (Luke 24:44). How did the story of Job make you think about the Messiah? You might think about Satan's attack on Job, Job's suffering, Job's longing for an arbiter and a redeemer or something else.

Write

Write a review of the book of Job. In the first paragraph say what the main questions in the book of Job are. Then describe how the story of

Job answers those questions. In the second paragraph explain what wisdom is, where it comes from and what it does. List a few wise things you will want to remember the next time you are suffering. In the third paragraph describe how you can help your friends when they are suffering. Finally, end your review with a prayer to Jesus your Redeemer. Thank him that he understands how you feel when you suffer. Tell him how you would like him to help you when you suffer.

Proverbs

407. Proverbs – Introduction

Pray. Then Read, Think and <u>Mark</u>.

Read your study Bible's introduction to Proverbs. Think about the questions for each of the following sections. <u>Mark</u> the answers and other things that seem important.

for the ESV Study Bible
- Author and Date
    - o Read the first paragraph. Who were the authors of the Proverbs?
- Theme
    - o What is Proverbs' goal?
    - o What is wisdom founded on?
    - o What does wisdom do?
- Purpose, Occasion, and Background
    - o Read the first sentence of the third paragraph ("First, the OT ..."). How does the Old Testament present God's redemption?
    - o Read the fourth paragraph ("Nevertheless ...").
    - o What do the Law and the Prophets emphasize?
    - o What does Proverbs emphasize?
    - o Read the fifth paragraph ("A key term ..."). What is wisdom?
- Key Themes
    - o Read the first paragraph. What all do the proverbs talk about?
    - o Read the five key themes. What is a life lived according to God's will like?
- Character Types in Proverbs
    - o Read the first two paragraphs. What does the wise person do?

- o Read the third paragraph. Is the fool stupid or unintelligent? What is the fool like?
- o Read the fourth paragraph. What is the simple person like?
- Literary Features
  - o Read the third paragraph. How does a proverb work?
  - o Read the sixth paragraph ("In some cases ...").
  - o What is the best example of two proverbs that seem to contradict each other?
  - o Should you interpret proverbs the same way you do laws?
  - o Read the seventh paragraph ("Proverbs of necessity ...").
  - o What do proverbs focus on?
  - o Are the truths in the proverbs always true everywhere in every situation?
  - o Should you interpret proverbs the same way you do promises or prophecies?

for the NIV Study Bible

- Authors
  - o Read the first paragraph. Who were the authors of the Proverbs?
- The Nature of a Proverb
  - o Read the first paragraph.
  - o How should you not interpret the proverbs?
  - o Are the truths in the proverbs always true everywhere in every situation?
  - o Read the third paragraph.
  - o How long are most of the proverbs?
  - o What do most of the proverbs in chapters 10-15 express?
  - o How do the proverbs evaluate conduct: how do they talk about the goodness or the badness of acting a certain way?
  - o Read the fourth paragraph ("A common feature ..."). How do the proverbs use figurative language, phrases that make you picture a figure in your mind?
- Purpose and Teaching
  - o Read the first paragraph.
  - o What is the purpose of Proverbs?
  - o What happens when people get wisdom and avoid folly?
  - o What does Proverbs base its practical wisdom on?

- o Read the third paragraph. What all do the proverbs talk about?
- o Read the fourth paragraph ("Although Proverbs ..."). What does Proverbs teach about God?
- o Read the last paragraph ("In summary ...").
- o What is the theme of Proverbs?
- o What does the fear of the Lord include?
- o What is wisdom?
- Literary Structure
  - o Read the second paragraph.
  - o How does Proverbs personify wisdom and folly: how does it write about them as if they were people?
  - o How do men entice or tempt the young man to folly?
  - o How do women entice the young man to folly?
  - o Read the last paragraph.
  - o What is the wife of noble character the epitome (the perfect example) of?
  - o Why does Proverbs end by talking about the ideal wife?

Write

Write your own introduction to Proverbs. In the first paragraph, say who the authors of Proverbs were. State the purpose of Proverbs. Describe Proverbs' theme. Write about what the basis of Proverbs or the beginning of wisdom is. In the second paragraph, explain what a proverb is like, how long it usually is and how it works. Tell why proverbs talk about the consequences of different types of behavior. Describe what kind of truths the proverbs teach. Say how you should and should not interpret the proverbs. Finally, outline Proverbs under eight headings.

A.   (1:1-7)
B.   (1:8-9:18)
C.   (10:1-22:16)
D.   (22:17-24:22)
E.   (24:23-34)
F.   (25-29)
G.   (30)
H.   (31)

408. Proverbs 1:1-33

a. What are the three main purposes of Proverbs (1:2, 3, 4)? Who should listen to the proverbs (1:4-5)? What do knowledge and wisdom begin with (1:7)? Write out verse seven in your notebook.

b. Who speaks to whom (1:8-19)? What might sinful men entice the son to do (1:10-16)? What will happen to people like them (1:17-19)?

c. Then who speaks in 1:20-33? Why will Wisdom not answer the simple and fools when they call for help (1:24-32, especially verse 29)? What does Wisdom promise to those who do listen to her (1:23, 33)?

409. Proverbs 2:1-3:12

a. What does the parent tell the son to do for wisdom (2:1-4)? Then what will Yahweh give the son (2:5-6)? And then what else will the son understand (2:9-10)?

b. From what kind of men will discretion and understanding deliver the son (2:11-15)? From what kind of woman will wisdom deliver the son (2:16-19)? What will wisdom and the fear of Yahweh prepare the son to do (2:5-6, 9-10, 20-21)?

c. What all does the parent tell the son to do with his heart (3:1, 3, 5; see 2:2, 5, 10)? Whose commands is this parent following (2:21-3:5; see Deuteronomy 6:4-9, 20-25)? When Yahweh disciplines someone, how is he treating that person (Proverbs 3:11-12; see 2 Samuel 7:8, 12, 14-15)?

410. Proverbs 3:13-4:27

a. Why is wisdom better than silver, gold and jewels (3:13-17)? Even though Yahweh God put humans out of the garden long before, what does the parent tell the son he can get if he takes hold of wisdom (see 3:18 and the cross-reference to Genesis)? What two kinds of people does the parent contrast three times (Proverbs 3:32-34)?

b. Who teaches whom (4:1-4)? What was most important to the father's father (4:5-8)? What does wisdom give (3:16-18, 22-25; 4:10, 12-13; see 3:2)?

c. What words show you that the parent is beginning a new appeal to his son (3:21; 4:1, 10, 20)? Why should the son guard his heart (4:23)? What guard can the son put in his heart to protect it (4:20-22)?

411.   Proverbs 5:1-6:19

a.   What are an adulterous woman and her speech like at first and in the end (5:3-4)? What does a man who goes to the adulteress's house give up (5:8-11)? In the end, what happens to him (5:5-6, 11-14, 22-23)?

b.   Does that mean the son should have no pleasure with a woman (5:15-20)? In fact, how does the father want the son to feel about the son's wife (5:18-19)? Why should the son drink water from his own well and keep his water for himself and his wife (5:15-17, 21)?

c.   When you put up security for someone, you promise that, if the other person does not pay back the money he borrowed or do what he promised he would do, you will do it for him instead. What does the father think about putting up security for someone else (6:1-5)? While the sluggard rests lazily, what does not rest (6:9-11)? Which kind of person does the seven things Yahweh hates (6:12-19)?

412.   Proverbs 6:20-7:27

a.   What is the adulterous woman like (6:24-25)? How dangerous is it to sleep with another man's wife (6:24, 27-29)? Why is it so dangerous (6:26, 29, 34-35)?

b.   How does the adulterous woman treat the simple young man (7:10-12, 22-23)? What all does the adulterous woman do to get the young man to come with her (7:13, 14-15, 16-17, 18, 19-20, 21)? Had the simple young man planned to go to the adulterous woman (7:6-9, 22)-23)?

c.   What happens to men who follow the adulterous woman (7:23, 26-27)? What will keep the son from being captivated by the adulterous woman (6:20-25, 32; 7:1-5, 24)? Why might the parent have told his son this story (6:20-22; 7:3, 22-24; see Deuteronomy 6:4-8)?

413.   Proverbs 8:1-36

a.   What are wisdom's words like (8:6-9)? How is wisdom useful to kings and rulers (8:12-16)? Why is wisdom so valuable (8:10-11, 17-21)?

b.   When and how did wisdom begin (8:22-26)? How was wisdom useful to Yahweh (8:27-30)? How does wisdom feel about Yahweh's world, especially humans (8:30-31)?

c.   What does wisdom tell the sons to do (8:32-34)? What will wisdom give the sons who seek her (8:17-18, 21, 35)? Why might many of the early Christian teachers have thought that writing about wisdom was another way of talking about Jesus (8:22-25; see John 1:1-5; 17:5; Colossians 1:15-16)?

414.   Proverbs 9:1-18

a.   How is the food that Wisdom offers like and unlike the food that Folly offers (9:2, 5, 17)? How are the words they say when they call out alike and unlike (9:4, 16)? How is what happens to people who go into Wisdom's house different from what happens to those who go into Folly's house (9:6, 18)?

b.   Why will Wisdom not bother to correct a mocker (9:7-8)? But what will wise and righteous people do when you rebuke or reprove them (9:8-9)? Can you live your life in a way that you will have no consequences for how you live (9:12)?

c.   Where does wisdom begin her teaching (9:10; see 1:7)? What are a couple ways the prologue to Proverbs has taught you to fear Yahweh (see 1:8-9:18)? Now that you've read through the prologue, what are you ready to learn (see 1:6; 10:1)?

415.   Proverbs 10:1-11:13

a.   What all about the first proverb reminds you of the prologue to Proverbs (10:1)? What two things does the first proverb compare (10:1)? What does it make you want to do (10:1)?

b.   Write out 10:12. Now analyze it: study the parts carefully. Which words in the second line are the opposites of *hatred* and *stirs up* in the first line? Which word in the second line is similar to *conflict* or *strife* in the first line? How do hatred and love take very similar things (conflict, strife, wrongs and offenses) and turn them into very different situations?

c.   What do the three proverbs in 10:18-21 talk about? How should you use your words (10:18-21)? How should you not use your words (10:18-21)?

416.   Proverbs 11:14-12:28

a.   What does 11:16 seem to teach about how to get wealth or riches? How do the next few verses give you another way of thinking about what happens to ruthless, violent people (11:17-19, 21)? And what does 11:28 remind you about riches?

b.   Write out 12:1 and analyze it. Look carefully at how the two lines are parallel. (1) Find and label parallel words in each line. For example, you could write *A* over *loves* in the first line and over its opposite *hates* in the second line. Then you could write *B* over *discipline* in the first line and over the similar word *correction* or *reproof* in the second line. (2) Think about how each line works. How does discipline give you knowledge? And how does hating correction or reproof leave you stupid? (3) Then think about how the two lines work together, and write what the proverb teaches you.

c.   Choose another proverb and analyze it as you analyzed 12:1. Write it out, then (1) find and label parallel words. (2) Think about how each line works. And (3) think about how the two lines work together, and write what the proverb teaches you.

417.   Proverbs 13:1-14:7

a.   Choose a proverb and analyze it. Write it out, then (1) find and label parallel words. (2) Think about how each line works. (3) Think about how the two lines work together. Then write what the proverb teaches you.

b.   Choose another proverb and analyze it. If you need extra help, check to see if there is a study note for the verse you chose.

c.   Choose a third proverb and analyze it.

418.   Proverbs 14:8-15:17

a.   In which verses does Solomon write about Yahweh? Scan quickly through the passage looking for "the LORD" or "God." Don't miss "Maker" in 14:31. List the references for those verses. What all does Yahweh know (15:3, 11)? What all does Yahweh do for those who fear him (14:9, 26-27; 15:8-9)?

b.   Choose another topic and list the verses that talk about it. You might choose words (14:9, 23, 25; 15:1, 2 etc.), poverty (14:20-21, 23-24, 31; 15:6 etc.), folly (14:8-9, 15-16, 18, 24, 29, 33; 15:2 etc.) or another topic. Note a couple wise things you want to remember.

c.   Choose a proverb and analyze it. Write it out, then (1) find and label parallel words. (2) Think about how each line works. (3) Think about how the two lines work together. Then write what the proverb teaches you. If you need extra help, check to see if there is a study note for the verse you chose.

Every day: (1) Follow your bookmark and pray. (2) Read and <u>mark</u> the passage.

419. Proverbs 15:18-16:9

a. What is the first word in the second line in most of the proverbs in chapters 10-15? For example, check 10:1; 15:1, 18, 25, 29. Is that also the first word in the second line in most of the proverbs in chapters 16-22? For example, check 16:3, 4, 6, 7, 8; 22:16. How do the two lines of 15:29 work together?

b. Analyze 16:4. Write it out, then (1) find and label parallel words. (2) Think about how each line works. Then (3) think about how the two lines work together: does the second line talk about something different from what the first line talked about, or does the second line tell you even more about the thing the first line was talking about?

c. Analyze 16:7. Write it out. Are there any parallel words in the two lines? How does each line work? How do the two lines work together?

420. Proverbs 16:10-17:19

a. Choose a topic and list the verses that talk about it. You might choose kings (16:10-15), money (16:16, 19; 17:2, 8, 16, 18), friendships and conflicts (16:28; 17:1, 9-14, 17, 19) or another topic. Note a couple wise things you want to remember.

b. Choose your favorite proverb from today's reading and analyze it. Write it out, then (1) find and label any parallel words. (2) Think about how each line works. (3) Think about how the two lines work together. Then write what the proverb teaches you.

c. Study another topic or analyze another proverb.

421. Proverbs 17:20-18:21

a. Study the topic of words. List the verses that talk about words. What kind of people does 18:2 make you think of? What do you want to do to use your words more wisely?

b. Choose your favorite proverb from today's reading and analyze it. Write it out, then (1) find and label any parallel words. (2) Think about how each line works. (3) Think about how the two lines work together. Then write what the proverb teaches you.

c. Study another topic or analyze another proverb.

422. Proverbs 18:22-20:4

a. Choose a topic and list the verses that talk about it. You might choose wives and husbands (18:22; 19:13-14, 22), poverty (18:23-24; 19:1, 4, 6-7, 10, 17, 22), anger (19:11-12; 20:2-3) or another topic. Note a couple wise things you want to remember.

b. Choose your favorite proverb from today's reading and analyze it. Write it out, then (1) find and label any parallel words. (2) Think about how each line works. (3) Think about how the two lines work together. Then write what the proverb teaches you.

c. Study another topic or analyze another proverb.

423. Proverbs 20:5-21:8

a. Choose a topic and list the verses that talk about it. You might choose plans and action (20:5-6, 8, 12, 18-19, 26-27; 21:1-2), faithfulness and righteousness (20:6-7, 11, 28; 21:2-3, 8) or another topic. Note a couple wise things you want to remember.

b. Choose your favorite proverb from today's reading and analyze it. Write it out, then (1) find and label any parallel words. (2) Think about how each line works. (3) Think about how the two lines work together. Then write what the proverb teaches you.

c. Study another topic or analyze another proverb.

424. Proverbs 21:9-22:16

a. Choose a topic and list the verses that talk about it. You might choose the quarrelsome wife (21:9, 19), the mocker (21:11, 24; 22:10), righteousness (21:12-15, 21, 26, 29) children (22:6, 15) or another topic. Note a couple wise things you want to remember.

b. Choose your favorite proverb from today's reading and analyze it. Write it out, then (1) find and label any parallel words. (2) Think about how each line works. (3) Think about how the two lines work together. Then write what the proverb teaches you.

c. Study another topic or analyze another proverb.

425. Proverbs 22:17-23:28

a. Whose teaching are the first several "Sayings of the Wise" similar to (22:17-23:11)? See the study note for 22:17-24:22. If someone who doesn't fear Yahweh teaches something wise, is it still wise (see Acts 7:22)? What do you think the important difference between Amenemope's Instructions and the Sayings of the Wise might be (Proverbs 22:19)?

b. What does Yahweh do for the poor and the fatherless (22:22-23, 28; 23:10-11)? What should you not want too much (23:1-5, 17-18)? What should you do instead (22:19; 23:2, 4, 17)?

c. Will disciplining a child, even with a rod, take his life or save it (23:13-14)? What does the wise teacher want his son to be like (23:15-17, 19, 22-26)? How does the wise teacher teach his son (23:12, 13-14, 26)?

426. Proverbs 23:29-24:34

a. What happens to people who linger or tarry long over wine (23:29-30)? What happens to their bodies and their senses (23:33-35)? In the end, what is too much wine like (23:32)?

b. What should wise people do when they hear there are people being led away to death (24:11-12)? What all will make them strong enough to do that (24:5-6, 10, 16, 19-21)? Why should you not pretend that you did not know they were being taken away (24:12; see Romans 2:6-11, 16)?

c. How should the judge and the witness speak (Proverbs 24:24-26, 28-29)? What should wise people do with their fields and homes (24:27, 30-34; see 24:3-4)? Who else says these exact words (see 24:33-34 and follow the cross-reference)?

427. Proverbs 25:1-27

a. What is the first word in 25:12, 13, 14, 25, 26; see 25:3, 18, 19, 20? How do the two lines in each of those proverbs work together? For example, how does the third line in 25:13 help you understand how the first two lines work together?

b. How should you speak with your neighbor (25:8-12)? How should you treat your enemy (25:21-22)? Are these proverbs wise only for Yahweh's people in the old covenant, or do they teach his people in the new covenant also? Follow the cross-references for 25:21-22 to the New Testament.

c. Choose your favorite proverb from today's reading and analyze it. Write it out, then (1) find and label any parallel words. (2) Think about how each line works. (3) Think about how the two lines work together. Then write what the proverb teaches you.

428. Proverbs 25:28-26:28

a. Why should you not answer a fool according to his folly (see 26:4 and the study note)? Why should you answer a fool according to his folly (see 26:5 and the study note)? How do these two proverbs side-by-side show you in what ways you should and should not interpret proverbs? See your introduction to Proverbs.

b. What are fools like (26:1-11)? What do sluggards do (26:13-15)? How do these proverbs about fools and sluggards fit together (25:28; 26:12, 16)?

c. Choose your favorite proverb from today's reading and analyze it. Write it out, then (1) find and label any parallel words. (2) Think about how each line works. (3) Think about how the two lines work together. Then write what the proverb teaches you.

429. Proverbs 27:1-28:12

a. What sort of people lead a nation best (28:2, 12)? How can they get wisdom and understanding to lead well (28:2, 4-5, 7)? And what will Yahweh do about wicked people in the land (28:8-10)?

b. Choose your favorite proverb from today's reading and analyze it. Write it out, then (1) find and label any parallel words. (2) Think about how each line works. (3) Think about how the two lines work together. Then write what the proverb teaches you.

c. Study a topic (like words or friendship) or analyze another proverb.

430. Proverbs 28:13-29:27

a. What is it like when foolish, wicked leaders rule (28:15-16, 28; 29:2, 4, 7, 12)? What is it like when wise, righteous leaders rule (28:16; 29:2, 4, 7, 14)? But, regardless of what sort of leader rules over them, where may people find hope (28:14; 29:13, 25-26)?

b. How should normal people live (28:13-14, 18-20, 25-27; 29:7, 11, 18, 23, 25)? How should friends treat each other (28:23)? How should parents treat their children (29:15-17)

c. Choose your favorite proverb from today's reading and analyze it. Write it out, then (1) find and label any parallel words. (2) Think about how each line works. (3) Think about how the two lines work together. Then write what the proverb teaches you.

431. Proverbs 30:1-33

a. Why does Agur think he has not learned wisdom (30:2-4)? Who else asked questions like these (30:4)? See the ESV study note for 30:2-6 or the NIV study note for 30:4. What does Agur think about God (30:3-9)?

b. What about those four creatures is too amazing for Agur to understand (see 30:18-19 and the study note)? What does Agur think is special about the next four creatures (30:24-28)? What lessons might people learn as they watch those animals closely?

c. Choose your favorite proverb from today's reading and analyze it. Write it out, then (1) find and label any parallel words. (2) Think about how each line works. (3) Think about how the two lines work together. Then write what the proverb teaches you.

432. Proverbs 31:1-31

a. How does King Lemuel's mother feel about her son (31:1-2)? What should Lemuel and other kings not do (31:2-7)? What should they do (31:8-9)?

b. How does the noble or excellent wife do her work (31:13-22, 24-27, 31)? How does her family feel about her (31:11-12, 21-23, 27-29)? How does she feel about Yahweh and his instruction (31:25-26, 30; see 14:26)?

c. Whom does the noble wife sound like (31:10, 12, 15, 17, 20, 22, 25-27, 30; see 1:7, 8, 20, 26; 3:1-10, 13-18; 8:1-21; 9:2; 18:22; 21:21)? Where can you read a story about a noble woman like this (31:10, 29)? Follow the cross-reference for 31:10 to Ruth. Which other mothers feared Yahweh and taught their children wisdom, love and faithfulness (Proverbs 31:1, 26; see 2 Kings 22:1-2; 2 Chronicles 35:26-27; Luke 2:51-52; 2 Timothy 1:5; 3:14-17)?

---

(3) Think about and answer the questions. (4) Return to your bookmark.

433. Proverbs – Review

Pray. Think through the following points.

You've now read through all of Proverbs. Today you will think back over the book.

 a. Reread your own introduction to Proverbs.

 b. What was the purpose and theme of Proverbs? What is wisdom? What do you think it means that wisdom begins with the fear of Yahweh?

 c. Look back through Proverbs. Note the words and verses you marked. What things seemed important to Solomon and the other wise teachers?

 d. What things were important to you? What was your very favorite proverb?

 e. Look back at your answers to question *d* each day. What were some things you discovered on your own?

 f. Think back through your answers to question *f* each day. What are some key ways God is teaching you to change the way you love, think or live?

 g. Has reading Proverbs made you want to be wise? What do you want your life to look like five years from now? Until then, what are some ways you want to think, speak or act more wisely?

 h. Jesus told his disciples that everything written about him in the Scriptures had to be fulfilled (Luke 24:44). How did Proverbs make you think about the Messiah? You might think about wisdom, righteousness, the king or something else.

Write

Write a review of Proverbs. In the first paragraph, explain what wisdom is, where it starts and how you can get it. In the second paragraph, describe how you feel about wisdom and being wise. Tell what you would like to be like. List a couple ways you want to think, speak or act more wisely. In the third paragraph, write out your favorite proverb. Explain what it means and say why it is your favorite. Finally, end your review with a prayer to Jesus. Thank him for his example of living a wise life. Thank him for teaching and giving wisdom. Ask him to help you in the particular ways you want to become more wise.

Ecclesiastes

434.   Ecclesiastes – Introduction

Pray. Then Read, Think and <u>Mark</u>.

Read your study Bible's introduction to Ecclesiastes. Think about the questions for each of the following sections. <u>Mark</u> the answers and other things that seem important.

for the ESV Study Bible

- Author, Title, and Date
    - o   Read the first paragraph.
    - o   In Ecclesiastes 1:1, what Hebrew (Hb.) word does the speaker use to say who he is and what he does?
    - o   How is that word often translated?
    - o   Read the third paragraph. Who do many people think wrote Ecclesiastes?
- Theme and Interpretation of Ecclesiastes
    - o   Read the first sentence of the first paragraph. What is the theme of Ecclesiastes?
    - o   Read the first sentence of the second paragraph ("According to ..."). What does the Preacher muse on or think about?
    - o   Read the last paragraph.
    - o   What does every human being want to find out but cannot?
    - o   So what do faithful people do?
- Purpose, Occasion, and Background
    - o   What is Ecclesiastes concerned with? What is its purpose?
- Key Themes
    - o   Read the first theme.
    - o   What is the Preacher painfully aware of?
    - o   Which New Testament author also writes about how the creation is subjected to futility?

- o Read the second theme.
- o The ESV uses the English word "vanity" to translate the Hebrew word *hevel* (*hebel*). What is the literal meaning of *hevel*?
- o What different things does the word *hevel* indicate or express?
- o Read the fourth theme. How does the Preacher feel about his work?
- o Read the fifth theme.
- o What gifts does God give humans?
- o What should we do with those gifts?

- History of Salvation Summary
  - o What do people not have to understand?

for the NIV Study Bible

- Author and Date
  - o Who may be the author of Ecclesiastes?
  - o What is the writer's title?
  - o What Hebrew word does that title translate?

- Purpose and Teaching
  - o Read the first paragraph.
  - o What does the author of Ecclesiastes consider?
  - o What is he concerned to spell out? That is, what does he want to explain?
  - o Read the second paragraph. What can human wisdom not find out?
  - o Read the sixth paragraph ("1. Humans cannot ..."). What can humans not achieve?
  - o Read the seventh paragraph ("2. Wisdom is ..."). Even though wisdom is God's gift, what can it not do?
  - o Read the eighth paragraph ("3. Experience confronts ..."). An anomaly is something that is different from the way it should be. What is the greatest anomaly?
  - o Read the thirteenth, fourteenth and fifteenth paragraphs. What are the first two things that wisdom counsels people to do?
  - o Read the last paragraph ("To sum up ..."). In what three ways does Ecclesiastes instruct humans how to live joyfully?

- Now read the study note for 1:2. The NIV uses the English word "meaningless" to translate the Hebrew word *hevel*. What is the original meaning of *hevel*?

Write

Write your own introduction to Ecclesiastes. Mention who probably wrote Ecclesiastes. Say what Hebrew title he used for himself and what that title means in English. Tell what the author considers or muses on. Explain why the author uses the Hebrew word *hevel* to describe human life. Describe some of the things human wisdom cannot do. Summarize what the author says humans should do. Then say how this advice fits together with the theme of Ecclesiastes.

435. Ecclesiastes 1:1-2:26

   a. Why does the Convener (Teacher or Preacher) say everything is a vapor or breath (meaningless or vain) (1:2-3)? What all does the Convener say about himself (1:12, 16; 2:9)? What did the Convener study or seek: what did he want to see (1:13; 2:3)?

   b. What makes the world and the things that happen in it like a vapor (1:4-11)? What makes being wise like a vapor (2:14-16)? What makes toil or work like vapor (2:18-23)?

   c. How did the Convener feel at first about his search and his toil (2:9-10)? Then what makes him start to hate life and his toil (2:11, 16-23)? So what should people do about their toil (2:24-26)?

436. Ecclesiastes 3:1-22

   a. What are the things that God has given humans to do (3:1-10)? How does God arrange those things and their times (3:1, 10-11)? So what is the best thing for humans to do (3:12-13)?

   b. What two things are eternal (3:11, 14)? But what can humans not get or know (3:9, 11, 14)? So what should humans do (3:14, 17)?

   c. How are humans like animals (3:18-21)? So what is the best thing for humans to do (3:22)? What does the Convener think they should not try to do (3:22)?

437. Ecclesiastes 4:1-5:7

   a. How do people feel about and treat each other (4:1-4; see 3:16)? What have people who have not yet been born not yet had to see (4:1-3)? Whose hands make them happier: fools who fold their hands together, busy workers who envy their neighbors and keep trying to get more or calm workers who do their work quietly (4:4-6)?

b. How are two people working together better than one person working alone (4:7-12)? How is the poor, wise youth better than the old, foolish king (4:13-16)? But what are all the things that people do like (4:4, 7, 16)?

c. What sacrifice do fools offer to God when they go to his house (5:1-4, 6)? How should people act when they go to God's house (5:2, 5-7)? Where is God, and where are humans (5:2)?

438. Ecclesiastes 5:8-6:12

a. What does the Convener, who is king over Israel, know about how people and officials treat the poor (5:8-9; see 3:16; 4:1-4)? When people love money, what are their lives like (5:10-17)? If someone toils for the wind, what does he carry with him when he dies (5:15-17)?

b. What is good to do (5:18-19)? What all does God give (5:19)? What does that kind of person not do very often (5:20)?

c. Does God give all those gifts to everyone (6:1-3, 6)? What advantage does a stillborn child have over that kind of man (6:3-6)? Does the Convener think he has found out everything about what it is good for people to do while they live (6:10-12; see 1:13; 2:3, 24-25; 3:12-13, 22; 5:18-20)?

439. Ecclesiastes 7:1-8:17

a. Why are mourning and sadness better for people than feasting and laughter (7:21-6; see 6:12)? What else is good for people (7:8-9)? What is God's work like (7:13-14)?

b. As he thinks about everything he has seen in his vapor life, how does the Convener think people should live (7:15-18)? Can even upright, righteous people always do good and never sin (7:20, 29)? In what different ways does wisdom protect people and preserve their lives (7:11-12, 19; 8:1, 5-6)?

c. Who all should punish the wicked, but sometimes don't punish them (8:3-5, 9-14)? Why is eating, drinking and being glad the best thing people can do (8:15)? But what can humans never get by their toil (8:16-17; see 7:14, 23-25, 27-28)?

440. Ecclesiastes 9:1-10:20

a. What all is in God's hands (9:1)? What else keeps humans from making sure that things happen the way they want them to (9:11; 10:8-11)? And then what happens to every human (9:2-4, 12)?

b. In what different ways should people enjoy life (9:7-9; see 10:19)? Why should people enjoy their vapor life (9:9)? What does the Convener say happens in Sheol, the place of the dead (9:10)?

c. What is wisdom better than (9:13-18)? How do fools and their folly mess things up (10:1-3, 12-15)? What sorts of mistakes do kings make (10:4, 5-7, 16)?

441. Ecclesiastes 11:1-12:14

a. What things will happen sooner or later, one way or another (11:1-3, 6)? What can no human know (11:5)? So how should people do their work (11:1-2, 4, 6)?

b. What should young people especially do (11:8-10)? But as they live that way, what should they remember (11:8-9; 12:1)? What different word pictures does the Convener use to show young people what old age is like (12:1-7)?

c. At the end of the book, what all does the Convener say is vapor of vapors (11:8, 10; 12:8)? Who gives wise words to the Convener and other wise people to share with others (12:11)? See the ESV study note or the NIV translation note. What is the conclusion of the matter (12:13)? Write out verse 13 in your notebook.

442. Ecclesiastes – Review

Pray. Think through the following points.

You've now read through Ecclesiastes. Today you will think back over the book.

a. Reread your own introduction to the book. What did the Convener want to find out? What was the theme of Ecclesiastes?

b. Look back through Ecclesiastes. Note the words and verses you marked. What things seemed important to the Convener?

c. What things were important to you?

d. Look back at your answers to question *d* each day. What were some things you discovered on your own?

e. Read through Psalm 39, a psalm written by Solomon's father David. What all does David say is breath or vapor (Psalm 39:5, 6, 11)? Whom does David talk to about his vapor life (Psalm 39:4:7-13)? What does David tell him (Psalm 39:7, 12)?

f.   Read Romans 8:18-39. Since God subjected the creation to fu-
tility or frustration, what does Paul say the creation and
God's children are waiting for (Romans 8:19-23)? What will
happen to God's children when they die (Romans 8:31-34, 38-
39)?

g.   Think back through your answers to question *f* each day.
What are some key ways God is teaching you to change the
way you love, think or live?

h.   Jesus told his disciples that everything written about him in
the Scriptures had to be fulfilled (Luke 24:44). How did Ecclesiastes make you think about the Messiah? You might
think about David's son who was a wise king, the Shepherd
who gives wisdom, the hope that Jesus' resurrection gives us
or something else.

Write

Write a review of Ecclesiastes. In the first paragraph, state the theme
of Ecclesiastes. Explain how the Convener feels about his vapor life.
Then summarize the Convener's advice about what people should do
with their vapor lives. In the second paragraph, compare what the
Convener did with his vapor life with what King David did with his.
In the third paragraph, describe what happened to Jesus at the end of
his life and then after that. Explain how Jesus' resurrection gives us
more hope than the Convener had. Finally, end your review with a
prayer to King Jesus, the wise Shepherd. Thank him for his short life
on earth and the hope that his resurrection gives you. And tell him
how you want to live your vapor life.

Song of Songs

443.   Song of Songs – Introduction

Pray. Then Read, Think and <u>Mark</u>.

Read the following sections in your study Bible's introduction to the Song of Songs and think about the questions. <u>Mark</u> the answers and other things that seem important.

for the ESV Study Bible

- Author and Date
  - o   Read the first two paragraphs.
  - o   The description "grammatically ambiguous" means that because of the way Song of Songs 1:1 is written (its grammar), the word *Solomon's* can have more than one meaning. Does Song of Songs 1:1 have to mean that Solomon wrote the Song?
  - o   What makes Solomon a bad example of married love for Israel?
- Theme, Title, and Interpretation
  - o   Read the first sentence of the first paragraph.
  - o   What kind of poetry does the Song of Songs contain?
  - o   What does the Song express or talk about?
- Purpose, Occasion, and Background
  - o   Read the second paragraph.
  - o   What kind of literature is the Song grouped with?
  - o   What other wisdom passage is parallel to the Song?
  - o   In that passage, and in the two chapters after it, who teaches whom about what?
- Literary Features and Structure
  - o   Read the last paragraph ("The woman is ...").
  - o   Whom does the woman address?
  - o   How does she feel about her beloved?
- Alternative Interpretations
  - o   Read the first two paragraphs.

     o   What was the main or dominant way people inter-
preted the Song?

     o   Even if you interpret the Song another way, what can
it still help you appreciate?

     o   Read the third paragraph. An anthology is a collec-
tion of writings. When some interpreters view the
Song as an anthology, do they think that the parts of
the Song of Songs tell a narrative or story that has a
plot?

for the NIV Study Bible

- Title
  - o   What can the title "Solomon's Song of Songs" mean?
  - o   Does it have to mean that Solomon was the author
of the Song of Songs?
- Interpretation
  - o   Read the first paragraph.
  - o   What other writings appear to be the closest parallels to the Song?
  - o   In those passages, who teaches whom about what?
  - o   So what kind of literature is the Song?
  - o   Read the second paragraph.
  - o   For a long time, how did most people view the Song?
  - o   What does the Song use extensively, that is, use a
lot?
- Theme and Theology
  - o   Read the first paragraph. How does the woman describe love?
- Literary Features
  - o   Read the first paragraph.
  - o   What does the poet evoke: that is, how does he make
you feel?
  - o   What does he avoid?
  - o   Read the second paragraph. Do all interpreters think
that the parts of the Song of Songs tell a single, con-
tinuing story?
  - o   Read the third paragraph. In the Song, whose voice
is dominant? That is, who sings the most, and whose
experience of love does the Song talk about most?

Write

Write your own introduction to the Song of Songs. In the first paragraph, explain what the word *Solomon's* in the title can mean. State
the theme of the Song. Say what sort of writing the Song is. Mention

passages in the Bible that are parallel to the Song, and describe who teaches whom about what in those passages. In the second paragraph, explain how most people in history have interpreted the Song. Tell how most people interpret the Song today.

444. Song of Songs 1:1-2:7

   a. Which vineyards has the darling kept and not kept (see 1:6 and the study note)? How is the way the beloved sees the darling different from the way she sees herself (1:5-6, 8, 10, 15; see 2:1)? What does the darling call her beloved (1:4, 7-8, 12)?

   b. How do the darling and the beloved feel about each other (1:2-4, 7-10, 13-16; 2:2-6)? What delightful things do they look, smell and taste like (1:3, 12-15; 2:1-3, 5)? Where else in the Scriptures have you read about a woman and a man in love with each other in a green garden with lovely flowers and fruitful trees (1:14, 16-17; 2:1-3)?

   c. Do the darling and the beloved talk to and treat each other as though they are already married (1:2, 4, 12-13, 16-17; 2:3-6)? How the daughters of Jerusalem feel about the darling and her beloved (1:3-4, 11)? So what very serious instruction does the darling give these girls (2:7)?

445. Song of Songs 2:8-3:5

   a. What kinds of words does the beloved use as he calls his darling (2:8-13)? How does he describe her (2:14)? What do foxes do (see 2:15 and the study note)?

   b. Who belongs to whom (2:16)? What does the darling say her beloved is like (2:9, 16-17)? Now what does she want him to do (2:16-17)?

   c. When the darling cannot find her beloved, where, for the first time in the Song, does she find herself (3:1-3; see 1:8, 14, 16-17; 2:1-3, 8, 12-17)? Would these verses make more sense if they were the darling's description of a really bad dream (3:1-4)? As soon as she describes how strongly she feels about her beloved, what does the darling tell the daughters of Jerusalem (3:5)?

446. Song of Songs 3:6-5:1

   a. As she sings to the daughters of Jerusalem, how does the darling's description of King Solomon feel different from her description of her beloved (3:6; see 1:2-3, 14, 16-17; 2:3, 9, 16-17)?

Though Solomon is a wealthy and glorious king, why does the darling say Solomon has around him 60 mighty men with swords (3:7-8, 11)? How many weddings do the daughters of Jerusalem probably know Solomon has had (3:10-11; see 6:8 and 1 Kings 11:1-3)?

b. If the darling's neck is like the tower of David, what are the courses or rows of stone and the thousand shields (Song of Songs 4:4)? Where does the beloved call the darling to come from (see 4:8 and the study note)? What does it mean that the darling keeps her garden locked (4:12)?

c. How do the beloved and the darling feel about each other, their bodies and their love (4:9-5:1)? As the daughters listen to the song, how do they feel (5:1)? When the darling and the beloved are alone together, what are the delights of their love like (4:10-5:1; see Genesis 1:29; 2:8-9, 15-16, 18, 21-25)?

447. Song of Songs 5:2-6:3

a. At first, how do the beloved and the darling feel (5:2-3)? When the darling cannot find her beloved, who finds her where (5:6-7)? Has the darling had this kind of bad dream-like experience before (5:2-7; see 3:1-4)?

b. How does the darling describe to the daughters of Jerusalem the way she really feels about her beloved (5:4, 8; see 5:3)? When she wants to show that her beloved is better than others, what does the darling describe (5:9-16)? What senses does the darling use to talk about her beloved (5:9-16)?

c. In the end, how is the beloved found (5:16-6:2)? What does the darling call the beloved (5:16; 6:3)? What does the beloved call his darling (5:2)?

448. Song of Songs 6:4-8:4

a. When the beloved compares his darling to the many queens, concubines and young women, what does he say is special about her (6:8-9)? What surprises the darling (6:11-12)? What do other people think about the darling (6:9-10, 13; see 5:9; 6:1)?

b. Who does the beloved think made the darling's thighs well (7:1)? What about the darling's body does the beloved find majestic or awesome (6:4, 10; 7:1, 4-5, 7)? What about her body does he find beautiful and pleasing (6:4-6, 10; 7:1-3, 6-9)?

c. What does the darling tell her beloved when she knows that he desires her (see 7:10-13 and the study note for 7:10)? Why does the darling wish the beloved were her (little) brother (see 8:1-2 and the study notes)? Who teaches whom (8:2, 4)?

449. Song of Songs 8:5-14

a. Whose example does the darling follow (8:2, 5)? What is real love between a woman and a man like (8:6)? Who lights the blazing flame of love (8:6)? For the NIV, see the translation note.

b. What have the daughters of Jerusalem learned about love (8:8-9)? Whose example are they following (8:8-10; see 4:4, 12)? Since the darling says that she is like a wall, does that mean that her life is dull or that her love has no real pleasure (8:5-6, 10)?

c. How does the darling feel about Solomon and the way he loves (8:7, 11-12)? Since the darling's companions have listened carefully to her, who wants the darling's attention now (8:13)? How does the darling end her song, the best of songs (8:14)?

450. Song of Songs – Review

Pray. Think through the following points.

You've now listened to the whole Song of Songs. Today you will think back over the book.

a. Reread your own introduction to the Song of Songs. In what ways was the darling's wise instruction of the daughters of Jerusalem like Solomon's instruction of his son (Proverbs 5-7)?

b. How does the darling sing her song in a way that makes you think about Adam and Eve in love in the garden of Eden? How delightful does the darling think real love can be?

c. How does Yahweh describe his relationship with Israel (see Hosea 1-2, especially Hosea 2:14-23)? How does Paul describe Jesus' relationship with the church, the gathering of all his people (see Ephesians 5:23-33)? How does John describe the Bride (see Revelation 21:2, 9-27; 22:1-5, 17, 20)?

d. Look back through the Song of Songs. Note the words and verses you marked. What things seemed important to the darling?

e. What things were important to you?

f. Look back at your answers to question *d* each day. What were some things you discovered on your own?

g. Think back through your answers to question *f* each day. What are some key ways God is teaching you to change the way you love, think or live?

h. Jesus told his disciples that everything written about him in the Scriptures had to be fulfilled (Luke 24:44). How did the Song of Songs make you think about the Messiah? You might think about how Christ loves his people or about something else.

Write

Write a review of the Song of Songs. In the first paragraph, show how the darling taught wisdom to the daughters of Jerusalem. Describe where she says real love between a woman and a man comes from and how good it can be. In the second paragraph, note a few lessons you've learned about love. In the third paragraph, explain how the love of the darling and the beloved for each other is like God's love for his people. Finally, end your review with a prayer to our Bridegroom Jesus. Thank him for loving us to the death. Tell him how you love him. Ask him to help you live wisely as you love or as you wait for love.

PART FOUR

NEW TESTAMENT

Matthew

451. Matthew - Introduction

Pray. Then Read, Think and Mark.

An introduction gets you ready to read a book. It usually tells you who wrote the book, when and for whom. It points out the important themes you should look out for and summarizes the book's message.

Read your study Bible's introduction to Matthew's Gospel. Think about the questions for each of the following sections. Mark the answers and other things that seem important.

for the ESV Study Bible

- Author and Title
  - Read the first paragraph. Who is the human author of this Gospel?
  - Read the last paragraph.
  - What was the author's other name?
  - Where was he from? What did he do?
- Theme
  - What is the theme of Matthew's Gospel?
- Purpose, Occasion, and Background
  - Read the first paragraph.
  - What does Matthew want to demonstrate in his Gospel?
  - For whom does Matthew write?
- Literary Features
  - In the second paragraph, read the first two sentences. What is "the most notable literary feature of the book's format"?
- Key Themes
  - What are some of the key themes in Matthew?
  - What can Jesus' five discourses be viewed as?
  - What chapters are they in?

for the NIV Study Bible

- Author
    - o Who is the human author of this Gospel?
    - o What was his other name? What did he do?
- Recipients
    - o For whom does Matthew write?
- Purpose
    - o What is Matthew's main purpose?
    - o How does he do it?
- Structure
    - o Read the first paragraph. How does Matthew struc-
       ture his Gospel?

Write

Write your own introduction to Matthew's Gospel. Tell who the author is, what he did and what his other name was. State Matthew's
basic theme and purpose. Say who Matthew's readers are. Describe
what he wants to show them. Explain how he structures his Gospel.

452.   Matthew 1:1-2:23

Follow your bookmark and then answer these questions:

  a. How would you say "Jesus" in Hebrew (see the note for 1:21)?
      What does that name mean? Remember to read "the LORD"
      as "Yahweh." What does the word Immanuel mean (1:23)?
      Why does this take place (1:22)? Which prophet does Mat-
      thew quote here (1:22-23)?
  b. What does the word *Messiah* or *Christ* mean (1:1; see the
      translation note)? What promise did Yahweh give David
      (1:1)? Follow the cross-reference to 2 Samuel 7:12-16. Which
      prophet do the priests and teachers quote (Matthew 2:5-6)?
      What did he say the son of David would do (2:6)?
  c. Which prophet's word is fulfilled in 2:14-15? Whom had Yah-
      weh called his son (2:15)? Follow the first cross-reference for
      son. Who is Matthew showing that Jesus is?

Return to your bookmark and do d through g.

453.   Matthew 3:1-4:25

Follow your bookmark and then answer these questions:

  a. With whom had Yahweh said he would be "well pleased"
      (3:17; follow the first cross-reference)? What did Yahweh say
      he would put on his chosen servant (see Isaiah 42:1)? What

happens to Jesus when he goes up out of the water (Matthew 3:16-17)?

b. Where does Jesus go when he comes out of the water (4:1)? How long does he stay there (4:2)? Who else came through water and then spent a 40-long period in the wilderness (see 4:2 and the study note)? From which story does Jesus quote when he resists Satan (see 4:4, 7, 10 and the study notes)? Who is Matthew showing that Jesus is?

c. Which prophet spoke of a great light dawning in Galilee (4:14-16)? Who would the light be, and what would he do (see Isaiah 9:6-7)? What is Jesus' message (Matthew 4:17)?

Return to your bookmark and do d through g.

454. Matthew 5:1-48

Follow your bookmark and then answer these questions:

a. What sorts of people are blessed or happy (5:3-11)? How does God make them happy (5:3-12)?

b. Who else went through water, into the wilderness and up onto a mountain to give God's instruction to God's people (5:1-2)? What has Jesus come to do and not to do (5:17)? What does Jesus require of his followers (5:20)?

c. What have the scribes taught (5:21)? If someone follows the scribes' teaching how may he or she fail to fulfill the righteousness God requires (5:22)? If you are tempted to be angry with another, what does Jesus tell you to do (5:24, 25)?

Return to your bookmark and do d through g.

455. Matthew 6:1-7:29

Follow your bookmark and then answer these questions:

a. Where is your Father (6:1)? What does he see and do (6:4, 6, 18)? How can you store up for yourself treasures in heaven (6:20)?

b. Why should you not worry (6:8, 25-30)? What you should you seek first (6:33)? What will you receive (7:7-8)? What else will you get (6:33)? What should you pray for, in order (6:10-11)?

c. Who enters the kingdom of heaven (7:21; 5:20)? What principle sums up the Law and the Prophets (7:12)? What do we want done to us (6:12)? What should we do to others (6:12; 7:1-5)? Does being righteous mean someone does not sin and does not need the Father's forgiveness (6:14-15)?

(3) Think about and answer the questions. (4) Return to your bookmark.

456. Matthew 8:1-9:38

a. What does the leper believe about Jesus (8:2)? Is his belief true (8:3)? What does Jesus tell the man to do (8:4)? What gift has Moses commanded people to bring to the priest for their cleansing? Follow the cross-reference for "the gift Moses commanded." Did the Law have any way to heal people from their disease, or did it just say what to do to declare them clean when they had already been healed (Leviticus 13:1-46; 14:1-32)? How does Jesus fulfill the Law of Moses and do even more (Matthew 8:3-4)?

b. In the Old Testament, who was asleep in a boat during a furious storm (8:24)? In each story, whom do the sailors call on to save them (Jonah 1:14-15; Matthew 8:25)? What sort of man is this (Jonah 1:16; Matthew 8:27)?

c. What does Jesus want more: mercy or sacrifice (Matthew 9:13)? Which prophet does Jesus quote (9:13)? What sort of mercy does Yahweh desire (see Hosea 6:6 and study note)? What does Yahweh promise his sinful people (see Hosea 14:1-2, 4)? What sort of people come to Jesus when he calls them (Matthew 9:9-13)?

457. Matthew 10:1-42

a. What message does Jesus send the disciples to proclaim (10:7)? What does the kingdom look like as it comes near (10:8)?

b. How will many people respond (10:17-18, 22)? How should the disciples respond (10:19, 26, 28)? Whom should they fear (10:28)? But what does he do for the disciples (10:19-20, 29-31)?

c. Where does Jesus tell the disciples to go (10:5, 6, 11, 23)? After Jesus instructs the twelve, where does he go (11:1)? What does Jesus demand of anyone who wants to follow him (10:37-38)? So what does Jesus say he brings when he comes (10:34)?

458. Matthew 11:1-12:50

a. Is Jesus the one who was to come (11:5)? Follow the cross-reference or study note for *poor*. In the following verse in the prophecy, what will Lord Yahweh's anointed proclaim (see Isaiah 61:2)? Do the towns of Israel welcome Jesus' and the disciples' message and repent (Matthew 10:40; 11:1, 19-20)? What does the Son of Man declare when he comes to these towns (10:14-15, 23; 11:20-24)?

b. What does God desire more: mercy or sacrifice (12:7)? Since the Law forbids people to work on the Sabbath, would priests be able to offer sacrifices on the Sabbath if God did not show them mercy and allow them to offer sacrifices (12:5)? What is God more concerned with: showing mercy to people or keeping the Law (12:3-4, 13)? List in order the things the Pharisees are most concerned with: caring for people, caring for their animals, keeping the Sabbath (12:11-14).

c. Whose service is more important than service in the temple (12:6)? Whose death, resurrection and preaching will be greater than Jonah's (12:39-41)? Whose wisdom is greater than Solomon's (21:42)?

459. Matthew 13:1-52

a. To whom does Jesus tell many things in parables (13:2-3, 34)? To whom does Jesus explain the meaning of the parables (13:10, 16, 36)? What do parables do (13:35)? Why does Jesus speak in parables (13:11-13)?

b. Which soil is each of the following types of people like (13:19-23)?
   • People who hear but do not understand
   • People who are excited but do not persevere
   • People who hear but are distracted by life
   • People who hear and understand

c. In which "field" do the man and the enemy sow seed (13:24-25, 37-39)? Where do the angels (messengers) pull the weeds out from (13:41)? What happens to the good seed and plants (13:43)?

460. Matthew 13:53-15:28

a. In Greek, "It is I" is literally "I am" (14:27). Who does Jesus say he is (14:27)? Who does Peter believe Jesus is (14:28-29)? How is Peter able to walk on the water (14:29)? Who do the disciples say Jesus is (14:33)?

b. Which parts of the body are the Pharisees more concerned about (15:2, 8, 17)? Which part of the body is God more concerned about (15:8, 18-19)? What comes out of the Pharisees' mouths (15:5, 9)?

c. What comes out of the mouth of an unclean, Canaanite woman (15:22)? Where does this Gentile "dog" say she is (15:27)? After the Son of David feeds the children of Israel, are there enough crumbs left over to feed believing Gentiles too (14:20; 15:27-28)?

461. Matthew 15:29-17:27

a. What did the prophet Isaiah say would happen when Yahweh came to his people (see Isaiah 35:5-6)? How many signs is Jesus giving (Matthew 15:30-31; 16:1-4)? What is the "sign of Jonah" (see 16:4 and follow the cross-reference)?

b. Read the study note for 16:18 to answer the following questions. What do *Peter* and *rock* have to do with each other? Who does Paul say the foundation of the church is (see Ephesians 2:20)? For whom will Peter open the doors into the kingdom of heaven (see Acts 2:9-11, 40-41; 5:12-16; 8:14-17; 10:1, 44-48)?

c. Who sees "the Son of Man in his kingdom" (16:28; 17:1-2)? Whose Son is he (17:5)? Why does Jesus not need to pay the temple tax (17:25-26)?

462. Matthew 18:1-19:15

a. What are little children like (18:2-3)? Who are like the little ones (18:6)? Whom does the Father not want to perish (18:14)?

b. What does a man do when one of his sheep wanders away (18:12-13)? What should Jesus' followers do if one of their brothers or sisters sins (18:15)? What should they do when the brother or sister listens and comes back (18:18, 35)?

c. For what reason would the Jewish teacher Hillel allow a man to divorce his wife (see the study note for 19:3)? Why should a man not divorce his wife (19:4-6)? What is a man doing if he divorces his wife and marries another woman (19:9)?

463. Matthew 19:16-20:34

a. Which command is the man not actually keeping (19:18-19, 21)? What does Jesus demand of his followers (follow the cross-reference for *perfect* in 19:21)? What does that look like (see 6:14-15; 7:12)?

b. Does the landowner have the right to do what he wants with his own money (20:15)? Does the landowner give any worker less than what he deserved (20:4)? Is the landowner being unjust, just or generous (20:2, 4, 5, 9, 13)? What right does God have (20:15-16)?

c. What special role does Jesus promise his followers (19:28)? What extra honor do James and John want (20:20-21)? How may one of Jesus' followers become great (20:26-27)? Who is the greatest (20:28)?

464. Matthew 21:1-22:14

a. Which Old Testament prophet also accused the Israelites of turning God's temple into a den of robbers (21:13)? Why do robbers go to their den (see Jeremiah 7:9-10)? What does Yahweh do to his wicked people when they defile his dwelling (see Jeremiah 7:12-15)?

b. What does Jesus want the fig tree to do for him (Matthew 21:19)? What does the fig tree have on it (21:19)? What does the father want his sons to do for him (21:31)?

c. What does the king do to those who reject his invitation again and again (22:7; see 21:43)? Then whom does the king invite (22:9-10; see 21:31-32, 41)? What must the "bad and good" people who come to the banquet do (22:10-12)?

465. Matthew 22:15-23:39

a. Whose likeness (or portrait) and inscription are on the coin (22:20)? Whose likeness is on the Pharisees, the Herodians and all humans (22:21)? Why does David call his Son, the Messiah, "Lord" (22:43-45; see 1:1, 20-23)?

b. How great are the two greatest commandments (22:40)? What more important, weightier matters of the Law do the scribes and Pharisees neglect (23:23)? How must Jesus' followers fulfill the Law and the Prophets (see 7:12)? How will their righteousness surpass the righteousness of the scribes and Pharisees (see 5:20)?

c. How do the Pharisees appear to other people (23:28)? What are they like on the inside (23:25, 28)? What will they do (23:32, 34)? What will happen to them (23:33, 35-36, 38)?

466. Matthew 24:1-25:30

a. What will happen to Jesus' followers (24:9)? What does Jesus send his messengers to do (23:34; 24:14, 31; 28:18-20)? In about A.D. 60, where does the apostle Paul say the gospel has been preached and believed (see Colossians 1:6, 23)?

(3) Think about and answer the questions. (4) Return to your bookmark. 277

b. When exactly will these things happen (24:36)? By when will all these things happen (24:34)? Is Jesus talking about the end of the world (24:21)?

c. Which servant gains the most gold (25:16-18)? What does the master praise the first two servants for (25:21, 23)? What does the master condemn the third servant for (25:26)?

467. Matthew 25:31-26:35

a. Whom will the Son of Man judge (25:31)? What does Jesus judge (25:35-36, 40, 42-43, 45)? In an earlier sermon, what type of people did Jesus call "blessed" and then tell them they would inherit the kingdom (25:34)?

b. Which scripture does Jesus quote when he says, "The poor you will always have with you" (26:11)? How should God's people treat the poor (see Deuteronomy 15:7-11)? Which command is greater even than the command to love our neighbors as ourselves (Matthew 26:11-13)?

c. Follow the first cross-reference for "blood of the covenant" (26:28). What did Moses do with the blood of the covenant (see Exodus 24:6-8)? What does Jesus say is his blood of the covenant (Matthew 26:27-28)?

468. Matthew 26:36-27:10

a. How does Jesus feel about what he knows is about to happen (26:38-39)? Could Jesus have escaped from the crowd and saved his life (26:53)? Why doesn't he (26:42, 54, 56)?

b. Who does Jesus say the high priest says he is (26:63-64)?

c. Which prophets' words do Judas and the thirty pieces of silver fulfill (see the study note for 27:9-10)? In Zechariah's prophecy, what did Yahweh tell the shepherd to do (see Zechariah 11:4, 7)? How much does the flock appreciate the shepherd (see Zechariah 11:8, 12-13 and study note)?

469. Matthew 27:11-28:20

a. In whose place does Jesus Christ die (27:15-17)? The name *Jesus Barabbas* means "Yahweh-saves the-son-of-a-father." Among humans, who all are children of their fathers? Whom all does Jesus' death save (1:21)?

b. What or who was on the other side of the curtain in the temple (27:51)? (Follow the first cross-reference for "curtain of the temple.") When Jesus gives up his spirit, where does it go and what does he do (27:51)? (Follow the reference in the study note to Hebrews.) Who then tears the curtain (27:51)?

c. Who had prophesied that all authority would be given to the Son of Man (follow the cross-reference for 28:18)? What did he say people of every nation and language would do (see Daniel 7:14)? What does Jesus tell his followers to do to make the prophecy come true (Matthew 28:19-20)?

470. Matthew – Review

Pray. Think through the following points.

a. Reread your own introduction to the book.
b. What was Matthew's basic theme and purpose in writing his Gospel?
c. How does Matthew structure his Gospel? In the story (or narrative) portions, how has Matthew shown you that Jesus really is "the Messiah, the son of David, the son of Abraham" (1:1)?
d. In the teaching portions, how has Matthew taught you to obey everything Jesus commanded him (28:20)?
e. Flip through the rest of Matthew's Gospel, looking for the verses you marked. What seemed important to Matthew?
f. What was important to you?
g. Look back at your answers to question *d* each day. What were some things you discovered on your own?
h. Think back through your answers to question *f* each day. What are some key ways God is teaching you to change the way you love, think and live?

Write

Write a review of Matthew's Gospel. In the first paragraph or two, state Matthew's main theme and purpose and how he brings them out in his Gospel. In the next paragraph, write about the things that seemed most important to you and how God is changing you. End your review with a prayer to Jesus the Messiah, the son of David and son of Abraham. Talk with him about who you think he is and how you want to follow him.

Mark

471.   Mark – Introduction

Pray. Then Read, Think and <u>Mark</u>.

Read your study Bible's introduction to Mark's Gospel. Think about the questions for each of the following sections. <u>Mark</u> the answers and other things that seem important.

for the ESV Study Bible

- Author and Title
    - o   Read the first sentence.
    - o   Who is the human author of Mark?
    - o   Who taught him and told him about Jesus?
- Date and Place of Writing
    - o   Read the first sentence. When and where was Mark most likely written?
- Theme
    - o   What is Mark's "ultimate purpose and theme"?
    - o   What is Mark's "central effort"?
    - o   What is discipleship, and what does it involve?
- Key Themes
    - o   What are some of the key themes in Mark's Gospel?
- Literary Features
    - o   Read the first two sentences of the first paragraph. What is Mark's Gospel like?
    - o   Read the second paragraph. What is the best way to "negotiate" or find a way through Mark's Gospel?

for the NIV Study Bible

- Author
    - o   Who is the human author of Mark?
    - o   Who taught him and told him about Jesus?

- Date of Composition
  - When may Mark's Gospel have been written?
- Place of Origin
  - Where may Mark's Gospel have been written?
- Occasion and Purpose
  - What may have been happening when Mark wrote his Gospel?
  - What may he be preparing his readers for?
  - How does he prepare them?
- Emphases
  - What are some of the emphases in Mark's Gospel?

Write

Write your own introduction to Mark's Gospel. Tell who wrote the book and who taught him. State Mark's purpose. Explain how some of Mark's key themes or emphases support his purpose. For example, how does discipleship relate to suffering and Jesus the Messiah?

472. Mark 1:1-2:22

a. *Christ* or *Messiah* means Anointed. In Psalm 2, who is Yahweh's Anointed (see Psalm 2:2, 6)? What does Yahweh say to him (see Psalm 2:7)? What does the voice from heaven say to Jesus (Mark 1:11)?

b. Which Old Testament verse does Mark quote or cite to describe John (1:3)? What good news does the voice proclaim (see Isaiah 40:9)? On the way, who leads whom from where to where? Follow the cross-reference for "valley" in Isaiah 40:4 (see Isaiah 49:5, 8-13). What does Isaiah tell Israel they must do to get on the way (see Isaiah 55:6-7)? What does John proclaim (Mark 1:4)? What does Jesus proclaim (Mark 1:14-15)?

c. Over what all does Jesus show his authority and power (1:23-27, 31-34; 2:10-12)? Over whom does Jesus have authority (1:17-20; 2:14)? Whom does Jesus cleanse (1:23, 41-42)?

473. Mark 2:23-4:34

a. Who rejects Jesus (2:24; 3:6, 21, 22)? From which regions do people follow Jesus (3:8)? To whom has Yahweh given this land (see Genesis 15:18-21)? How many apostles does Jesus appoint (Mark 3:14)? When else were there twelve leaders for God's people (see Ezekiel 47:13-14)?

b. *Beelzebul* is a Greek way of writing *Baal-Zebul,* the Canaanite title for Baal the Prince. What do the teachers of the law say Baal-Zebul is prince of (3:22)? *Demons* is the Greek word for deities or the gods of the nations. What does Jesus call Baal-Zebul (3:23)? What will Jesus and his Twelve do to Baal and his princedom (3:15, 27)?

c. How does Jesus teach the crowds (4:2)? How do parables work: how do you make sense of them? See the study note for 4:2. Why does Jesus speak in parables (4:11-12)? Who gets the point of the parables (4:9, 34)?

474. Mark 4:35-6:6

a. In each of the first two stories: What or who opposes Jesus (4:37; 5:6)? Is there danger (4:38; 5:2-5)? How does Jesus respond (4:39; 5:8, 13)? What happens to the opposition (4:39; 5:13, 15)? How do the people respond (4:41; 5:15, 17, 20)? "Who is this" (4:41; 5:7)?

b. What do the next two stories have to do with each other (5:21-43)? How long has the woman been suffering to bleeding (5:25)? How old is the little girl (5:42)? What heals the woman (5:34)? What does Jesus tell Jairus (5:36)?

c. What do the people of Jesus' hometown hear and see (6:2)? What do they feel (6:3)? What can Jesus *not* do (6:5)? Now who is amazed (6:6)?

475. Mark 6:7-7:30

a. Who is Herod? See study note for 6:14 and follow the reference to the note on Matthew 14:1. What happens to a holy and righteous servant (Mark 6:27)? What can it cost to follow Jesus faithfully?

b. Why does Mark mention that the grass is green (6:39)? What does Jesus make the people do (6:39)? What are the people beside (6:34)? What do the people still want (6:42)? Who does Mark show Jesus is (see Psalm 23)?

c. What do human rules and tradition lead to (Mark 7:7-8)? What does God care about (7:8-9, 19)? What makes people unclean (7:18-23)? What does Jesus do for an "unclean" Greek woman (7:29-30)?

476. Mark 7:31-9:29

a. Who all are deaf or blind (7:32; 8:17-18, 22)? What do the disciples not see or hear: what do they not get (8:17-20)? How many baskets of pieces were left over when Jesus fed 5,000 men in Jewish territory (6:32-44; 8:19)? How many baskets of pieces (crumbs) were left over when Jesus fed 4,000 people among the nations (8:1-10, 20)? Does Jesus have enough "bread" for everyone, Jew and Gentile, and plenty left over? Now do you see (8:21)?

b. Who appear with Jesus on the mountain (9:5)? What did God give through the first man? What role did the second man have? What do the Law and the Prophets say about the Son of Man (8:31; 9:12)? What must anyone do who wants to follow the Son of Man (8:34)?

c. Why can the disciples not drive the spirit from the boy (9:18-19, 29)? What does Jesus tell the boy's father (9:23)? What does the father say (9:24)? What happens (9:26-27)?

477. Mark 9:30-10:45

a. What do the disciples want (9:34; 10:37)? How does a disciple become a great leader (9:43-44)? How does Jesus say he will do that (9:45)? How do the disciples feel about Jesus' judgment and death (9:32; 10:32)?

b. Who can keep the commandments and become good like God (10:18-19)? Who then can be saved (10:26-27)? What makes the impossible possible (10:27; see 9:23)? What one thing does the rich man lack (10:21-22)? What do the disciples have (10:28)?

c. What is God joining together (10:29-30)? Of the things Jesus' disciples give up for Jesus, what will they not get many of in return (10:29-30)? How does someone enter the Father's new family (9:36-37; 10:13-16)?

478. Mark 10:46-12:12

a. What does Bartimaeus call Jesus (10:47-48)? As Jesus approaches Jerusalem, what do the people say is coming (11:10)? What does "Hosanna" mean (see 11:9 and the study note)? Who do the people think Jesus is? What do they want him to do (11:9-10)?

b. Who is meant to be in the outer courts of the temple (11:15, 17; see the study notes)? What verse from Isaiah does Jesus quote (11:17)? What does Yahweh promise the foreigners who join themselves to Yahweh (see Isaiah 56:3, 5-7)? Whom all is Lord Yahweh gathering (see Isaiah 56:8)?

c. What parable in Isaiah is Jesus referring to (Mark 12:1-9)? In that parable, who was the vineyard (see Isaiah 5:7)? What did the vineyard not do (see Isaiah 5:4)? What happened to them (see Isaiah 5:5-6)? In Jesus' parable, who are the tenants (Mark 12:1, 12)? What do they do wrong (12:3-5, 8)? What will happen to them (12:9-11)?

479. Mark 12:13-13:37

a. Who leaves the temple (13:1)? What does he say will happen to it (13:2)? What are the disciples' two questions (13:4)? What is Jesus' answer to the first question: When will "all these things" happen (13:30)?

b. Which passage from Isaiah does Jesus quote in 13:24-25 (see the cross-reference)? When Isaiah said the sun, moon and stars would be darkened, whom was he prophesying about (see Isaiah 13:1, 10)? What will happen to Babylon (see Isaiah 13:9, 11, 17, 19)? How does Isaiah describe the king of Babylon (see Isaiah 14:4, 12)?

c. Where will people claim the Messiah (Christ) is (Mark 13:21-22)? Which prophet does Jesus quote in 13:26 (see cross-reference or study note)? In Daniel's vision, where is the one like a son of man coming to (see Daniel 7:13)? What will happen in heaven (see Daniel 7:14)? Then what will happen on earth (Mark 13:2, 30)?

480. Mark 14:1-52

a. What does the woman do for Jesus (14:3)? How does Jesus describe what she does (14:6)? What is the woman preparing Jesus' body for (14:8)? Where does Jesus already know the gospel will be preached (14:9)?

b. Which Old Testament passage prescribes the first Passover (14:12)? What must the animal be like (see Exodus 12:5)? What does Jesus call the bread (Mark 14:22)? What does Jesus call the cup (14:23-24)? Where is the lamb?

c. Which Old Testament prophet does Jesus quote to warn the disciples (14:27)? What does Yahweh do with some of the sheep (see Zechariah 13:9)? What do these sheep do afterward (see Zechariah 13:9)? How is Zechariah's prophecy fulfilled (Mark 14:43, 49-50)?

481. Mark 14:53-16:8

a. What does the high priest expect the Messiah (Christ), the Son of "the Blessed One" to do (14:61)? Who else does Jesus say he is (14:62)? What other Old Testament passages does he refer to (see the study note for 14:62)? By what title is Jesus mocked and executed (15:9, 17-18, 26, 32)?

b. How does Jesus respond to the charges against him (14:60-61; 15:4-5)? What prophecy is Jesus fulfilling (see study notes for 14:61; 15:5)? Read through that whole section of Isaiah's prophecy (Isaiah 52:13-53:12). Which verses in this section of Isaiah's prophecy (Isaiah 52:13-53:12) foretell that the Messiah will have to suffer many things, be rejected, be killed and rise again (Mark 8:31; 9:31)?

c. What are the two temples of God (15:29-30)? What has one temple done to the other (11:15-17, 27-33; 12:35)? What happens to one (15:37)? Then what happens to the other temple (15:38)? What happens to the first temple (16:6)? What will happen to the other (13:1-2)?

482. Mark – Review

Pray. Think through the following points.

a. Reread your own introduction to the book.
b. What was Mark's main theme or purpose in writing his Gospel?
c. At the beginning and the end of his Gospel, Mark calls Jesus "the Messiah (Christ), the Son of God" (1:1; 14:61). Where else does Mark show Jesus to be the Anointed, the Son of God?
d. What does Mark show the Son of Man choosing and suffering? What does Mark say and show about the nature of discipleship?
e. Flip through the rest of Mark's Gospel, looking for the verses you marked. What seemed important to Mark?
f. What was important to you?
g. Look back at your answers to question *d* each day. What were some things you discovered on your own?
h. Now that you have seen how Jesus lived, died and rose, what do you say (15:38)?
i. Think back through your answers to question *f* each day. What are some key ways God is teaching you to change the way you love, think and live?

Write

Write a review of Mark's Gospel. In the first paragraph or two, state Mark's main theme or purpose and how he brings it out in his Gospel. In the next paragraph, write about the things that seemed most important to you and how God is changing you. End your review with a prayer of praise to Jesus the Messiah, the Son of God. Talk with him about whether and how you want to follow him.

Luke

483. Luke - Introduction

Pray. Then Read, Think and <u>Mark</u>.

Read your study Bible's introduction to Luke's Gospel. Think about the questions for each of the following sections. <u>Mark</u> the answers and other things that seem important.

for the ESV Study Bible

- Author
    - Who wrote this Gospel?
    - What else did he write (his "second work")?
- Theme
    - Why did Luke write his Gospel?
- Purpose, Occasion, and Background
    - To whom did Luke address his two works?
    - What are a couple of Luke's goals in writing?
    - Where did Luke get the material for his Gospel?
- Literary Features
    - Read the beginning and end of the last paragraph. What verse expresses the unity of Luke's Gospel?
- Key Themes
    - What are some of Luke's key themes?

for the NIV Study Bible

- Author
    - Who wrote this Gospel?
    - What else did he write (as a "companion volume")?
    - In a letter to the Corinthian believers in A.D. 55, Paul describes someone "praised by all the churches for his service to the gospel" (2 Corinthians 8:18). Which person and gospel may that have been (see the study note for 2 Corinthians 8:18)?

- Recipient and Purpose
  - o Read the first paragraph. Who may have published Luke's Gospel (had it copied and distributed)?
  - o Read the second paragraph. What were Luke's purposes as he wrote his Gospel? That is, what did he want to do?
- Characteristics
  - o What are some of Luke's "characteristic themes"?
- Sources
  - o What sources did Luke use as he wrote his Gospel?
- Plan
  - o What is the main theme of Luke's Gospel?
  - o What is a key verse?

Write

Write your own introduction to Luke's Gospel in your notebook. Tell who the author is, how he got his material and to whom he wrote. State Luke's purpose in writing. Summarize a few of Luke's themes and cite a key verse.

484. Luke 1:1-80

a. What is Luke's Gospel an orderly account of (1:1)? From whom and how has Luke gotten his information (1:1-3)? What kind of details does Luke include to show that these things are certainly true (1:4, 5, 26-27; 2:1-4)?

b. *Zechariah* means "Yahweh has remembered," and *Elizabeth* means "My El has sworn." To which righteous old couple in Genesis did Yahweh promise a child (1:6-7, 13)? What promises does the LORD, the God of Israel, remember (1:54-55, 69, 72-73)? What is the Lord on his way to do (1:71-72, 74, 77, 79)?

c. *John* means "Yahweh shows grace or favor." How does Gabriel greet Mary (Luke 1:28)? Compare the prayer of *Hannah* ("Grace" or "Favor") with the song of Mary: How do they open their prayers (see 1 Samuel 2:1-2; Luke 1:46-49)?

485. Luke 2:1-52

a. Why does Joseph go to the town of David (2:4)? Who is the Lord's Anointed, Lord in the town of David (2:11, 26; see Psalm 2:2, 6)? Who is Jesus' father (Luke 2:48, 49; see 1 Samuel 2:12-14)?

b. Which prophet promised that Israel would be consoled and Jerusalem redeemed (Luke 2:25, 38)? Follow the cross-reference for "the consolation of Israel" (2:25). Compare Isaiah's prophecy with Luke's fulfillment. Who returns to Zion (see Isaiah 52:8; Luke 2:22)? What do the nations see (see Isaiah 52:10; Luke 2:30-32)?

c. Anna's name means "grace" or "favor"; *Phanuel* means "before the face of El"; *Asher* means "happy." Where does Anna live (2:36-37)? What (or who) makes her happy (Luke 2:37; see Psalm 1:1-2)? On whom does God's favor rest (Luke 2:8, 14, 28-29, 36-38, 40, 52)?

486. Luke 3:1-4:13

a. What year was the fifteenth year of the reign of Tiberius Caesar in the provinces (see the study note for 3:1)? Write those dates beside 3:1 in the margin of your Bible. About how old was Jesus when he began his ministry (3:23)? About what year was he born? Double-check your answer with the study note for 2:2. Write those dates in the margin beside 2:1.

b. Who is on his way (3:4)? How does John say to prepare the way for him (3:3, 8)? What does good fruit look like (3:10-14)?

c. Who fills Jesus and leads him into the wilderness (4:1)? What does he lead Jesus to remember and say (4:4, 8, 12)? List what else he has done so far in Luke's Gospel (1:14, 17, 35, 41, 67, 80; 2:26-27; 3:22).

487. Luke 4:14-5:39

a. Who anoints Jesus and makes him the Messiah or Christ (3:21-23; 4:1, 14, 18)? What four things does he anoint Jesus to proclaim (4:18-19)? What is the good news about God's kingdom (4:18-19, 43)?

b. What types of things oppress people (4:33, 38, 40, 41; 5:12, 15, 18, 23)? How does Jesus set them free (4:35, 39, 41; 5:13, 20, 24)? What do Jesus' words have (4:32, 36; 5:17, 24)?

c. Who gives Jesus power and authority (4:14, 18; 5:17)? Why does Jesus go away alone to pray (4:42; 5:16)?

488. Luke 6:1-49

a. What does Jesus do when people are watching him closely to see if he will break their rules (6:8, 10)? Why was it okay for David and why is it okay for Jesus to break the normal rules? (Check the story in 1 Samuel 21:1-6; then read Luke 6:9.) Whose son is Jesus (Luke 1:32)?

(3) Think about and answer the questions. (4) Return to your bookmark.

b. Who leads his people on a level way (6:17; see 3:4-6)? What did Yahweh promise to do in the time of his favor (see Isaiah 49:8-13)? Where do people come from, and what do they want Jesus to do (Luke 6:18-19)?

c. How must we love our enemies (6:31, 35)? What do we want others to do for us (6:36-38)? Whom should we not judge, and whom should we (6:42)?

489.   Luke 7:1-50

a. Is the centurion an Israelite (7:1, 9)? What does the centurion believe Jesus has authority over (7:7-8)? What amazes Jesus (7:9)?

b. What did Isaiah say the Anointed Messiah, "the one who was to come," would do (4:18-19)? What does Jesus do (7:22)? Through which prophets did Yahweh say he would send a messenger ahead of him? See the cross-reference for 7:27; see also Luke 1:17, 76.

c. Who judges rightly (7:29, 35)? Why do sinners love Jesus so much (7:34, 37-38, 44-50)? How much does Jesus care about appearing to be righteous (7:34, 39)?

490.   Luke 8:1-56

a. Who travels with Jesus (8:1-3)? Who are his daughters (8:48, 54)? What do Jesus' family members do (8:1, 3, 21, 48)?

b. What is the difference between hearing and "hearing" (8:10, 12-15, 18, 21)? Who hears and obeys (8:25, 54-55)? Who hears, perseveres and produces a crop (8:15, 49-56)?

c. What lamp does Jesus light and hide (8:10, 16-17)? Who will bring the lamp out and show it to others (8:16-18)? Where does Jesus want to be revealed (8:26, 38-39)? Where does he want to stay hidden (8:40, 56)?

491.   Luke 9:1-50

a. Who is the Son of Man (9:20-21)? What will happen to the woman's offspring when he crushes the serpent's head (see Genesis 3:15)? What will happen to the Son of Man (Luke 9:22, 44)?

b. What does God choose his Son to do (9:35)? Follow the cross-reference for "chosen"; see also Isaiah 49:5-6. What will the Servant do when he leads the people out (see Isaiah 49:9-

10; Luke 9:10-17)? What will happen to the Servant (see Isaiah 52:13-53:12; Luke 9:21-22)?

c. What "departure" do Moses and Elijah talk with Jesus about (9:31; see the translation note)? When Moses led a "departure," entered a cloud on a mountain and saw the glory of God, what did he write and lead the people to make (see Exodus 25:8-9)? When Peter, John and James tell others what they have seen, what will they write (Luke 9:25-36; see John 1:14; 1 John 1:1-3)?

492.   Luke 9:51-10:42

a. When a pair of Jesus' followers enters a town, what is coming near the people (10:8-9, 11)? When people reject Jesus' messengers, whom are they rejecting (10:16)? How does the Son reveal the Father to the seventy-two (10:17, 19, 21-22)?

b. How do people in one Samaritan village treat Jesus (9:52)? When does the Samaritan become the traveler's neighbor (10:33)? What does the Samaritan do when loves his neighbor (10:33, 34, 37)?

c. When Jesus "sets his face" resolutely to go to Jerusalem, which Scripture is he fulfilling (see 9:51 and the study note)? When people want to follow King Jesus and serve in God's kingdom, what must they leave behind (9:57-62)? What one thing is needed (10:39-42)?

493.   Luke 11:1-54

a. To whom should we pray (11:2)? How should we ask (11:5, 8, 9-10)? What will he do (11:9-10, 13)? But who and where are we (11:2, 7, 13)?

b. What does the stronger man do to the strong man (11:21-22)? What does Jesus do to Beelzebul, that is Satan (11:14, 20)? What do people cleansed of an unclean spirit need (11:13, 24-26, 35-36)?

c. What should the Pharisees do to and from the inside (11:41, 42)? What kind of burdens do the scribes (experts in the law) give the people, and how could they have helped them (11:42, 46)? Why does Jesus refer to the deaths of Abel and Zechariah (see 11:51 and the study note)?

494. Luke 12:1-13:21

a. Who knows that you need food and clothes (12:6-7, 22-24, 27-28, 30)? What should you do and not do (12:29, 31)? What will the Father give you (12:31-32)?

b. What is the "present time" the crowd must interpret and recognize (12:40, 46-48, 49)? On which fig tree has Jesus not found fruit for three years (see 13:6-7 and the study note; see also 3:8-9)? What must the people do (12:58; 13:3)?

c. Whom would the synagogue leader set loose and not set loose (13:14-16)? How do the Pharisees and scribes keep the small parts of the law but neglect justice and love, load people down with burdens and not help them (11:42, 46; 13:14)? From which oppressor does Jesus set the daughter of Abraham free (4:18; 13:16)?

495. Luke 13:22-15:31

a. What must Jesus' followers hate; that is, what must they love less than they love Jesus (14:26)? What is it like when someone gives up everything to follow Jesus (14:32-33)?

b. Though many seek and knock, what does the master of the house say (13:25, 27)? What must they do to enter (11:4, 9-10, 13; 13:3)? What does the younger son do (15:18-21)?

c. Whom would the Pharisees and scribes lift up (14:5)? Whom does Jesus lift up (exalt) and eat with (14:11-13, 21; 15:2)? Whom does Jesus not eat with (14:18-20, 24; 15:28-30)?

496. Luke 16:1-17:37

a. What will happen when you are faithful with worldly (or unrighteous) wealth (16:9, 11)? How can you be faithful with worldly wealth (12:32-33, 42-43; 14:13-14)? Why was the rich man not welcomed into eternal dwellings (16:9, 21-23)?

b. When will the kingdom of God come (see 17:20-21 and the study note)? Now that the kingdom of God is being preached, may you forget about the Law and the Prophets (16:16-18)? Did the rich man listen to Moses and the Prophets (16:29, 31)?

c. What must you do when your brother or sister sins against you (17:3)? What must you do when he or she repents; what is your duty as a servant (17:3-4, 9-10)? If this is so hard that it's almost impossible, how can you do it (17:5-6)?

497. Luke 18:1-19:27

a. To whom will God give justice (18:7-8)? Whom does God justify or declare righteous (18:13-14)? Whom does the rich ruler not trust (12:27-33; 18:22-25)? How are children like the widow and the tax collector and unlike the rich ruler (18:17)?

b. What happened to someone else from Bethlehem who was going up to Jerusalem and was delivered over (Luke 18:31-32; see Judges 19:1, 10, 12, 22, 25-26)? What did David prophesy would happen to the Anointed (Luke 18:32; see Psalm 22:6-7, 12-13, 16)? What happened to Lord Yahweh's faithful servant (Luke 8:32-33; see Isaiah 50:6)? Who else "rose from the dead" on the third day (Luke 18:33; see Jonah 1:17)?

c. Who sees, and who does not see (Luke 18:34, 35-37)? How does a rich man enter the kingdom of God (Luke 18:25; 19:8)? How does God make the impossible possible (18:27; 19:5, 10)?

498. Luke 19:28-20:47

a. What does the crowd of disciples call Jesus (19:38)? Whose house does Jesus say the temple is (19:46)? By what authority does Jesus do these things (20:3-4, 8)?

b. In the parable of the tenants, who are the owner, the tenants, the servants and the son (20:9-13)? Who is the stone the builders reject (20:14-15, 17)? When will God give "the vineyard" to other tenants (19:41-44; 20:16)?

c. Is the Messiah David's son (20:41)? To whom does Yahweh say, "Sit at my right hand until I make your enemies a footstool for your feet" (20:42-43)? What makes the Messiah so great that David calls him "my Lord" (20:44)?

499. Luke 21:1-22:38

a. What will the people do to Jesus' followers (21:12, 16-17)? What will God do to the people (21:20-24)? What should Jesus' followers raise their heads and look for when they see Jerusalem surrounded (21:20, 28)?

b. Who is the first to be betrayed, brought before priests and kings and put to death (21:12, 16; 22:2-4)? When will Jesus eat the Passover and drink wine again (22:16, 18)?

c. Who leads Judas to betray Jesus (22:3-4)? What has Satan asked for (22:31)? What has Jesus prayed for (22:32)?

500. Luke 22:39-23:25

    a. Why does Jesus tell the disciples to pray (22:39, 46)? To whom does Jesus pray, and what does he ask for (22:42)? How is Jesus' prayer like the prayer he taught the disciples (see Matthew 6:9-13; Luke 11:2-4)?

    b. What did Jesus say would happen to him (18:32)? What did Jesus say Peter would do (22:34)? What happens (22:57, 58, 60-61, 62-64; 23:1, 11)?

    c. Who do the chief priests and the teachers of the law say Jesus is (22:70)? Who does Pilate say Jesus is (23:3)? What crime does the crowd accuse Jesus of (23:21, 23)?

501. Luke 23:26-24:53

    a. Who is Jesus (23:35)? What must happen to God's Chosen Servant? Follow the cross-reference for "Chosen One"; see also Isaiah 52:13; 53:4-12. What may Jesus have told the two disciples on the road to Emmaus (Luke 24:26-27)?

    b. What is the name of the man who wraps Jesus' body in linen cloth and lays him in a tomb (23:50, 53)? Who all rests on the Sabbath (23:53, 56)? Who are the first people to tell the message "Jesus is risen!" (24:1, 6, 10)?

    c. What all does Jesus open (24:31, 32, 45)? With which eyewitnesses of the things that were fulfilled did Luke talk (1:1-2; 24:44-48)? What do the disciples do when Jesus is taken up to heaven (24:52-53)?

Acts

502.   Acts – Introduction

Pray. Then Read, Think and <u>Mark</u>.

Read your study Bible's introduction to Acts. Think about the questions for each of the following sections. <u>Mark</u> the answers and other things that seem important.

for the ESV Study Bible

- Opening paragraph
    - o   What is the main purpose of Acts?
    - o   With which other book does Acts belong?
    - o   To whom is Acts addressed?
- Author
    - o   Read the first paragraph. Who wrote Acts?
- Date
    - o   Read the last sentence. When was Acts probably written?
- Theme
    - o   Who empowers the believers?
    - o   What do they do?
- Distinctive Features
    - o   Read the first paragraph.
    - o   With which two men does Acts deal primarily?
    - o   Whose ministry do the events of their ministries remind you about? See also Key Theme 14.
    - o   Read the third paragraph. What is the most distinctive feature in Acts?
- Key Themes
    - o   Under what general category can the major themes of Acts be placed?
    - o   In which verse is it set forth?
    - o   What are the first five themes?

for the NIV Study Bible

- Author
  - Read the first paragraph. Who wrote Acts?

- Date
  - When may Acts have been written?

- Recipient
  - To whom is Acts addressed?
  - With which other book does Acts belong?

- Theme and Purpose
  - Read the first paragraph. Which verse summarizes the theme of Acts? What is the theme?
  - Read the fourth purpose.
  - What does the church succeed in doing?
  - How does the church triumph?

- Plan and Outline
  - Read the first paragraph. Around what four things does the design of Acts revolve?

Write

Write your own introduction to Acts. Tell who the author is, to whom he wrote and what book Acts belongs with. State Luke's purpose (ESV) or theme (NIV) and the verse that sets it forth. Describe the spread of the gospel and the church: who, what, where and how. Summarize some of Acts' main themes.

503. Acts 1:1-2:47

a. What happens after Jesus is taken up to heaven (Luke 22:69; Acts 1:9; 2:33)? How does Peter know that is what has happened (Acts 2:34)? Who taught Peter to interpret the Bible this way (Luke 24:44-49; Acts 1:3)?

b. Where will the disciples be Jesus' witnesses (Luke 24:46-48; Acts 1:8; see Isaiah 55:4-7)? What is the Father's promise that Jesus sends (Luke 24:49; Acts 1:4-5, 8; 2:33)? How does the Holy Spirit give the disciples power to witness to the nations (Luke 24:47-49; Acts 1:8; 2:4, 5-11)?

c. What did John preach and promise (Acts 1:5; see Luke 1:77; 3:3, 16)? What must be preached to all nations (Luke 24:47)? What did Yahweh promise to those in Zion who repent of their sins (see Isaiah 59:20-21; Acts 2:38)?

504. Acts 3:1-4:37

a. What did Moses say the people must do to the prophet the Lord their God raises up (4:22)? What did Samuel and Nathan the prophets say about the Messiah (see 3:24 and the study note)? Why did God send his servant to the Israelites first (4:25-26)?

b. What did the leaders of Israel do to Jesus (4:10-11)? Which nations and kings plotted against Jesus the Anointed (4:25-27)? Who planned beforehand, or predestined, that they would do this evil (2:23; 4:28)?

c. How does God help his servants (4:29-31)? What other grace does he give them (4:33-34)? Who taught the disciples to live like this (4:32-35; see Acts 2:42-47; Luke 12:22-34)?

505. Acts 5:1-6:7

a. How does Joseph encourage the believers (4:35-37)? What do Ananias and Sapphira do (5:3, 9)? What does the Lord do (5:5, 10)?

b. Where do the apostles do many signs and wonders (5:12, 15-16; 3:7-8, 11)? Why do the priests and Sadducees oppose the apostles' teaching (5:17; see 4:1-2; 23:8)? Who told the apostles they would suffer for the Name (Acts 5:41; see Luke 21:12-13)?

c. What do the apostles never stop proclaiming (Acts 5:42)? What are the seven men like, and where are they from (6:3, 5)? What happens when the apostles give themselves to prayer and the service of God's word (6:4, 7)?

506. Acts 6:8-7:60

a. Who cannot stand against Stephen's wisdom (Acts 6:10; see Luke 21:12-15;)? Whose face does Stephen's face shine like (Acts 6:15; 7:38; see Exodus 34:29-35)? What does Stephen see as he dies (Acts 7:55-56; see Luke 22:69)?

b. What two things do the foreign Jews say Stephen has said (Acts 6:14)? Before Solomon built a house for him, where did God dwell (7:2, 30-31, 44-47)? What did the prophet Isaiah say about the Lord's dwelling (7:48-50)?

c. Whom did the Israelites reject (7:9, 27-29)? Through which leader did God save the Israelites (7:10-15, 34-36)? Which leader has the Sanhedrin rejected (Acts 7:52, 55-56; Luke 22:69-71)?

(3) Think about and answer the questions. (4) Return to your bookmark.

507.   Acts 8:1-40

a.   What do the Holy Spirit's signs make the people do (8:6, 8, 13)? Who must come before believers in Samaria receive the Holy Spirit (8:14-17; see Matthew 16:18-19)? How is the Holy Spirit different from other spirits and powers (8:6-7, 13, 20)?

b.   What passage is the Ethiopian eunuch reading (8:28, 32-33)? What did Yahweh promise in Isaiah 55:5-7? To whom did he give special promises in Isaiah 56:3-8 (see Deuteronomy 23:1)?

c.   How does God take the good news from Jerusalem to Judea and Samaria (Acts 8:1, 4)? How does God take the good news to the Ethiopian eunuch (8:26, 29-30)? What does the good news give those who believe (8:8, 39)?

508.   Acts 9:1-43

a.   Use your study Bible's timeline of events in Paul's life to write the following years in the margins of your Bible.

    ○   Beside 7:1, write the year Saul probably witnessed Stephen's stoning.

    ○   Beside 9:1, write the year Saul probably went to Damascus.

    ○   Beside 9:23, write the year Saul probably went to Jerusalem.

b.   Who does Saul know the voice is (9:4-5a)? What will Saul do (9:15-16)? What does Saul see now (9:17-18, 20, 22)?

c.   Who does Peter act like (9:39-41; see Luke 8:51-55)? What do Jesus and Peter say to the little girl and the woman (Acts 9:40; see Mark 5:41)?

509.   Acts 10:1-11:18

a.   How did Yahweh teach the Israelites to be holy, different from the other peoples (see Deuteronomy 14:2-3, 8, 10, 12, 21)? What kinds of animals are in the large sheet (Acts 10:11)? What does God tell Peter (10:13, 15)?

b.   What kind of person is Peter staying with in Joppa (see 9:43 and the study note)? What kinds of animals are in the sheet (10:12)? What kinds of nations does God accept (10:34)?

c.   What kinds of nations do the apostles and believers not accept (11:1-3)? Who gave Peter a vision, told Peter to go with the men, told Cornelius to send for Peter and came on Cornelius and his household (11:5-10, 12, 13-14, 15)? How do the apostles and believers respond to what God has done (11:18)?

James

510. James – Introduction

Pray. Then Read, Think and <u>Mark</u>.

Read your study Bible's introduction to James' letter. Think about the questions for each of the following sections. <u>Mark</u> the answers and other things that seem important.

for the ESV Study Bible

- Author
    - o Read the first paragraph. Who wrote James?
- Date
    - o When was James most likely written?
- Theme
    - o What is James' primary theme?
    - o What two conflicts does he write about?
    - o What does James challenge his readers to seek?
- Purpose, Occasion, and Background
    - o To whom did James write?
    - o What was happening to them?
- Literary Features
    - o Read the first two sentences.
    - o What is James a collection of?
    - o What Old Testament books is James' genre (or style) like?

for the NIV Study Bible

- Author
    - o Read the first paragraph.
    - o What is the name of the person who wrote James (1:1)?
    - o Which James is he?
- Date
    - o When did James probably write this letter?

- Recipients
  - o To whom did James write?
  - o What was happening to them?
  - o How and why did James write?
- Distinctive Characteristics
  - o What are the first, second, fourth and fifth distinctive characteristics of James?

Write

Write your own introduction to James. Tell who the author is and when he wrote his letter. Say whom he wrote to, and describe what was happening in their lives. State James' emphasis or primary theme. Describe James' style and identify the Old Testament books his style is like.

511. James 1:1-5:20

a. What does pure religion do (1:27)? Which law does pure religion keep (2:8, 12-13)? Which of our neighbors does God especially choose and hear (2:5; 5:4)?

b. Why did God credit righteousness to Abraham; that is why did God count Abraham righteous (2:23)? How did Abraham fulfill God's counting him righteous (2:21, 23)? If you have faith that does not act, is your faith complete and faithful (2:17, 20, 22)?

c. How does temptation begin (1:13-14)? What causes fights and quarrels among you (4:1-2)? What does the wisdom that comes from heaven above make you like (3:13, 17)?

512. Acts 11:19-13:12

a. What leads a great number of Greeks to believe and turn to the Lord (11:20-21)? What does Barnabas' name mean, and what does he do when he comes to Antioch (see 4:36; 11:22-24)? What are the disciples in Antioch called (11:26)?

b. How does the Lord protect Peter and other believers (12:7-11, 23)? Who is conquering kingdoms (12:24)? Who is the James Peter tells the believers to tell about his rescue (see 12:17 and the study note)?

c. What all does the Holy Spirit do for Barnabas and Saul (11:24; 13:2, 4, 9)? Whom is Saul speaking to when Luke calls Saul by a different name (13:7, 9)? What do the Lord's apostles say to sorcerers (13:6, 8-11; 8:9, 18-24)?

513. Acts 13:13-14:28

a. When Paul speaks to Jews in Antioch, what story does he tell them (13:17-23)? How did God fulfill his promise to David (13:32-37)? What words of the prophets did Jesus fulfill so that he could forgive sins and declare believers right (see Isaiah 53:7-9, 11)?

b. What did the prophet Habakkuk say would happen to Israelites who scoff (Acts 13:41; see Habakkuk 1:5-6)? How do many Jews respond to Paul's message (Acts 13:45, 50; 14:2, 5, 19)? What did Isaiah say Yahweh's servant would do (Acts 13:47; Isaiah 49:5-6)?

c. When Paul speaks to non-Jews in Lystra, how does he identify God; that is, who does he say God is (14:15)? What does this God do for the nations (14:17)? What does Barnabas do for the new disciples (14:22-23)?

---

(3) Think about and answer the questions. (4) Return to your bookmark.

Galatians

514.   Galatians – Introduction

Pray. Then Read, Think and <u>Mark</u>.

Read your study Bible's introduction to Galatians. Think about the questions for each of the following sections. <u>Mark</u> the answers and other things that seem important.

for the ESV Study Bible

- Author
  - Who wrote Galatians?
- Date
  - When did Paul probably write this letter?
- Theme
  - What happens in the new covenant?
  - What is the heart of the gospel?
- Purpose, Occasion, and Background
  - Read the first paragraph.
  - What do the false teachers require the believers in Galatia to do?
  - What may the false teachers want to escape?
- Key Themes
  - What are the fifth and sixth key themes?

for the NIV Study Bible

- Author
  - Who wrote Galatians?
- Date
  - Read "2. The South Galatian theory." When did Paul probably write this letter?
- Occasion and Purpose
  - Who are the Judaizers?
  - What do they teach?

   o   What may they be trying to avoid?
   o   According to Paul, how are people justified?
   o   How are believers to live out their new lives?
 • Theological Teaching
   o   What does obedience come from?

Write

Write your own introduction to Galatians. Tell who the author is and when and to whom he wrote his letter. Say who the false teachers are. Describe their teaching, and suggest what they may be trying to avoid. State Paul's main theme, and summarize his argument against the false teachers.

515.   Galatians 1:1-4:7

a.   Who sent Paul and gave him his gospel (1:1, 11-12)? When Paul met with James, Cephas and John, what did they add to his message (2:6-8)? Why did Cephas stop eating with Gentiles (2:12-13)?

b.   How are Abraham and the Jews justified or counted righteous (2:15-16; 3:6)? Who are blessed along with Abraham and become his children (3:7-9)? How do they receive the blessing (3:2, 14)?

c.   What did the law do for us (3:23)? Who become the children of God (3:26-28)? How do Paul and the children of God live (2:20; 4:6)?

516.   Galatians 4:8-6:18

a.   If the Gentile believers allow themselves to be circumcised, what will happen to them (5:2-4)? What value does circumcision have (5:6)? In the new creation, who is the Israel of God (3:7-8, 26-29; 4:6-7, 31; 6:15-16)?

b.   How do we wait for righteousness (5:5)? What is the only thing that counts (5:6)? How do we obey the truth (5:6-7, 14)?

c.   Who sets us free (5:1, 18)? What happens to people who use their freedom to act any way their flesh (or sinful nature) wants (5:13, 19-21)? What happens when we live by the Spirit (5:16, 22-25)?

517. Acts 15:1-16:5

a. What do the believers who belong to the party of the Pharisees say the believers from other nations must do (15:1, 5)? How does Peter know God accepts believers from other nations (15:8-9)? How are Jewish and non-Jewish believers saved (15:11)?

b. When the LORD rebuilds David's tent (the kingdom of Israel), what else does he promise will happen (15:16-17; see Amos 9:11-12)? With whom was God making a covenant when he first told people not to eat blood (Acts 15:20; Genesis 9:4, 17)? How do the apostles and elders make this decision (15:2, 6, 7, 12, 13, 28)?

c. What happens when the Gentile believers hear the message from the apostles and elders (15:30-32; 16:4-5)? Who is Timothy's mother (16:1)? Why does Paul circumcise Timothy (16:1-3)?

518. Acts 16:6-18:17

a. In what different ways does the Holy Spirit send Paul from one place to the next (16:6-7, 9-10; 17:10, 14)? To which kinds of people do Paul and Silas preach the good news (16:14; 17:2-3, 10-11, 17, 22; 18:4)? Who believe and who are baptized (16:15, 33-34; 18:8)?

b. Which kinds of people oppose the gospel (16:19; 17:5, 13; 18:6, 12-13)? Which kingdoms is the kingdom of Jesus the Anointed Messiah conquering (16:20-21, 38-39; 17:2-4, 6-7, 12, 34; 18:8, 13)? Whose words are being fulfilled (see Luke 21:12-16)?

c. When he speaks to the philosophers in Athens, what Athenian title does Paul use for God (Acts 17:23)? Though Paul uses their words to teach about the Creator, which god were the Greek poets talking about (see 17:28 and the study note)? Why does God command all people everywhere to repent (17:30-31)?

1 and 2 Thessalonians

519.   Thessalonians – Introduction

Pray. Then Read, Think and <u>Mark</u>.

Read your study Bible's introduction to 1 and 2 Thessalonians. Think about the questions for each of the following sections. <u>Mark</u> the answers and other things that seem important.

for the ESV Study Bible

- 1 Thessalonians: Author and Title
  - o Read the first sentence. Who wrote 1 Thessalonians?
- 2 Thessalonians: Author and Title
  - o Read the first sentence. Who wrote 2 Thessalonians?
- 1 Thessalonians: Date
  - o Read the first sentence. When and from where was 1 Thessalonians written?
- 2 Thessalonians: Date
  - o When and from where was 2 Thessalonians written?
- 1 Thessalonians: Theme
  - o What is the most prominent theme in Thessalonians?
- 1 Thessalonians: Purpose, Occasion, and Background
  - o Read the eighth paragraph ("When Paul heard...").
  - o What are Paul's two main purposes?
  - o Read the ninth paragraph.
  - o How does Paul seek to encourage the Thessalonians?
  - o To what two things does Paul call the new believers?

for the NIV Study Bible

- 1 Thessalonians: Author, Date and Place of Writing
  - o Read the first sentence. Who wrote 1 Thessalonians?
  - o Read the first sentence of the second paragraph. When and from where was 1 Thessalonians written?

- 2 Thessalonians: Author, Date and Place of Writing
    - Read the first sentence. Who wrote 2 Thessalonians?
    - Read the second paragraph. When and from where was 2 Thessalonians written?
- 1 Thessalonians: Purpose
    - What are Paul's three purposes in writing these letters?
- 1 Thessalonians: Theme
    - What subject seems to be predominant in both letters?
    - Eschatology is the study of the end, that is, of last things.

Write

Write your own introduction to 1 and 2 Thessalonians. Tell who the author is, where he is and when and to whom he writes. List Paul's main purposes in writing these letters. State the main theme of the two letters.

520.   1 Thessalonians 1:1-5:28

a. How did the Thessalonian believers become imitators of the Lord, of Paul and of the churches in Judea (1:6; 2:14-15)? What does Timothy say to encourage the Thessalonian believers in their faith (3:1-5)? What good news does Timothy bring back to Paul (3:6)?

b. What should believers be like when our Lord Jesus comes (3:13)? What will the Lord do to those who commit sexual sins (4:3-6)? What should the believers' daily life be like (4:11-12)?

c. Whom will God bring with Jesus when he comes down from heaven (4:14, 16)? Who all will meet the Lord in the air when he comes (4:14-17)? What should we do with Paul's teaching about Christ's coming (4:18)?

521.   2 Thessalonians 1:1-3:18

a. What is happening to the believers in Thessalonica (1:3-6; 3:2)? What will the Lord Jesus do to those who do not believe and obey his good news (1:6, 8, 9; 2:10, 12)? What will the Lord do for the believers until then (1:11-12; 3:4-5, 16)?

b. What will happen before the coming of the Lord Jesus and the day of the Lord (2:1-3)? What will the man of lawlessness do (2:4, 9-10)? Who will kill and destroy the man of lawlessness (2:8)?

c. What was Paul, Silas and Timothy's daily life like when they were in Thessalonica (3:7-9)? What was their rule (3:10)? What should our lives be like (3:13)?

522.   **Acts 18:18-20:3**

a.   It's helpful to know when the events in Paul's life are happening. Write the following years or names of his letters in the margins beside the following verses:
   - Beside 18:1 write "51"
   - Beside 18:5 write "1 Thess."
   - Beside 18:11 write "52" and "2 Thess."
   - Beside 18:23 write "53"
   - Beside 19:10 write "55"
   - Beside 19:21 write "1 Cor."

b.   What do Priscilla and Aquila explain to Apollos (18:26)? What do people receive when they believe and are baptized into Jesus' name (18:25; 19:1-6)? Who all hear the word of the Lord (19:10)?

c.   How is the Lord's power greater than the power of Sceva's sons and the power of the magicians (19:11-20)? What is the silversmith Demetrius worried about (19:24, 27)? How does Paul describe this power struggle (see 1 Corinthians 15:32; 2 Corinthians 1:8)?

I Corinthians

523. I Corinthians – Introduction

Pray. Then Read, Think and <u>Mark</u>.

Read your study Bible's introduction to 1 Corinthians. Think about the questions for each of the following sections. <u>Mark</u> the answers and other things that seem important.

for the ESV Study Bible

- Author and Title
  - Who wrote 1 Corinthians?

- Date
  - Where was he when he wrote 1 Corinthians?
  - What verses in Acts mention that time?

- Theme
  - What did Paul want the believers in Corinth to do?

- Purpose, Occasion, and Background
  - Read the first paragraph. What mingles in Corinth?
  - Read the third paragraph.
  - What did Paul deal with in his first letter to the believers in Corinth?
  - How did Paul find out about what was happening among the believers in Corinth?
  - Read the fourth paragraph ("In response to ..."). What was the root of the believers' disunity?
  - Read the fifth paragraph ("At the root ..."). What must God's people be like?

- The Ancient City of Corinth
  - Read the fourth paragraph ("In Paul's day ...").
  - What dotted the city?
  - What was common in this port city?

for the NIV Study Bible

- Author and Date
    - Who wrote 1 Corinthians?
    - When did he write it?
    - Where was he when he wrote it?
- The City of Corinth
    - Read the first two paragraphs. Where is Corinth? (See Map 13 in the back of your study Bible.)
    - Read paragraph 3 "Its religion." What kinds of temples were in Corinth?
    - Read paragraph 4 "Its immorality." What other big problem was common in Corinth?
- Occasion and Purpose
    - Read the first paragraph. How did Paul find out about the conditions in the church in Corinth?
    - Read the second paragraph. What did Paul write about in his first letter to the believers in Corinth?
    - Read the third and fourth paragraphs.
    - What were Paul's purposes for writing?
- Theme
    - What is the theme of 1 Corinthians?

Write

Write your own introduction to 1 Corinthians. Tell who the author is, where he is and when he writes. Describe the first letter he wrote them and what he heard later on. Connect their problems with problems in the city of Corinth. State Paul's theme and summarize his purposes for writing this letter. Outline 1 Corinthians under eight headings.

524.   I Corinthians 1:1-4:21

a. What do the people God has called think about the message of Christ's cross (1:24)? How does Paul tell his message (2:4, 13)? What does the Spirit do for believers (2:11, 12, 16)?

b. What are the believers in Corinth quarreling about (3:3-5)? How many temples are there (3:16-17)? What is the foundation of the temple (3:10-11)?

c. What do you have that you can boast about (4:7)? What has God done to the apostles (4:9-12)? What should the Corinthian believers do with the Apostle Paul's life (4:16-17)?

525. 1 Corinthians 5:1-7:40

    a.   From which Old Testament book does Paul quote to instruct believers how to live together in community (5:13)? Who should judge disputes between believers (6:1)? What is Paul's judgment about a sexually immoral man in the church gathering (5:4-5, 12-13)?

    b.   What must the Corinthian believers be careful not to be deceived about (6:9-10)? What are believers' bodies (6:15)? Where is the temple in Corinth (6:19-20)?

    c.   What should believers who are married do (7:2-5, 10-11)? What should believers who are not married do (7:8-9)? Why does Paul advise believers who are not yet married to stay unmarried (7:26, 28, 29, 31)?

526. 1 Corinthians 8:1-11:1

    a.   What rule sums up Paul's instruction in chapters 8-11 (10:31)? Why does Paul give thanks for anything he eats (8:6; 10:25, 26, 30)? How else does Paul eat or drink (or not eat or drink) for the glory of God (8:13; 10:24, 32-33)?

    b.   What happened to our ancestors even though they were baptized and ate and drank spiritual food and drink (10:1-7)? When people eat or drink food or drink sacrificed to an idol, with whom are they participating (10:20-21)? Which food should you not eat when an unbeliever invites you to dinner (10:27-28)?

    c.   Against whom did our ancestors grumble? Follow the cross-references for "and were killed (or destroyed)" in 10:9-10. Whom do some grumble against (1 Corinthians 9:2-3)? Why should we, like Paul, not use our rights (9:12, 15, 19-23; 10:32-11:1)?

527. 1 Corinthians 11:2-12:31

    a.   Who is a man's head, and who is a woman's head (11:3)? Who is a man's glory, and what is a woman's glory (11:7, 15)? How should a man pray, and how should a woman pray (11:4, 5, 13)?

    b.   What must we discern when we eat the bread and drink the cup (11:29)? What is the body of Christ (10:16, 17; 11:23-24, 29; 12:13, 27)? How should we eat (10:31; 11:33)?

    c.   How many spirits, lords, gods and bodies are there (8:6; 12:4-6, 11, 13, 20)? How many body parts and kinds of gifts and services are there (12:4-6, 12, 14, 20, 27)? What is the purpose of the many parts and gifts (12:7, 14-20)?

528. I Corinthians 13:1-14:40

a. What are the greatest spiritual gifts and acts worth if you have no love (12:31-13:3)? When we see face to face and know fully, what will we still need (13:18-10, 12)? List out the things love is and does (13:4-8).

b. How do Paul and others speak, pray and sing in tongues (14:2, 14-15)? How are those who prophesy greater than those who speak in tongues (14:1-5)? What should believers do with prophecy and speaking in tongues (14:1, 39)?

c. Which three types of speaking does Paul write about in 14:27, 28, 29-32? Who all may prophesy (11:4, 5; 14:31)? What does the Law say about who should have taught and led whom in the Garden of Eden (1 Corinthians 14:34; see Genesis 2:15-17, 22, 24; 3:6, 12, 17)?

529. I Corinthians 15:1-16:24

a. If there is no resurrection of the dead, then who could not have been raised (15:12-13)? But what are the four parts of the gospel that Paul preached and the Corinthian believers received (15:3-5)? After he was raised, to whom all did Christ appear (15:5-8)?

b. How long must Christ keep reigning (15:24-25)? How does Christ destroy his last enemy (15:26, 51-57)? What will happen after we are all made alive (15:22-24, 27-28)?

c. Why do Paul, Sosthenes and other believers endanger themselves every hour (15:29-32, 57-58)? Is Paul's work in Ephesus going well, or is it hard (16:8-9)? How should we do everything we do (15:14, 22, 24)?

2 Corinthians

530. 2 Corinthians - Introduction

Pray. Then Read, Think and <u>Mark</u>.

Read your study Bible's introduction to 2 Corinthians. Think about the questions for each of the following sections. <u>Mark</u> the answers and other things that seem important.

for the ESV Study Bible
- Author and Title
    - Who wrote 2 Corinthians?
    - How many letters did he probably write to the believers in Corinth?
    - To whom does he write this letter?
- Date
    - When and from where did Paul write 2 Corinthians?
    - Flip back to Acts 20:2. In the margin write "2 Cor."
- Theme
    - What is the central theme of 2 Corinthians?
- Purpose, Occasion, and Background
    - Read the first two paragraphs.
    - Did Paul's first two letters or his quick trip to Corinth help the believers there accept Paul as an apostle and his message as true?
    - What was Paul's next letter like?
    - Who probably took that letter to Corinth?
    - Read the third paragraph ("To Paul's great joy...").
    - Whom did Paul meet in Macedonia?
    - What were some people in the church in Corinth still doing?
    - Read the last paragraph ("Paul's letter..."). What were Paul's three overlapping purposes?

for the NIV Study Bible

- Author
    - o Who wrote 2 Corinthians?
- Recipients
    - o To whom does he write this letter?
- Date
    - o When and from where did Paul write 2 Corinthians?
    - o Flip back to Acts 20:2. In the margin write "2 Cor."
- Occasion
    - o Read the first paragraph.
    - o How many letters did Paul probably write to the believers in Corinth?
    - o Where was Paul when he wrote 1 Corinthians?
    - o After Paul wrote 1 Corinthians, who came to Corinth?
    - o What did they challenge?
    - o Read the second paragraph.
    - o Did Paul's first two letters or his quick trip to Corinth help the believers there accept Paul as an apostle and his message as true?
    - o What was Paul's next letter like?
    - o Who probably took that letter to Corinth?
    - o Read the third paragraph.
    - o When Paul left Ephesus, where did he go?
    - o Whom did he meet there?
    - o What news did he bring?
    - o Read the fourth paragraph. What were some people in the church in Corinth still doing?
- Purposes
    - o Read purposes 3, 6, 7, 8 and 9. What is the true nature of Christian ministry; what is it really like?

Write

Write your own introduction to 2 Corinthians. Tell who the author is, where he is and when he writes. Describe what has happened since he wrote his first two letters to them and what some of them are still doing. State Paul's theme and purposes in writing this letter. Outline 2 Corinthians under three or four headings.

531. 2 Corinthians 1:1-3:18

a. What trouble did Paul experience in Asia (2 Corinthians 1:8; see Acts 19)? Why did this suffering happen (2 Corinthians

1:5-6, 9)? What is God like, and what does he do for us (1:3-4)?

b. How does Paul behave and make his plans (1:12, 15, 17)? Why did Paul decide to leave Troas, even though the Lord had opened a door for him (2:12-13)? From a different perspective, how is Paul led (2:14)?

c. What happened to Moses' face (3:7)? Follow the cross-reference for *glory*. How are Israelites in Paul's day like the Israelites' in Moses' day (2 Corinthians 3:14-15)? What happens to believers who look at the Lord's glory (3:18)?

532.   2 Corinthians 4:1-7:16

a. What glorious treasure do we keep in clay jars (4:6)? What happens to clay jars as they carry the glorious treasure (4:8-9; 6:4-10)? What does this show (4:7, 10)?

b. When will we be clothed in our "heavenly dwelling" (5:1-5, 8)? When is the new creation and the day of salvation (5:17; 6:2)? What happens when we are reconciled to God, when we make peace with God (5:19-21)?

c. Why must the captives touch no unclean thing as they come out (see 2 Corinthians 6:17 and follow the cross-reference to Isaiah)? What does God say the people will be (2 Corinthians 6:16, 18)? What unclean things does Paul tell the Corinthian believers to separate themselves from (2 Corinthians 6:14-16; 7:1)?

533.   2 Corinthians 8:1-9:15

a. What have the believers in Achaia promised (9:2, 5)? Why is Paul sending Titus and two other brothers to Corinth ahead of him (8:6; 9:2-5)? How is Paul handling the money carefully (8:19-21)?

b. Who gives people seed before they plant and bread after they harvest (9:10)? Why does God give some people plenty (8:14; 9:8-11)? What happens when they give (9:12-15)?

c. How did our Lord Jesus Christ give (8:9)? How did the Macedonian believers give (8:1-5)? How should the believers in Achaia give (9:6-7)?

534. 2 Corinthians 10:1-13:14

a. Who have spoken against Paul and put him down (11:5-6, 12-14; 12:11)? What does Paul fight against (10:4-5)? How does he fight against them (10:5)?

b. How does Paul speak in chapters 11 and 12 (11:16-18, 21; 12:1, 11)? What does Paul boast about to show that he really is an apostle (11:23-30; 12:5, 9, 10)? Why did God give Paul a thorn in his flesh (12:7-9)?

c. What is Paul fighting for in the church in Corinth (10:6; 11:2; 12:20-21; 13:2, 10)? How does Paul show his love for the believers in Corinth (11:7-9, 11; 12:13-15, 19; 13:9-10)? How does Paul close this letter (13:11-14)?

Romans

535.   Romans – Introduction

Pray. Then Read, Think and <u>Mark</u>.

Read your study Bible's introduction to Romans. Think about the questions for each of the following sections. <u>Mark</u> the answers and other things that seem important.

for the ESV Study Bible

- Author and Title
  - Who wrote Romans?
- Date
  - When and from where did Paul write Romans?
  - Flip back to Acts 20:3 and write "Rom." in the margin.
- Theme
  - What is the theme of Romans?
- Purpose, Occasion, and Background
  - Read the second paragraph. What particular issues does Paul want to address?
  - Read the third and fourth paragraphs. When did the church in Rome start, and how did it grow?
  - Read the fifth paragraph ("Paul's selection ..."). For what two reasons did Paul write Romans?
  - Read the last paragraph. What does Paul want the Gentiles to come to in order to bring glory to God?
- Key Themes
  - Read themes 1, 2, 5, 6, 8, 9 and 11.

for the NIV Study Bible

- Author
  - Who wrote Romans?

- Date and Place of Writing
  - When and from where did Paul write Romans?

- Recipients
  - What types of people are in the church at Rome?

- Major Theme
  - What is the major theme of Romans?
  - *Justification* means being declared righteous.

- Purpose
  - What are Paul's three purposes in writing Romans?

- Occasion
  - Where was Paul when he wrote Romans?
  - Flip back to Acts 20:3 and write "Rom." in the margin.

- Content
  - How did God provide salvation?
  - How do we receive salvation?
  - How does God provide to free believers from sin, law and death?

Write

Write your own introduction to Romans. Tell who the author is, where he is and when he writes. Explain what types of people are in the church in Rome. State the theme of Romans and Paul's purposes for writing. Summarize the content or themes of Romans. Outline Romans under eight or nine headings. Use the word "righteousness" whenever it fits.

536. Romans 1:1-3:20

a. To what does Paul call the Gentile nations (1:5)? Paul's thesis (the summary of his main point) is in 1:16-17. Copy it out. Then circle these key words: faith, believe, righteous.

b. What do all people know about God (1:19-20, 21, 32)? What do all people know about the way they act (1:32; 2:1, 14-15)? By what standards does God judge Jews and the other nations (2:12)?

c. Who will be declared righteous (2:13)? But does the law help people live righteously, or does it show them that they are sinful and unrighteous (3:20)? So will anyone be able to keep the law enough for God to declare him or her righteous (justify him) (3:20)?

Every day: (1) Follow your bookmark and pray. (2) Read and <u>mark</u> *the passage.*

537. Romans 3:21-5:11

a. If people cannot keep the law enough to be declared right-eous, how can someone get righteousness (3:22)? Who is the atonement, propitiation or covering for sins (3:25)? What does *justify* mean (4:2-3)

b. Did Abraham have to be circumcised in order to be justified (4:9-11)? To whom does God credit righteousness (4:3, 22-24)? Whose father is Abraham (4:11-12, 16-18)?

c. What other gracious gifts does God give us when we believe and he justifies us (5:1, 2, 5, 11; see 2:7, 10)? How has God shown us how great his love for us is (5:8)? How does God save us from the wrath he is revealing against human wick-edness (1:18; 5:9-10)?

538. Romans 5:12-8:39

a. What are the different effects of Adam's one act and Christ's one act (5:18-19)? How does being united with Christ change the way we live (6:3-4, 6-7, 8, 10-11)? What does obedience from the heart lead to (6:16-17, 19, 22)?

b. Why does Paul call himself "wretched" (7:24; see 7:18-23)? What happens when we walk or live according to the Spirit (8:4)? So how can you live righteously (8:4, 5-6, 9-10, 13)?

c. What will happen to the creation when God's children are revealed (8:14-21)? For what good purpose is God working all things together (8:28-29)? What must we remember when we suffer through hard or painful times (8:18, 28, 35, 37-39)?

539. Romans 9:1-11:36

a. Which of Abraham's descendants are counted as his off-spring (9:6-13; see 4:11-12, 16)? What does salvation depend on (9:8, 11, 15-16, 18)? What rights does God have over the "clay pots" he has made (9:19-23; see Genesis 2:7)?

b. How did the people of Israel try to get to righteousness (Romans 9:31-32; 10:3)? How do you get righteousness (9:30; 10:4, 6, 8-10)? Was it because they did not hear and understand that the Israelites did not believe (10:16, 18, 19, 21)?

c. Whom has God not rejected (11:2, 5, 7)? Why does God bind everyone in disobedience and sin (11:32)? What does Paul do when he finishes trying to explain the great wisdom of God's ways (11:33-36)?

540. Romans 12:1-15:13

a. Why should we offer our bodies to God as a living sacrifice (12:1; see 3:22-25; 5:1-9; 8:1-4, 32, 38-39 etc.)? How do we renew our mind (12:2; see 8:5-6)? What does a transformed life look like (12:2, 9; 13:8-10)?

b. Why do some people with weak faith eat only vegetables and no meat (14:2, 6, 14; see Daniel 1:8 and the study note there)? What must all believers do (Romans 14:5, 19, 23)? What is the rule that tells us whether and how to accept or welcome another person (15:7)?

c. What promises did God give Abraham and the patriarchs (15:8; see 4:13, 16-18)? With whom have the Gentile believers from other nations joined (15:10, 12)? How do Jews and Gentiles and weak and strong live together as God's holy people (12:3-5, 9-10, 16, 18; 13:8; 14:17-19; 15:5-7, 13)?

541. Romans 15:14-16:27

a. Just like a priest, what does Paul prepare the Gentile nations to be (15:16-17)? What must Gentile believers do (1:5; 15:18; 16:26)? Who does all this great work (1:5; 15:15-19)?

b. Where does Paul want to proclaim the good news about Christ (15:20-22)? How can the saints in Rome help Paul (1:10-13; 15:24, 29-32)? What phrase describes who believers are and how they live (16:2, 8, 11, 12, 13)?

c. Under whose feet did God promise to crush Satan the serpent? Follow the cross-reference for "will soon crush" (16:20). So how will God crush Satan under our feet (Romans 16:20; see 12:4-5)? Then what will happen for God in his creation (Genesis 3:17-19; Romans 8:17-23; 11:36; 16:25-27)?

542. Romans – Review

Pray. Think through the following points.

You've now read all of Romans. Today you will think back over the book.

a. Reread your own introduction to the book.

b. What was the theme of Romans? What were Paul's purposes for writing this letter?

c. Look back through the book. Note the words and verses you marked. What are the main things God was teaching the saints in Rome? How do these things help Jews and Gentiles in the church live in peace with each other?

d. Look again at your outline of the book. Then read your summary (your answer to question *g*) for each day's reading. What all was Paul saying about faith and righteousness?
e. What things seemed important to you?
f. Look back at your answers to question *d* each day. What were some things you discovered on your own?
g. Think back through your answers to question *f* each day. What are some key ways God is teaching you to change the way you love, think or live?

Write

Write a review of Romans. In the first paragraph state the theme of the book and summarize what Paul says about faith and righteousness. In the second paragraph explain how Paul's teaching will help different kinds of believers live in peace with each other. In the third paragraph, write about the things that seemed most important to you and how God is changing you. End your review with a prayer that glorifies God for his mercy to the nations ... and to you.

543. Acts 20:3-21:26

    a. When do believers gather to break bread (20:6-7)? What do elders do in the church (20:17-18, 28)? How do believers relate to each other (20:7, 11, 17, 32, 36-38; 21:1, 4-6, 7, 8-9, 12-14, 16, 17)?

    b. Through whom does the Holy Spirit speak to Paul (20:23; 21:4, 9, 10-11)? What does the Holy Spirit compel Paul to do (20:22-23; 21:13)? What does Paul keep doing in order to finish the course of his race (20:20, 21, 24, 25, 26, 27, 31, 36)?

    c. What do James and the elders in Jerusalem do when Paul tells them about what God has done among the Gentiles (21:20)? How does Paul live among believers from other nations and teach them to live (Acts 21:25; see 1 Corinthians 9:19, 21-23; Galatians 2:3)? How does Paul live among Jewish believers and teach them to live (Acts 16:1-5; 18:18; 21:21-24; see 1 Corinthians 9:19-20, 22-23)?

544. Acts 21:27-23:11

    a. What are the Jews from Asia worried about (21:28)? Who is supposed to be allowed into the temple courts (21:28-29; see Mark 11:15-18)? What does Paul say to make the crowd shout, "Rid the earth of him!" (Acts 22:21-22)?

    b. Where is Paul from, and what language does he speak (21:37, 39, 40; 22:3, 27-28)? How does Paul describe the way he once lived (22:3)? Why does Paul call himself a Pharisee and say he hopes in the resurrection of the dead (23:6-8)?

    c. How does Paul get opportunities to testify about Jesus (21:33, 39-40; 22:1, 30; 23:11; see Luke 21:12-15)? What exactly do the Jews accuse Paul of (22:30; 23:9)? Who else was accused by a mob in Jerusalem, tried by the Sanhedrin and held by the Romans (see Luke 22:47, 54, 66; 23:1-5)?

545. Acts 23:12-24:27

    a. Who threatens Paul, and who protects him (23:12-15, 16, 23; see Romans 15:31)? What is the commander or tribune's verdict (23:29)? What three things does Ananias accuse Paul of (24:5-6)?

    b. How does Paul respond to Ananias's charges (24:12-13, 18)? How does Paul describe his faith: How is it similar to and different from the "faith" of his Jewish accusers (24:14-15)? What is "the Way" (24:14, 22)? Look at your answers to questions 484b and 486b.

Every day: (1) Follow your bookmark and pray. (2) Read and mark the passage.

c. What does Paul say that frightens the governor Felix (24:24-25)? What does Paul call Jesus (24:24; see Acts 17:30-31; Romans 1:4; 2:16)? Why does Paul end up being held for two years (24:26-27)?

546. Acts 25:1-26:32

a. What is no one able to do about Paul (23:28-29; 25:18-20, 25-27)? What is the verdict of the governor and the king (25:25; 26:31)? How does Paul get opportunities to testify about Jesus to two governors, a king and Caesar (23:11, 26-30; 25:6-7, 10-12; 26:16-17, 22)?

b. What does Paul call the Pharisees (26:5; see 24:5, 14)? What is God's promise to the ancestors that the twelve tribes are hoping to see fulfilled (26:6-7, 8, 23; see 25:19)? How does Paul describe his message (26:22-23; see Luke 24:44-48)?

c. What did the Lord send Paul to do for the Gentiles (26:18)? What is Paul's message (26:20; see Luke 3:3, 8)? What is Paul's prayer for King Agrippa and everyone listening to him (26:29)?

547. Acts 27:1-28:31

a. What opposes Paul now (27:7, 14-18, 20, 41)? Why must Paul survive (27:24)? What did God give or grant Paul (27:24)?

b. Which gods are unable to stop God's servant Paul (27:20; 28:4-6, 11)? How does God have the good news declared among the islands (27:26; 28:1, 8-9)? Whose prayer does God answer (28:15; see Romans 16:30-32)?

c. What is the hope of Israel (Acts 28:20)? See your answer to question 544b. What does King Jesus fulfill (28:23)? Which scripture do the unbelieving Jews fulfill (28:24-27)?

548. Luke-Acts – Review

Pray. Think through the following points.

You've now read both of Luke's volumes. Today you will think back over Luke's Gospel and Acts.

a. Reread your own introduction to each book (lessons 483 and 502).

b. What were the purpose and key themes of Luke's Gospel? What were the purpose and themes of Acts?

c. Meditate on Luke 24:13-27, 44-49. What are the main things God was doing through Jesus and through the apostles?

    d.   Look back through both books. Note the words and verses you marked. What things seemed important to you?

    e.   Look back at your answers to question *d* each day (lessons 484-501, 503-509, 512, 513, 517, 518, 522, 543-547). What were some things you discovered on your own?

    f.   Think back through your answers to question *f* each day. What are some key ways God is teaching you to change the way you love, think or live?

Write

Write a review of Luke-Acts. In the first paragraph tell who the author is and state the purpose of each book. In the second paragraph list some of the themes in the two books and explain how the two books fit together. In the third paragraph, write about the things that seemed most important to you and how God is changing you. End your review with a prayer of praise to Jesus, the Lord's Anointed, the fulfillment of all the Scriptures and the king of the nations.

Ephesians

549.　Ephesians – Introduction

Pray. Then Read, Think and <u>Mark</u>.

Read your study Bible's introduction to Ephesians. Think about the questions for each of the following sections. <u>Mark</u> the answers and other things that seem important.

for the ESV Study Bible

- Author and Title
    - Read the second paragraph. Who wrote Ephesians?
    - Read the fifth paragraph ("Moreover ..."). What type of letter may Ephesians have been?
    - Read the last paragraph. To which churches was Ephesians written?
- Date
    - When did Paul write Ephesians? Where was he?
- Theme
    - What are the two main themes of Ephesians?
- Purpose, Occasion, and Background
    - What was the city of Ephesus fascinated with?
    - Follow the reference in parentheses (Acts 19:19).
    - To whom did Paul preach in Ephesus (Acts 19:8-10)?
    - What kinds of things did God do through Paul (Acts 19:11-12, 17)?
    - What did many believers confess and then destroy (Acts 19:18-19)?
    - Whom did Paul's teaching and power threaten (Acts 19:27)?

for the NIV Study Bible

- Author, Date and Place of Writing
    - Who wrote Ephesians?
    - When did he write? Where was he?

- What type of letter is Ephesians?
- To which churches was it written?
- The City of Ephesus
  - Which famous temple was in Ephesus?
  - Follow the references back to Acts 19.
  - To whom did Paul preach in Ephesus (Acts 19:8-10)?
  - What kinds of things did God do through Paul (Acts 19:11-12, 17)?
  - What did many believers confess and then destroy (Acts 19:18-19)?
  - Whom did Paul's teaching and power threaten (Acts 19:27)?
- Theological Message
  - Read the first paragraph. What did Paul want his readers to understand and appreciate?
  - Read the second paragraph. What is the "climax of God's purpose"?

Write

Write your own introduction to Ephesians. Tell who the author is, where he is and when he writes. Describe the city of Ephesus. Summarize what happened when Paul was in Ephesus. (Cite the references to Acts 19 in parentheses.) State the themes of Ephesians.

550. Ephesians 1:1-3:21

a. What has God blessed the saints with (1:3)? What is it about God that makes him want to bless us (1:4, 5, 6, 8; 2:4, 5, 8)? For what purpose does God bless us (1:6, 12, 14; 2:7)?

b. Whom are the believers, the blessings and God's work in (1:1, 3, 4 etc.)? Underline every time Paul writes "in Christ" or "with Christ" in chapters 1-3. What is God's will for all things (1:9-10)? What has God put under Christ's feet (1:20-22)?

c. How is God building his temple (2:13-16, 19-22; 3:16-18)? What will God make known through the church (3:10-11, 20-21)? What does God's Spirit fill the temple with (1:19; 2:22; 3:16-17, 19-20)?

551. Ephesians 4:1-6:24

a. In the psalm Paul quotes from, where was the Lord going from and to (Ephesians 4:8; see Psalm 68:7-8, 18, 29)? At those times, what did he give gifts to people to do (see Exodus 35:30-36:3; 2 Chronicles 2:1, 13-14)? What are our gifted leaders equipping us to build up (Ephesians 4:11-12, 15-16)?

b. What must we put off and put on (2:3, 10; 4:22-24)? Whom must we be and live like (4:24, 32; 5:1, 2, 25)? What ways must we walk or live in (5:2, 8, 15)?

c. Whom must we be strong in (6:10)? Underline every time Paul writes "in Christ" or "in the Lord" in chapters 4-6. Whose armor must we put on (6:13, 17)?

Colossians

552.   Colossians – Introduction

Pray. Then Read, Think and <u>Mark</u>.

Read your study Bible's introduction to Colossians. Think about the questions for each of the following sections. <u>Mark</u> the answers and other things that seem important.

for the ESV Study Bible

- Date
    - o   Who wrote Colossians?
    - o   When did he write? Where was he?
    - o   What else did he write then?
- Theme
    - o   What is the theme of Colossians?
- Purpose, Occasion, and Background
    - o   Read the first paragraph. Who carried the gospel to Colossae? When?
    - o   Read the first sentence in the third paragraph ("The fact that ..."). What are some of the distinctively Jewish elements in the false teaching?
    - o   Read the fifth paragraph ("The best explanation ...").
    - o   What did the dangerous teaching in Colossae come from?
    - o   What was a central feature of that belief?
    - o   Read the sixth paragraph ("What likely happened ..."). What might a spiritual leader have taught about himself and about Christ?
- Key Themes
    - o   What are the first and fourth key themes?

for the NIV Study Bible

- Author, Date and Place of Writing
    - o   Read the second paragraph. Who wrote Colossians?

- ○ When did he write? Where was he?
- ○ What else did he write then?
- • Colossae: The Town and the Church
  - ○ Read the second paragraph. Who carried the gospel to Colossae? When?
- • The Colossian Heresy
  - ○ What are the first four elements of the false teaching in Colossae?
- • Purpose and Theme
  - ○ Why did Paul write Colossians? What is his purpose?
  - ○ What is the theme of Colossians?

Write

Write your own introduction to Colossians. Tell who wrote Colossians, when and from where. Summarize the history of the church in Colossae—who carried the gospel there—and connect it with a verse in Acts. Explain the false teaching in Colossae and list some of its elements. Then state the purpose and theme of Colossians.

553. Colossians 1:1-4:18

a. How do people qualify (or get) to be pleasing to God (1:12-14, 21-22)? In what ways is the Son preeminent in (or first ahead of) all things (1:15-20)? What is God's gloriously rich mystery (1:27)?

b. How is Christ superior to philosophy (2:3-4, 8-9)? How is Christ superior to the old ways of being holy (1:22; 2:11-17)? How is Christ superior to the cosmic elements, rules and regulations (2:8-10, 15, 20-23)?

c. Where should Christians live their lives (2:6-7)? Why should you set your heart and your mind on things above (2:20; 3:1-2)? Then what should you put off and put on (3:5-8, 9-12)?

Philemon

554.   Philemon – Introduction; 1-25

Pray. Then Read, Think and <u>Mark</u>.

Read your study Bible's introduction to Paul's letter to Philemon. Think about the questions for each of the following sections. <u>Mark</u> the answers and other things that seem important.

for the ESV Study Bible

- Date
    - o   Who wrote Philemon?
    - o   When did he write? Where was he?
    - o   What else did he write then?
- Theme
    - o   What is the theme of Philemon?
- Purpose, Occasion, and Background
    - o   Read the first paragraph. Who is Philemon?
    - o   Read the second paragraph. What happened between Onesimus and Philemon?

for the NIV Study Bible

- Author, Date and Place of Writing
    - o   Who wrote Philemon?
    - o   When did he write? Where was he?
    - o   What else did he write then?
- Recipient, Background and Purpose
    - o   Who is Philemon?
    - o   What had happened between Onesimus and Philemon?

Now read Paul's letter to Philemon (1-25). <u>Mark</u> any words or sentences that seem important to you. Think about these questions.

- What does Paul call Philemon (and Timothy) (1, 7, 20)? What does Paul ask Philemon to treat Onesimus like (16, 17)? How has Onesimus changed (10-13, 16, 18; see also the study note for 10)?

Write

Write your own introduction to Paul's letter to Philemon. Summarize the story of Philemon, Onesimus and Paul. Explain the meaning of Onesimus's name and how Onesimus has changed. Then tell why Paul is writing Philemon, and describe what Philemon's relationship with Onesimus should be like.

(3) Think about and answer the questions. (4) Return to your bookmark.

Philippians

555. Philippians – Introduction

Pray. Then Read, Think and <u>Mark</u>.

Read your study Bible's introduction to Philippians. Think about the questions for each of the following sections. <u>Mark</u> the answers and other things that seem important.

for the ESV Study Bible

- Author and Title
    - o Who wrote Philippians?
- Date
    - o Where was the author when he wrote Philippians?
- Theme
    - o What is the chief theme of Philippians?
    - o What does the kind of life look like?
    - o Who are the best examples of that kind of life?
- Purpose, Occasion, and Background
    - o Read the second paragraph. What prompted Paul to write Philippians?
    - o Read the fourth paragraph ("Yet Paul's purpose ..."). What was Paul most concerned about?
- The Ancient City of Philippi
    - o What type of city was Philippi?
- Key Themes
    - o How can faithful Christians respond to suffering?
    - o How should Christians live together?
    - o What is the old covenant unable to do?

for the NIV Study Bible

- Author, Date and Place of Writing
    - o Who wrote Philippians?
    - o Where was he when he wrote it?

- Purpose
  - ○ What was Paul's primary purpose in writing this letter?
  - ○ What were his other desires?
- Recipients
  - ○ What were the citizens of Philippi proud about?
- Characteristics
  - ○ What kind of letter is Philippians?
  - ○ What does vigorous Christian living look like?

Write

Write your own introduction to Philippians. Tell who the author is, where he is and when he writes. Explain what has just happened and why Paul wants to write to the believers in Philippi. Describe the city of Philippi. State the important themes in Philippians. Explain how Christ is an example of the way believers should live.

556. Philippians 1:1-2:30

a. For Paul, what is the only point of life (1:21)? What has God granted us (1:29-30)? Whose example of suffering and struggling for Christ should the saints at Philippi follow (1:7, 13, 20, 27-30; 2:25, 27, 29-30)?

b. What is Paul's relationship with the saints at Philippi like (1:4-5, 7-8, 25-26)? How should the saints relate to each other (1:9, 27; 2:1-4, 14-15)? For what purpose does God keep working in the saints' lives (1:5, 9-11, 25-27; 2:12-13)?

c. What attitude of mind did Christ Jesus have (2:5-8)? What did God do to Christ Jesus after he humbled himself and suffered (2:9)? Whose knees will bow before Jesus, and whose tongues will confess "Lord Jesus Christ" (2:10-11; 4:22)?

557. Philippians 3:1-4:23

a. How do the evil dogs pursue righteousness (3:2, 4-6, 9)? How does Paul have righteousness (3:9)? Toward what goal does Paul press on (3:10-14, 20-21)?

b. What must all of us, even gospel workers, do (2:1-4; 4:1-3)? What must we always do (2:18, 28, 29; 3:1; 4:4)? When we worry, how does God give us peace (4:6-7)?

c. What does it mean to know Christ (3:8, 10; 4:1)? How did the Philippians share in Paul's troubles (2:25, 30; 4:10, 14-18)? With the Lord's strength, what can Paul do (4:11-13)?

Titus

558. Titus – Introduction; 1:1-3:15

Pray. Then Read, Think and <u>Mark</u>.

Read your study Bible's introduction to the letter to Titus. Think about the questions for each of the following sections. <u>Mark</u> the answers and other things that seem important.

for the ESV Study Bible
- Author and Title
    - o Who wrote Titus?
- Date
    - o About when did he write Titus?
- Theme
    - o What is the theme of Titus?
    - o What two things is this theme the basis for?
- Purpose, Occasion, and Background
    - o Read the first paragraph.
    - o Who started the churches in Crete?
    - o What did Paul leave Titus to do in Crete?
    - o Read the third paragraph. In the ancient world, what was Crete known for?

for the NIV Study Bible
- Author
    - o Who wrote Titus?
- Crete
    - o What was life in Crete like?
- Occasion and Purpose
    - o Who started the churches in Crete?
    - o What did Paul leave Titus to do in Crete?
    - o What three things did Paul want to give Titus in this letter?

- Place and Date of Writing
  - o When and from where did Paul write Titus?
- Distinctive Characteristics
  - o What did Paul emphasize again and again?

Now read Paul's letter to Titus (1:1-3:15). Mark any words (e.g. "good") or sentences that seem important to you. Think about these questions.

- What does grace teach (or train) us to do (2:11)? Why did Christ give himself for us (2:14)?
- Did God save us because of righteous works we had done (3:5)? What should people who have put their trust in God devote themselves to do (3:8, 14)?

Write

Write your own introduction to Titus. Name the author and the recipient. Summarize the history of the churches in Crete and Paul's reason for leaving Titus in Crete. Describe life in Crete. State the theme(s) of Titus. Choose something Paul teaches in chapter 2 or 3 and show how it connects with the theme.

Timothy

559. Timothy – Introduction

Pray. Then Read, Think and <u>Mark</u>.

Read your study Bible's introductions to the letters to Timothy. Think about the questions for each of the following sections. <u>Mark</u> the answers and other things that seem important.

for the ESV Study Bible

- 1 Timothy
    - o Author and Title
        - ▪ Read the first sentence. Who wrote 1 Timothy?
    - o Date
        - ▪ How many times was Paul imprisoned in Rome? What did he do in between?
        - ▪ About when did Paul write 1 Timothy?
    - o Theme
        - ▪ What is the theme of 1 Timothy?
    - o Purpose, Occasion, and Background
        - ▪ Read the first paragraph. What did Paul leave Timothy to do in Ephesus?
    - o Literary Features
        - ▪ Read the second paragraph. What is Paul's relationship with Timothy like?
        - ▪ What is the "overarching concern" of 1 Timothy?
- 2 Timothy
    - o Author and Title
        - ▪ Who wrote 2 Timothy?
    - o Date
        - ▪ About when does Paul write 2 Timothy?
    - o Theme
        - ▪ What is the theme of 2 Timothy?

- ○ Purpose, Occasion, and Background
  - ▪ Read the first paragraph. Why does Paul want Timothy to come?
  - ▪ What does Paul exhort Timothy to do?

for the NIV Study Bible

- 1 Timothy
  - ○ Author
    - ▪ Who wrote 1 and 2 Timothy?
  - ○ Background and Purpose
    - ▪ What did Paul leave Timothy to do in Ephesus?
    - ▪ Why did Paul write 1 Timothy
  - ○ Date
    - ▪ About when did Paul write 1 Timothy?
  - ○ Recipient
    - ▪ Read the second paragraph. When did Paul go on his fourth international journey?
    - ▪ What is Paul's relationship with Timothy like?
- 2 Timothy
  - ○ Reasons for Writing
    - ▪ Why does Paul want Timothy to come?
    - ▪ What does Paul admonish Timothy to do?

Write

Write your own introduction to 1 and 2 Timothy. Tell who wrote the letters. Explain why Paul leaves Timothy in Ephesus and why he writes his first letter. Tell where Paul is when he writes his second letter. Summarize Paul's exhortation. Finally, describe Paul's relationship with Timothy and why Paul wants him to come to him.

560. 1 Timothy 1:1-3:16

a. What do the false teachers in Ephesus want to teach (1:3-4)? What does Paul teach instead (1:5, 11, 14)? What does Christ Jesus do for sinners and through them (1:15-16)?

b. Why should we pray for all those in authority (2:1-4)? How many gods and mediators are there for all people (2:5-6)? What should men, women and children in the church be like (2:2, 8, 10, 15)?

c. What must a woman, an overseer and a deacon do with their children (2:15; 3:4, 12)? Compare 3:2-3 with 3:8-9. What must both overseers and deacons be like (3:2-3, 8-9)? Why has Paul left Timothy in Ephesus (1:3-4; 3:14-15)?

(3) Think about and answer the questions. (4) Return to your bookmark. 337

561.   1 Timothy 4:1-6:21

a.   Where does false teaching come from (4:1)? What do the false teachers teach (4:2-3, 7; 6:3-4, 20-21)? What does Paul teach instead (4:3-5; 5:14; 6:17-18)?

b.   What should people in the church treat each other like (5:1-2)? What good deeds or works should a woman do (5:10, 14-16)? Which Scriptures does Paul quote from to teach about honoring elders (5:17-18)?

c.   How should Timothy live and teach (1 Timothy 4:7-8, 10, 11-13, 15-16)? Then what will happen (4:10, 16)? What is God going to bring about or display (6:13-16)?

562.   2 Timothy 1:1-2:26

a.   In what ways did God help Timothy grow up to become an approved servant (1:5, 6, 7, 9, 13)? How does God's Spirit make us ready to suffer (1:7-8)? What is the gospel that is worth suffering for (1:10-11; 2:8-10)?

b.   Who teaches (or should teach) whom (1:5, 13; 2:2)? What three types of people should Timothy be like, and how should he be like them (2:3-6)? What reward will the commanding officer give the good soldier who has endured suffering (2:3-4, 12)?

c.   What are the false teachers in Ephesus like (2:14, 16, 18, 23, 26)? How should Timothy live (2:19-22)? How should Timothy teach (2:14, 15, 24-25)?

563.   2 Timothy 3:1-4:22

a.   Who oppose Paul, Timothy and their message (2:25-26; 3:8; 4:14-15, 17)? How is the Scripture useful or profitable (3:16-17)? How must Timothy prepare for Christ Jesus' appearing and kingdom (4:2, 5)?

b.   What is Paul's life like right now (1:12, 16; 2:9; 4:9-13)? What will happen to everyone who wants to live a godly life in Christ Jesus (3:12)? To whom will the Lord give a crown of righteousness (4:8)?

c.   What happened at Paul's first defense or hearing (4:16-17)? Whom all has the Lord rescued from the lion's mouth (4:17)? Follow the cross-references for "from the lion's mouth." What will the Lord receive (2 Timothy 4:18)?

Peter

564. Peter – Introduction

Pray. Then Read, Think and <u>Mark</u>.

Read your study Bible's introductions to Peter's letters. Think about the questions for each of the following sections. <u>Mark</u> the answers and other things that seem important.

for the ESV Study Bible

- 1 Peter
    - ○ Author and Title
        - ▪ Read the first paragraph. Who wrote 1 Peter?
    - ○ Date
        - ▪ About when did he write 1 Peter?
    - ○ Theme
        - ▪ What is the theme of 1 Peter?
    - ○ Purpose, Occasion, and Background
        - ▪ Read the first paragraph. What did Peter encourage his readers to do?
        - ▪ Read the second and third paragraphs. To whom did Peter write?
- 2 Peter
    - ○ Author and Title
        - ▪ Read the first paragraph. Who wrote 2 Peter?
    - ○ Date
        - ▪ About when was 2 Peter written? Where was the author when he wrote it?
    - ○ Theme
        - ▪ What does the grace of God in Christ do?
        - ▪ What does the Holy Spirit do?
    - ○ Purpose, Occasion, and Background
        - ▪ What does Peter want his readers to do?
        - ▪ What does Peter combat or fight against?

for the NIV Study Bible

- 1 Peter
    - Author and Date
        - Read the first paragraph. Who wrote 1 Peter?
        - Read the last paragraph. About when did he write 1 Peter?
    - Recipients
        - Follow the direction and read 1:1 and its study note. To whom was 1 Peter written?
    - Themes
        - What does 1 Peter have much to say about?
        - For what two purposes did Peter say he had written?
        - What are some other themes in 1 Peter?
- 2 Peter
    - Author
        - Read the first paragraph. Who wrote 2 Peter?
    - Date
        - Read the first paragraph. About when was 2 Peter written?
    - Purpose
        - What are Peter's three purposes in 2 Peter?

Write

Write your own introduction to 1 and 2 Peter. Tell who wrote the letters, where he is when he wrote them and to whom he wrote. In the second paragraph, state the theme and purposes of 1 Peter. In the third paragraph, explain the themes or purposes of 2 Peter.

565.   1 Peter 1:1-3:7

a. What hope does God give his elect (1:3-5, 13)? Why do these exiles have to suffer trials (1:6-7)? Whom were the prophets serving when they spoke (1:10-21)?

b. How should God's children live (1:14-17, 22-23; 2:2-3)? What has happened to those who rejected the living stone (2:4, 7-8)? When the prophets spoke, what did they call the people who would believe in Christ (1:10, 12; 2:5, 9-10; see the study note for 2:9)?

c. What example did Christ leave us (2:20-23)? How should all the foreigners and exiles live (2:12-13, 17)? How should wives and husbands follow Christ's example (3:1-7)?

566.   **1 Peter 3:8–5:13**

a.   What made Christ (and makes us) strong enough to suffer (2:23; 3:12; 4:1, 5, 19)? What has Christ done to the spirits and powers (3:18-19, 21-22)? What should you do about the devil (4:7; 5:8-9)?

b.   How should you speak when you are suffering (3:9, 10, 15-16)? Why shouldn't you think it's strange when you suffer (4:12; 5:9)? How should you feel when you suffer (4:13-14, 16)?

c.   What is God's will, and what does he call Christians to (2:15, 20-21; 3:17; 4:19)? Why should those who suffer entrust themselves to God (4:19; 5:10; see 1:3)? What happens after we share in Christ's sufferings (1:7; 3:18, 22; 4:13)?

567.   **2 Peter 1:1–3:18**

a.   What has God promised believers and called them to (1:4, 10)? So how should believers live (1:5-10)? How do we know the prophetic word is confirmed and reliable (1:19-21; 3:15-16)?

b.   What did the false teachers used to be like. (2:20-21)? What are they like now (2:2-3, 12-14)? What two things does Peter's list of God's ancient judgments prove to us (2:4-8, 9)?

c.   How will the day of the Lord be like the flood (3:4-7, 10)? How should we feel about the Lord not having come yet (3:4, 8-9, 15)? How should we live now (3:11-12, 14, 17-18)?

Jude

568.   Jude – Introduction; 1-25

Pray. Then Read, Think and <u>Mark</u>.

Read your study Bible's introduction to Jude's letter. Think about the questions for each of the following sections. <u>Mark</u> the answers and other things that seem important.

for the ESV Study Bible

- Author and Title
  - o   Who wrote Jude?
- Date
  - o   When was Jude written?
- Theme
  - o   What must the church and faithful people do?
- Purpose, Occasion, and Background
  - o   Read the first paragraph. What were the false teachers doing?

for the NIV Study Bible

- Author
  - o   Read the first paragraph. Who wrote Jude?
- Date
  - o   Read the second paragraph. When may Jude have been written?
- Occasion and Purpose
  - o   Read the first paragraph. What were the immoral men perverting (or twisting) God's grace into?
  - o   What did Jude think his readers must do?

Now read Jude's letter (1-25). <u>Mark</u> any words or sentences that seem important to you. Think about these questions.

- What happened to all the wicked angels and people Jude lists in 6-11? What did the Lord Jesus do for his people (4)? What must Jude's beloved friends do (20-21)? What is God able to do (24)?

- What book does Jude quote from (14-15)? See the study note for 14. Does that mean this book is Scripture? See also the study note for 9 or 8-10.

Write

Write your own introduction to Jude's letter. Tell who the author is. Describe the problem in the churches and what the believers must do. List the other books Jude refers to, and explain why he refers to them.

Hebrews

569.   Hebrews – Introduction

Pray. Then Read, Think and Mark.

Read your study Bible's introduction to Hebrews. Think about the questions for each of the following sections. Mark the answers and other things that seem important.

for the ESV Study Bible

- Author, Audience, and Title
    - o Read the first paragraph. Do we know who wrote Hebrews?
    - o Read the last paragraph.
    - o Whom did the author of Hebrews write this sermon for?
    - o What does the writer use frequently?
- Date
    - o Read the first paragraph. By what year was Hebrews probably written?
- Theme
    - o What is Christ greater than?
    - o So what should the readers do?
- Purpose, Occasion, and Background
    - o Read the second and third paragraphs.
    - o What do the warning passages do?
    - o What do the expository sections show (or argue for)?
- Key Themes
    - o Read the first two themes. Who is Jesus?
- History of Salvation Summary
    - o What has Christ done?
- Literary Features
    - o Read the last paragraph. What key words occur many times in the book?

for the NIV Study Bible

- Author
  - o Read the first sentence. Do we know who wrote Hebrews?
  - o Read the last paragraph. What does the author of Hebrews quote regularly?
- Date
  - o By what year was Hebrews written?
- Recipients
  - o To whom was this letter addressed?
  - o What were they tempted to do?
- Theme
  - o Read the first paragraph.
  - o What is the theme of Hebrews?
  - o What does the prologue (the words at the front of the book) present Christ as?
  - o What is Christ superior to?
  - o What key words occur many times in the book?
  - o Since these things are true of Christ, what can there be none of?
  - o What does the author warn the readers about?

Write

Write your own introduction to Hebrews. Describe the occasion by telling who the readers were and what they were being tempted to do. Then explain the argument. State the theme of Hebrews. Summarize what Hebrews shows Christ to be and how it does that. (Make sure to point out the key words.) Last, explain the book's warnings and show how they connect the book's argument with the readers' temptations.

570. Hebrews 1:1-4:13

a. In what way did God speak to the prophet Moses long ago (1:1; see 2:2 and the study note)? In what ways do the prophets say the Son is superior to the angels (1:2-4, 5, 8-13)? So why must we pay the most careful attention to God's message about salvation which his Son announced (1:2; 2:1-3)?

b. How does God put Jesus' enemies under his feet (1:2-3, 13; 2:8-9, 14-15)? How did Jesus become a merciful high priest (2:10, 14, 17-18)? How is Jesus like Moses but greater than him (3:2-6)?

c. What did God tell those people who started out by leaving Egypt but then were not faithful to the end (3:7-11, 14, 16-19)?

What is the connection between belief or unbelief and obedience or disobedience (3:8, 12, 18-19; 4:2)? How do we enter God's rest and rest from our work (4:3, 9-11)?

571. Hebrews 4:14-7:28

a. How did Jesus become the sort of high priest who can empathize with or feel like us (4:15-16; 5:7-9)? If someone begins following Christ and then stops (falls away), can he be brought back to repentance (6:4-6)? So how should believers live (4:14, 16; 5:9; 6:10-12)?

b. What was Melchizedek, and what do his names mean (7:1-2)? How is Jesus like Melchizedek (7:1-3, 15-17)? How is Jesus greater than the Levitical priests (7:4-10, 23-24, 27-28)?

c. Why is the former regulation or commandment set aside (7:11, 18-19)? What has Jesus done for the people, and what does he do now (7:25, 27)? So which covenant and priest should Jewish believers follow (7:19, 22, 25-26)?

572. Hebrews 8:1-10:18

a. What was the fault with the first covenant and the people (8:7-9)? What can the old covenant—its law and its ministry—not do (9:8-10; 10:1-4)? When did God promise the new covenant (see 8:8-12 and the study note)?

b. What was the tabernacle on earth (8:5; 9:23-24)? What sacrifice did Christ, our high priest, offer (9:12, 14, 23, 25, 26, 28)? Where did Christ offer his sacrifice (8:2; 9:11-12, 24)?

c. How many times did Christ offer his sacrifice (9:12, 25-28; 10:11-12, 14)? What does his sacrifice do (9:12, 14, 15, 26-28; 10:10, 14)? How does Christ's sacrifice fulfill the promise of the new covenant (10:12-17)?

573. Hebrews 10:19-13:25

a. How does the author apply the truths he's been writing about (10:19-24)? How can the believers be strong enough to persevere (10:35-39)? What did the believers wait for by faith (11:10, 13-16)?

b. How should we live (or run) now (12:1-2)? Why does God discipline his children (12:5-11)? How is Mt. Zion better than Mt. Sinai (12:18-29)?

c. What other instructions does the author give in chapter 13? What did God do for Jesus (13:20-21)?

574.   Hebrews – Review

Pray. Think through the following points.

  a.   Reread your own introduction to Hebrews.
  b.   What temptation or struggle were the readers facing? How does the author of Hebrews encourage and warn the believers?
  c.   Look back through the book. Note the words and verses you marked. What things seemed important to you?
  d.   Look back at your answers to question *d* each day. What were some things you discovered on your own?
  e.   Think back through your answers to question *f* each day. What are some key ways God is teaching you to change the way you love, think or live?

Write

Write a review of Hebrews. In the first paragraph describe the struggle the readers of Hebrews were facing and how the author of Hebrews encourages and warns them. In the second paragraph, write about the things that seemed most important to you and how God is changing you. End your review with a prayer of praise to Jesus for the many ways he is so much better than the old priests, the old covenant and the old sacrifices.

John's Gospel

575.   John — Introduction

Pray. Then Read, Think and <u>Mark</u>.

Read your study Bible's introduction to John's Gospel. Think about the questions for each of the following sections. <u>Mark</u> the answers and other things that seem important.

for the ESV Study Bible
- Author and Title
    - o   God is the main author of John. Who is the human author? <u>Underline</u> his name.
- Date and Place of Writing
    - o   Read the first sentence. When was John's Gospel most likely written?
- Theme
    - o   What is John's theme?
- Purpose, Occasion, and Background
    - o   Read the second paragraph.
    - o   What is John's purpose statement?
    - o   Where is it?
    - o   What is John's central contention (point or argument)?
- Literary Features
    - o   Read the second paragraph.
    - o   What images does John use to portray Jesus?
    - o   What is the first half of the book built around?

for the NIV Study Bible
- Author
    - o   God is the main author of John. Who is the human author? <u>Underline</u> his name.

- Date
  - ○ Read the first paragraph (ending in "... no later than 70"). When do most think John's Gospel was written?
- Purpose and Emphases
  - ○ Read the second paragraph (beginning with "John begins ..."). Who does John show Jesus to be?
  - ○ Read the third paragraph.
  - ○ What is John's central theme?
  - ○ What verse is it in?
  - ○ What is John's main purpose?
  - ○ What verse is it in?

Write

Write your own introduction to John's Gospel in your notebook. Tell who wrote the book and when. State John's purpose and the verse it is in. Describe how John wrote his Gospel to fulfill his purpose: who does John show Jesus to be?

576. John 1:1-2:12

a. What are the first three words of John's Gospel (1:1)? What other book of the Bible begins with those words? What other words in John 1 are also in Genesis 1? Look in John 1:3, 4, 5.

b. Make a chart with four columns. Head the columns with the labels "Verse," "Witness," "Title" and "OT." In each of the following verses, what title does the witness call Jesus? Which idea, promise or verse in the Old Testament is God's Spirit reminding the witness of? Look at the study note for each verse.

Verse	Witness	Title	OT
1:1	John the apostle	Word	Genesis 1:3
1:1	John the apostle	God	Genesis 1:1
1:14	John the apostle	Dwelling	
1:29, 35	John the Baptizer		
1:34			
1:41			
1:45			
1:49			Psalm 2:7
1:49			Psalm 2:6
1:51	Jesus		Daniel 7:13-14

c. In the old covenant and in the new covenant, who gave his people wine (see Deuteronomy 7:13; Jeremiah 31:12)? What does John call this first miracle (John 2:11)? What does this miracle reveal (2:11)?

577. John 2:13-4:42

a. Who first wrote, "Zeal for your house will consume me" (2:17)? Follow the cross-reference. What did that man want to build (see 2 Samuel 7:1-2)? Who did the LORD say would build a house for him (see 2 Samuel 7:12-13)? Who would the LORD be to that man (see 2 Samuel 7:14)? Now, in John's Gospel, who wants to build what (John 2:16, 19, 21)?

b. What must happen if someone is to see the kingdom of God (3:3)? How does rebirth happen (3:6, 8)? What do those who believe in the Son have (3:36)? What do those who reject the Son still have (3:36)?

c. Why do the Samaritans worship what they "do not know" (4:22)? Follow the cross-reference and read the story. Who does Jesus say he is (John 4:25-26; read Exodus 3:14 also)?

578. John 4:43-6:15

a. From which region to which region does Jesus travel (4:43-45)? What sort of people live in the first region? When did they start to believe in Jesus (4:39-42)? What sort of people live in the second region (4:45)? What does Jesus say they must have before they will believe (4:48)?

b. What does Jesus do on the Sabbath (5:9, 17)? Who else works on the Sabbath (5:17)? What other things do they have in common (5:19, 21, 23, 26)?

c. How does the Father testify about Jesus (5:37, 39)? How do Jesus' works testify about him (5:36, 39, 46)?

579. John 6:16-7:24

a. Who else walks on water (John 6:19; see Job 9:8)? Who else gives bread from heaven (John 6:32-33)? After walking on water, Jesus says (in Greek), "I am" (6:20). What does he say after giving bread from heaven (6:35, 41, 48, 51)?

b. What is the Father's will (6:40)? Who will look to Jesus (6:44, 65)? How does Jesus give them life (6:51, 53-58)?

c. Which miracle is Jesus talking about (see 7:21 and the study note)? Is it okay to circumcise a boy on the Sabbath (7:22)? How is circumcision like healing (7:23)? Is it okay for Jesus to do this work on the Sabbath (7:24)?

580. John 7:25-52; 8:12-58

a. Where do the people think the Messiah will come from (7:27, 41-43, 52)? Where is Jesus from (8:14)? In which dark land did Isaiah say a great light would shine (see Isaiah 9:1-2)? Who would the light be (see Isaiah 9:6)? What would the light do (see Isaiah 9:7)?

b. What does Jesus call the people to do (John 7:37)? Follow the first cross-reference for "come to me and drink." What did Yahweh tell the people to do and what did he promise them (see Isaiah 55:3)?

c. What does Jesus call himself (John 8:24, 28, 58)? Who else calls himself by this name? See the study note for 8:58 and follow the reference to the verse in Exodus. Who do you believe Jesus is?

581. John 9:1-10:42

a. Why did a bad thing happen to this man (9:2-3)? What does Jesus call himself (9:5)? In what ways does the Light of the World shine on the blind man (9:6-7, 30-33, 35-38)?

b. What does Jesus call himself (10:11)? Follow the cross-reference to the chapter in Ezekiel. How were Israel's shepherds caring for them (see Ezekiel 34:1-6)? What did Lord Yahweh promise to do for his sheep (see Ezekiel 34:11-16)? Who would be their shepherd (see Ezekiel 34:23)? What would the sheep know (see Ezekiel 34:30-31)?

c. Who believe and who do not believe (John 9:16, 24, 31-32, 35-38; 10:19-21, 41-42)? Why do some people believe in Jesus (10:27, 38)? Why do others not believe (10:25-26)?

582. John 11:1-12:19

a. For what two reasons is Lazarus sick and then dead (11:4, 15, 40)? What does Martha believe about her brother (11:24)? What does Jesus say about himself (11:25)? How does this sign fulfill Jesus' earlier promise (11:43-44; see 5:25-29)?

b. How does Caiaphas speak (11:51)? For whom had Isaiah said God's servant would die (see Isaiah 52:15; 53:5-6, 8)? Go back to John 11:52. Follow the first cross-reference for gathering the scattered children of God. What had Yahweh said his servant would do (see Isaiah 49:5-6)?

c. Which Old Testament verses does the crowd shout as Jesus approaches Jerusalem (John 12:13)? What do they call him? What does the psalmist want Yahweh to save him from (see

Psalm 118:10-11)? What verse does John use to describe Jesus' riding on the donkey (John 12:15)? What will the coming king do (see Zechariah 9:9-10)?

583. John 12:20-13:38

a. Which hour has come at last (12:23, 27-28)? What did Isaiah see (12:38-41)? Follow the cross-reference for "he saw Jesus' glory" (John 12:41). Why did the people not believe even though they had heard Isaiah and seen Jesus (12:39-40)?

b. Whose example is Jesus following (13:4-5; see 12:3)? What had Yahweh told Moses to put in the tabernacle between the tent of meeting and the altar (see Exodus 30:17-21)? Who did what there? What is Jesus preparing his disciples to be and do (John 13:7-10)?

c. How does Jesus show his love to the end (13:1)? Who is Jesus (13:3)? What does Jesus act like (13:4)? What does Jesus command his disciples to do (13:34)? What will the world know when they see Jesus' disciples loving each other (13:35)?

584. John 14:1-16:15

a. Who is in whom (14:10-11)? If the disciples love Jesus, what will they do (14:23)? Then what will the Father and Jesus do (14:23)? Then who will be in the disciples (14:17, 20)?

b. Then what will the disciples do (15:5, 7-8)? Who does all this work (14:10)? To what does Jesus compare this "being in" and "working" (15:5)?

c. What will the Spirit do for the disciples (14:26-27)? Whom does the world hate (15:18)? What do both the Spirit and the disciples do (15:26-27)? What does the Spirit do to the world (16:8-11)?

585. John 16:16-18:27

a. How does Jesus feel about his disciples: what is he trying to do for them (for example, in 16:33)? For whom does he pray (17:9)? What three things does he ask the Father to do for them (17:11, 13, 15, 17)?

b. For whom does Jesus pray next (17:20)? What two things does he ask the Father to do for us (17:21, 24)? What will the world believe and know when believers are one (17:21, 23)?

c. What does Jesus call himself (18:5, 6, 8)? When he calls himself this, what do the soldiers and officials do (18:6)?

Every day: (1) Follow your bookmark and pray. (2) Read and mark the passage.

586. John 18:28-19:42

a. What is Pilate's first question of Jesus (18:33)? What is Pilate's last statement about Jesus (19:19-22)? The Greek word for *Jew* is *Ioudaios*. Who betrays Jesus (18:2, 28-30)? In John 1:11, how does John foreshadow Jesus' betrayal: how does he make you feel like Jesus will be betrayed?

b. Why did the soldiers divide Jesus' clothes and cast lots for his garment (19:24)? What Old Testament verse does John quote? Who wrote that psalm? When? Read through Psalm 22 and list at least three other prophecies Jesus fulfills in his death.

c. What work does Jesus finish (John 19:30; see Psalm 22:31)? What verses does John quote in John 19:36-37? What does John show that Jesus is (19:36)? Whom had the house of David (the tribe of Judah) pierced in Zechariah 12:10? (Zechariah 12:1 tells you who the *I* in Zechariah 12:10 is.) Who is the son (Zechariah 12:10)? What happens on that day (Zechariah 13:1)?

587. John 20:1-21:25; 7:53-8:11

a. What happens to John, Mary, the disciples and Thomas before each of them believes (20:8, 14-16, 20, 26-28)? Why does John record Jesus' signs (20:30-31)? When did you first believe (20:29-31)?

b. Earlier, when someone's outer garment was off, what did Jesus tell Peter (13:4-10)? What does Peter do this time (21:7)? What did Peter do the last time he was near a charcoal fire? See the study note for 21:9 and follow the reference. How many times does Jesus ask Peter, "Do you love me?" (21:17)?

c. What is another thing Jesus probably did (21:25; see 7:53-8:11)? Do the oldest manuscripts or copies of John's Gospel include this story? What two things does Jesus tell the woman (8:11)? Does John's Gospel include other times when Jesus taught these two things? See the cross-references for 8:11.

588. John – Review

You've now read all of John's Gospel. Today you will think back over the book and write a review.

Pray. Think through the following points.

a. Reread your own introduction to the book.

b. What was John's purpose for writing his Gospel? How did he go about doing that?

c. Look again at John's prologue (1:1-18). What themes does John include in his opening to set the course for the rest of the book?

d. Flip through the rest of John's Gospel, looking for the verses you marked. What seemed important to John?

e. What was important to you?

f. Look back at your answers to question *d* each day. What were some things you discovered on your own?

g. Did John accomplish his purpose in your life as you read his Gospel?

h. What do you believe about Jesus?

i. Think back through your answers to question *f* each day. What are some key ways God is teaching you to change the way you love, think and live?

Write

Write a review of John's Gospel. In the first paragraph or two, state John's purpose and how he goes about achieving it. Give an example of one way John does that. In the next paragraph, write about the things that seemed most important to you and how God is changing you. End your review with a prayer of praise to Jesus the Messiah, God's Son, telling him what you believe about him.

John's Letters

589.   1-3 John – Introduction

Pray. Then Read, Think and <u>Mark</u>.

Read your study Bible's introductions to 1, 2 and 3 John. Think about the questions for each of the following sections. <u>Mark</u> the answers and other things that seem important.

for the ESV Study Bible

- Introduction to 1 John
    - o Author and Title
        - ▪ Read the first paragraph. Who wrote 1 John?
    - o Date
        - ▪ When was 1 John probably written?
    - o Theme
        - ▪ What three things does 1 John call readers back to?
    - o Literary Features
        - ▪ Read the second paragraph. What tests help us know if we are in Christ?

- Introduction to 2 John
    - o Author and Title
        - ▪ Who wrote 2 John?
    - o Purpose, Occasion, and Background
        - ▪ What did John urge his readers to do?
        - ▪ What practical counsel did he offer?

- Introduction to 3 John
    - o Author and Title
        - ▪ Who wrote 3 John?
    - o Theme
        - ▪ What is the theme of 3 John?

for the NIV Study Bible

- Introduction to 1 John
  - o Author
    - Read the first paragraph. Who wrote 1 John?
  - o Date
    - When was 1 John probably written?
  - o Occasion and Purpose
    - Read the second paragraph. What were John's two basic purposes?
    - What did John strike at?
    - How did he confirm his readers' faith?

- Introduction to 2 John
  - o Author
    - Who wrote 2 John?
  - o Occasion and Purpose
    - When John wrote this second letter, what we as he trying to urge?

- Introduction to 3 John
  - o Author
    - Who wrote 3 John?
  - o Occasion and Purpose
    - What two things did John write this letter to do?

Write

Write your own introduction to John's letters. Tell who wrote them and when. Summarize John's purposes and themes in 1 John. Describe what John urged his readers to do in 2 John. State the theme or purposes of 3 John.

590.   1 John 1:1-5:21

a. What does John write about (1:1-3)? Why does John write this letter (1:4; 5:13)? How can you know you are born of God, know Jesus and have eternal life (2:5-6; 3:14-15; 5:1, 13)?

b. What do the false teachers teach (1:8, 10; 2:22)? How many antichrists are there, and what do they do (2:18-22; 4:2-3)? What do we know is true (5:18-20)?

c. What is God like (1:5; 2:29; 4:8)? What must God's children be like (1:6-7; 2:29; 4:7, 11)? When we abide or remain in God, what happens (2:24, 27, 28; 3:6, 9, 24; 4:13, 15, 16)?

591.   2 John 1-13; 3 John 1-14

   a.   Who are the chosen (or elect) lady and her children (2 John 1, 13)? How are the chosen lady, her children and Gaius living (2 John 4; 3 John 3-4)? How should they live (2 John 5-6)?

   b.   How can the chosen lady and her children recognize the deceivers (2 John 7, 9-11; 3 John 11)? What should believers do for traveling teachers who speak the truth (3 John 5-8)? But what is Diotrephes doing (3 John 9-10)?

   c.   John uses many words in his second letter that remind us of his first letter. Underline them. Then think about why these things are so important to John.

Revelation

592. Revelation – Introduction

Pray. Then Read, Think and <u>Mark</u>.

Read your study Bible's introduction to Revelation. Think about the questions for each of the following sections. <u>Mark</u> the answers and other things that seem important.

for the ESV Study Bible

- Author and Title
    - o Read the first paragraph. Which Old Testament prophets' writings are the series of symbolic visions a lot like?
    - o Read the first two sentences of the third paragraph. Who did the early church fathers say wrote down Revelation?
- Date
    - o When did Irenaeus say John received the Revelation?
    - o So when do most scholars think John wrote down Revelation?
    - o When do some others think John wrote down Revelation?
- Genre
    - o Read the first paragraph. What kind of writing does Revelation call itself?
    - o Read the first sentence of the second paragraph. What does *apocalypse* mean?
- Theme
    - o Who is the cosmic conflict between?
    - o Who has won and will win the war?
    - o What did the visions that God granted John fortify the church to do?

- Purpose, Occasion, and Background
  - What four things threatened the churches in Asia (Turkey)?
- Literary Features
  - Read the second paragraph.
  - What is the most important thing to know about the literary form of the book of Revelation?
  - How did John portray characters and events?
- Schools of Interpretation
  - Read number 1. What does historicism think the order of the visions symbolizes?
  - Read the first two sentences of number 2. What does futurism think the order of the visions represents?
  - Read the first two sentences of number 3. What events does preterism think fulfilled the visions in Revelation?
  - Read the last sentence of number 4. According to idealism, what three things do the visions in Revelation point to?

for the NIV Study Bible

- Author
  - Who wrote down Revelation?
- Date
  - What were Christians entering when Revelation was written?
  - What were two periods when Christians were persecuted?
  - When do most interpreters think Revelation was written down?
- Occasion
  - What were Roman authorities making people do?
  - What had already happened to some Christians?
- Purpose
  - Why did John write down Revelation?
  - Who fights in the final showdown?
  - What must believers be ready to do?
  - How did John encourage them and give them hope?
- Literary Form
  - What kind of writing is Revelation?
  - What is that kind of writing like?
  - How can we know what the symbols mean?

- Interpretation
  - o What are four ways of interpreting the book of Revelation?

Write

Write your own introduction to Revelation. Tell who wrote down Revelation and when he probably wrote it down. Describe what was happening to Christians at that time. Show how those events are part of the battle between God and Satan. Tell what John tells the Christians to do. In the next paragraph name the genre that Revelation uses. End the introduction with a list of the four ways (or schools) of interpreting Revelation. Summarize each way in one sentence.

593.   Revelation 1:1-3:22

a. What are some similarities between Daniel's dream and visions and what John saw (Revelation 1:5-7, 13-14; see Daniel 7:9, 13, 14, 18, 27)? What is Jesus already, and what are the seven churches (Revelation 1:5-6, 9)? What is the mystery of the seven stars and the seven golden lampstands that John saw (1:12-13, 16, 20)?

b. Who are the *angels* of the seven churches (see 1:20 and the study note)? What is already happening in some churches and will happen to others (1:9; 2:3, 10, 13; 3:10)? How are the churches tempted (2:2, 6, 14-15, 20-23)?

c. What does Jesus say he will do (2:5, 16; 3:11, 20)? How will believers conquer and be victorious (2:7, 10-11, 17, 19, 25, 26; 3:3, 5, 10-12, 21)? What are some things the Son of God will give those who are victorious (2:7, 26-27; 3:12, 21)?

594.   Revelation 4:1-8:1

a. Who else saw God enthroned like this (see 4:1-6 and the study note for 4:5)? What did the other prophets who saw God's glory see and hear (see 4:6-8 and the study notes for 4:7-8)? Why is our Lord and God worthy (4:11)?

b. Which Old Testament characters spoke about the Lion of the tribe of Judah and the Root of David (follow the cross-references in 5:5)? Why is the Lamb worthy (Revelation 5:9-10, 12)? When did the Lamb receive power (5:13)? Look back at your notes for Matthew 24 and 28 (lessons 466 and 469).

c. What does it mean when terrible things happen on earth and in heaven (Revelation 6:12-14)? Look back at your notes for Matthew 24 (lesson 466). What seal is put on the foreheads of the servants of God (see Revelation 7:3 and the study note)? What happens to the saints and their brothers and sisters (6:9-11; 7:9, 13-14)?

595. Revelation 8:2-11:19

a. How does God answer the prayers of his saints (8:3-6)? What judgments in the Old Testament are the first four trumpets like (see 8:7-12 and the study notes)? Whom does God use to judge rebellious humans (9:1, 11)?

b. How do people respond after the plagues (9:20-21)? What must John do with the message on the scroll (10:2, 8-9, 11)? How is the message sweet, and how is it bitter (10:9-10)?

c. What happens to the two witnesses (11:7-8, 11-12)? Other than 7,000 people, what do the rest do (11:13)? When we see them worship, what do we know has started to happen (11:15, 17-18)?

596. Revelation 12:1-14:20

a. What is the "great red dragon" a sign of (12:2, 9)? How do the male child (the Lamb), Michael and his angels and the brothers and sisters throw the dragon down (12:7-9, 11)? Now what has come (12:10)?

b. What do the dragon and the first beast do (12:17; 13:7)? In Daniel's vision, what are the leopard, the bear and the lion signs of (Revelation 13:2; see Daniel 7:1-6)? What does the second beast do (Revelation 13:13)?

c. When does the Lamb finish the harvest that begins with the firstfruits of 144,000 (14:4, 14-16)? What will God do to those who worship the beast and receive its mark (14:9-11)? How must God's saints live (13:10; 14:12)?

597. Revelation 15:1-16:21

a. What things do both Moses and the victorious saints praise God for (15:3-4)? Follow the cross-references in the study note for 15:3. How are God's ways just and true (Revelation 15:3; 16:5-7)? Why will all nations come and worship God (15:4)?

b. When else has the temple been so full of the glory of God that no one could enter it (follow the cross-references for 15:8)? How are the second and third bowls like and unlike the second trumpet (Revelation 16:3-4; see 8:8-9)? What do people do after the fourth, fifth and seventh bowls (16:9, 11, 21)?

c. How are the sixth seal and the sixth trumpet like the sixth and seventh bowls (16:12-21; see 6:12-15; 9:13-16)? What does *Armageddon* mean, and what other battles have been fought there (see 16:16 and the study note)? What is our great hope (16:15)?

598. Revelation 17:1-19:10

a. What is "Babylon the Great, the Mother of Prostitutes" (17:5, 18)? What do the kings of the earth come across many waters to do with the prostitute (17:1-2, 15; 18:3, 9, 11-13, 23)? What is the prostitute drunk with (17:6; 18:24)?

b. Why do the ten horns and the beast (kings and empire) attack the prostitute (17:12, 16-17)? What must God's people do (18:4, 20)? At the end of these "woes," what has happened to Babylon (18:10, 17, 19, 21; see 11:14)?

c. Why does the great multitude shout "Hallelujah" (19:1-5)? How has the Bride made herself ready (19:7-8)? Compare the prostitute with the bride (17:1-6; 18:11-13; 19:7-8).

599. Revelation 19:11-22:21

a. Who kills the kings of the earth and their armies (19:11-13, 51-16, 21)? What do beheaded witnesses do for a thousand years (20:4-6)? Who defeats the devil and the armies of the nations (20:9)?

b. What are the dead judged according to (20:21)? Who is thrown into the lake of fire (19:20; 20:10, 14-15; 21:8)? What happens to people whose names are in the book of life (21:27; see 13:8; 17:8)?

c. What is the holy city Jerusalem (21:2, 9-10)? How does the holy city remind you of the tabernacle? See the study note for 21:16 and the ESV note or the NIV cross-reference for 21:19. How does the holy city remind you of the garden of Eden (22:1-5)?

600. Revelation – Review

Pray.

You've now finished reading Revelation ... and the New Testament ... and maybe even the whole Bible. Congratulations! Thank God for giving you his word, for helping you to read it and for blessing you.

Think through the following points.

a. Reread your own introduction to Revelation.
b. What was happening to believers in Asia Minor when John wrote down Revelation? What did Christ and John tell the believers to do?
c. Think back through the book. How does John use the stories and pictures of Revelation to encourage believers to be faithful even though they suffer so much?
d. Look back at the words and verses you marked. What things seemed important to you?
e. Look back at your answers to question *d* each day. What were some things you discovered on your own?
f. Think back through your answers to question *f* each day. What are some key ways God is teaching you to change the way you love, think or live? How has he encouraged you to be faithful?

Write

Write a review of Revelation. In the first paragraph describe what was happening to the churches in Asia Minor and how John encourages them to live. In the second paragraph, write about the things that seemed most important to you and how God has encouraged you to be his faithful witness. End your review with a prayer of praise to Jesus, the King of kings. Tell him how you want to live now and describe what it will be like to live with him forever in the new Jerusalem.

Bibliography

Along with God's people, I am heir to the teaching of the ancient church in the Nicene Creed, to whose faith I am committed.

From infancy my parents taught me the Holy Scriptures, which make me wise for salvation through faith in Christ Jesus. In this book, I in turn talk with my children that they may write God's word on their hearts and know and love him with all their life.

Dr. Dan Estes gave me a love for the scholarly study of God's word. Dr. Estes introduced me to Gordon Fee and Douglas Stuart's *How to Read the Bible for All It's Worth*. In writing the questions in this reading guide, I have found the most help in Drs. Fee and Stuart's outstanding *How to Read the Bible Book by Book: A Guided Tour*.

Dr. Raju Abraham gave me a "way of seeing" the Scriptures and pointed me to Jim Jordan, whose *Through New Eyes* had opened his. Mr. Jordan put me onto Peter Leithart's writing. Dr. Leithart has written *A House for My Name* and *The Four* as helpful, high school-level introductions to the Old Testament and the Gospels.

Dr. Tim Laniak and Dr. Rollin Grams taught me how to read the Scriptures as narrative and modeled and encouraged seeing the Old Testament fulfilled in the New. Each of them directed me to N.T. Wright's extraordinary work, especially *Jesus and the Victory of God*. Prof. Wright's *For Everyone* commentaries were especially helpful for understanding difficult passages. Finally, Dr. Scott Hafemann made me think even more carefully about how the whole Scripture fits together.

Appendix
Teacher's Guide

In writing *Treasures Old and New*, I have tried to keep my words simple enough for a twelve-year old to understand. Yet the questions they pose, and certainly the Scriptures to which they point, should be deep enough to challenge an adult. I have kept in mind that some readers will study through *Treasures Old and New* on their own and many others will do so as part of a class. As I have taught twelve-year olds in school, seventy-year olds in Sunday school and my own children at home I have been encouraged to see the fruit these questions have borne in my students. I pray this Teacher's Guide will help you as you lead your students to pray and read and think and talk their way through God's word.

Teacher's guides vary in their approach. Some give general principles, leaving plenty room for the teacher's own personality and creativity. Others prescribe specific practices, reassuring the uncertain teacher through every minute of a lesson. This guide includes some principles and many practices. All are suggestions; few, if any, are rules. The guide is a guide: use as much or as little of it as you want as God's Spirit forms within you the heart and mind and skill of an able teacher.

The First Few Classes

In the first few class sessions, work through the lesson in class. For example, on the first day of class, turn to lesson 1, Genesis - Introduction. Ask a student to read the first paragraph about what an introduction is and does. Then ask another to read the next paragraph. Direct the students to open their study Bibles to the introduction to Genesis. Ask a student to read the section about the title of Genesis. Then pose the question from lesson 1: "What does *Genesis* mean?" Let students find the answer in their study Bibles, report it to you and jot down a short note in their notebooks. Carry on like this through the whole introduction. Near the end of class, help the students to prepare an outline, and then send them home to write their own introduction.

On the second day of class, you can work with the students through lesson 2, Genesis 1:1-2:25. The lesson might run like this: Begin with prayer, asking God's Spirit to teach all of you and renew your minds as you study. Tell the students to open their study Bibles to Genesis 1. Ask one student to read the first two verses aloud. Then ask the next student the first question: "What four things are not yet good with the earth at the beginning?" If students struggle to find the four things (formless, empty, darkness and deep or waters), use questions to help them identify the words: "What is the earth like?" "Is that good yet?" etc. Once they've found all four words, direct the students to read one after another through the rest of chapter 1 one paragraph at a time. Then pose the next question—"What does God do to turn the chaos into goodness?"—and the questions in part b. The students will need to read Genesis 2:1-17 to answer the questions in part c. Then have them take turns reading 2:18-25.

Once they've answered questions a to c, direct them to turn to the back of the book and tear or cut out one of the bookmarks. Direct the students to complete parts d, e and f on their own. After a few minutes, ask several students what they wrote for d, several what they wrote for e and several for f. Then, as a class, brainstorm several words or phrases that might serve well as a title for the reading (part g). Finally, close the class with prayer.

You might follow this approach again for lesson three.

For lesson four, you might assign the students to complete each part in pairs. After the pairs have worked through part a, have them discuss their answers with the class. Carry on like this for the rest of the questions, including the bookmark.

Normal Classes

As soon as the students seem ready, have them complete the following day's assignment at home. As they read through the passage at home, they should pick up answers to first-order questions like "Who did what when and where?" The questions in Treasures Old and New should lead them to think through second-order questions as well: "How and why did they do it?", "How does this passage work?" and "What should I do?"

At the beginning of class, I usually glance at each student's notebook to see whether he completed the assignment. (In my classes, I give 100% for answering all the questions or 70% for answering most of them. If students have not completed the assignment, I tell them to listen carefully in class and note the answers as the other students share them. I then give 50% for any assignment completed late.)

After prayer, use first-order questions to review the content of the passage. Do the students show that they recognize the names of the characters? Can they summarize the basic plot of the story? Or can they state a simple outline of the parts of the psalm or the parts of the argument in a letter? For example, if I were doing lesson 5, Genesis 10:1-12:20, I might begin with questions like "What is chapter ten about?" "Then what happens in chapter eleven?" "And what is in the second half of chapter eleven?" "Whom is chapter twelve about?" "What do they do?" I would conclude the opening discussion by asking several students what their *g* for the lesson was, what they wrote as a title for the reading.

I would then use the questions in *Treasures Old and New* to lead a reflective discussion on the passage. I address questions directly to individual students, encouraging every student to think about the passage and engage the discussion. If no student knows the answer to a question, I try my best not to tell them the answer. Instead I point the class to a particular verse or word and use leading questions that suggest another way of thinking about the significance of a particular word or phrase. I want them to learn the skills of reading the Scriptures carefully.

If students have questions *about the passage,* I let the class discussion follow their lead. These may be questions they thought of the night before (question *e*) or questions that come up in the middle of the discussion. My real desire is to have the students meet God by his Spirit in the words of Scripture. And students learn best what they are already asking questions about. If a student asks me a question I can't answer, I am resolved not to make one up on the spot but rather to honor God and them with the truth. "That's a great question. I'm still working through that one myself." Then I go home and keep working on it.

I aim to leave a few minutes at the end of class for students to share their answers to question *f.* Creating and requiring an atmosphere of kindness and openness will give students the security to share more and more openly about what God is teaching them personally, even what they're struggling through. Bless the Spirit for speaking through his word and his people to his people!

Your most important contribution to the class, though, will be your own attitude. Your delight in God and desire to know him through his word will show and, by God's grace, spread like runny noses through a class of kindergarteners.

Assessment

In my classes I weight the elements of the class something like this:

- 30% - Daily Reading
  The regular habit of reading God's word daily is most important.
- 25% - Tests
  Well-written tests are a good way to make sure students are following along with the reading and the class discussions.
- 20% - Reviews
  Reviews help students focus their thoughts on what they're learning. They require reflection, synthesis, extension and application.
- 15% - Introductions
  Introductions are another constructive writing assignment but do not require the same complexity of thought.
- 10% - Scripture Memory

Further

It was my great joy to serve as Discipleship Director at Rocky Bayou Christian School in Niceville, Florida and think carefully through how to teach the Scriptures to children of all ages. For further suggestions of how to incorporate *Treasures Old and New* into a K-12 Bible curriculum, see etclark.edublogs.org.

Index of Lessons
in Canonical Order

Old Testament

New Testament

BOOKMARK
Treasures Old and New

Everyday...

Pray

Ask God's Spirit to teach you and renew your mind as you study.

Read and Mark

Write the reference to head the next section in your notebook. Read through the passage. <u>Mark</u> any words or sentences that seem important to you.

Think and Write

Skip two lines and write the answers to the three questions. Then answer these three:

    d.   Write at least one of your own ideas. It could be
        o   something you discovered or
        o   something you think is important.
    e.   Write at least one of your own questions. It could be
        o   something you don't understand or
        o   something you'd like to learn more about.
    f.   Write at least one way God is teaching you to change the way you love, think or live.
    g.   Go back below the reference and write a title for the day's reading.

Pray

Ask God's Spirit to help you obey what he is teaching you.

(In the unlikely event that you lose the other bookmark ☺, it's probably a good idea not to tear this one out as well.)

BOOKMARK

Treasures Old and New

Everyday...

Pray

Ask God's Spirit to teach you and renew your mind as you study.

Read and Mark

Write the reference to head the next section in your notebook. Read through the passage. <u>Mark</u> any words or sentences that seem important to you.

Think and Write

Skip two lines and write the answers to the three questions. Then answer these three:
    d. Write at least one of your own ideas. It could be
        • something you discovered or
        • something you think is important.
    e. Write at least one of your own questions. It could be
        • something you don't understand or
        • something you'd like to learn more about.
    f. Write at least one way God is teaching you to change the way you love, think or live.
    g. Go back below the reference and write a title for the day's reading.

Pray

Ask God's Spirit to help you obey what he is teaching you.